PRICEWATERHOUSECOOPERS

Illustrative financial statements –
IFRS and UK GAAP 2009

UK Accounting Consulting Services
PricewaterhouseCoopers LLP

© 2008 PricewaterhouseCoopers

Published by

CCH
a Wolters Kluwer business

145 London Road
Kingston-upon-Thames
Surrey
KT2 6SR
Tel: +44 (0) 844 561 8166
Fax: +44 (0) 208 247 1184
E-mail: customerservices@cch.co.uk
Website: www.cch.co.uk

This book has been prepared for general guidance on matters of interest only, and does not constitute professional advice. You should not act upon the information contained in this book without obtaining specific professional advice. Accordingly, to the extent permitted by law, PricewaterhouseCoopers LLP (and its members, employees and agents) and publisher accept no liability, and disclaim all responsibility, for the consequences of you or anyone else acting, or refraining from acting, in reliance on the information contained in this document or for any decision based on it, or for any consequential, special or similar damages even if advised of the possibility of such damages.

ISBN 978-1-84798-111-0

Printed and bound in Italy by Legoprint.
Typeset by YHT, London.

British Library Cataloguing-in-Publication Data.
A catalogue record for this book is available from the British Library.

© 2008 PricewaterhouseCoopers

No part of this publication may be reproduced, stored in any system, or transmitted in any form or by any means, electronic, mechanical, photocopying, recording, or otherwise without the prior permission of PricewaterhouseCoopers LLP.

Preface

This publication provides example sets of financial statements for the year ended 31 December 2008. These model financial statements will assist you in preparing financial statements by illustrating the required disclosure and presentation for UK groups and UK companies, whether you report under IFRS or UK GAAP.

IFRS GAAP plc for the UK
An example annual report including the consolidated financial statements of IFRS GAAP plc group of companies. The annual report has been prepared to show the disclosures and format that might be expected for a group of its size that prepares its financial statements in accordance with International Financial Reporting Standards (IFRS), UK law and listing rules requirements, for a fictional corporate entity (IFRS GAAP plc).

GAAP UK plc
An example annual report including the consolidated financial statements of the GAAP UK plc group of companies. The annual report has been prepared to show the disclosures and format that might be expected for a group of its size that prepares its financial statements in accordance with the Companies Act and UK Accounting Standards. GAAP UK plc is a fictitious unlisted company that is incorporated in the UK. It has a number of UK and overseas investments, including subsidiaries and joint ventures.

GAAP UK Limited
An example set of financial statements for UK GAAP Limited. These financial statements have been prepared to show how an unlisted UK company might prepare its financial statements in accordance with the Companies Act and UK Accounting Standards.

I would like to acknowledge with thanks the following people for their contribution to this publication:

Fran Bennett
Nicola Bruyns
Angela Green
Joanna Malvern
Dave Walters

I also thank Sherridan Stewart for her work in processing the text.

Peter Holgate
Senior Technical Partner
PricewaterhouseCoopers LLP
London
November 2008

Contents

IFRS GAAP plc — Year ended 31 December 2008

This publication provides an illustrative set of consolidated financial statements, prepared in accordance with International Financial Reporting Standards (IFRS), UK Company Law and Listing Rule requirements, for a fictional manufacturing, wholesale and retail group (IFRS GAAP plc).

IFRS GAAP plc is an existing preparer of IFRS consolidated financial statements; IFRS 1, 'First-time adoption of International Financial Reporting Standards', is not applicable.

For an illustrative set of financial statements for first-time adopters of IFRS, refer to the PricewaterhouseCoopers' publication 'Adopting IFRS: IFRS 1 – First time adoption of International Financial Reporting Standards'.

This publication is based on the requirements of IFRS standards and interpretations for financial years beginning on or after 1 January 2008. IFRS 8, 'Operating segments', has been adopted early.

We have attempted to create a realistic set of financial statements for a corporate entity. Certain types of transaction have been excluded, as they are not relevant to the group 's operations. The example disclosures for some of these additional items have been included in appendices III and IV.

The example disclosures should not be considered the only acceptable form of presentation. The form and content of each reporting entity 's financial statements are the responsibility of the entity's management. Alternative presentations to those proposed in this publication may be equally acceptable if they comply with the specific disclosure requirements prescribed in IFRS.

These illustrative financial statements are not a substitute for reading the standards and interpretations themselves or for professional judgement as to fairness of presentation. They do not cover all possible disclosures that IFRS requires. Further specific information may be required in order to ensure fair presentation under IFRS. We recommend that readers refer to the 2008 version of GAAPChecker (our automated checklist), as well as our publication IFRS Disclosure Checklist 2008.

Structure

Abbreviations

IFRS1p37	=	International Financial Reporting Standard [number], paragraph number.
7p22	=	International Accounting Standards [number], paragraph number.
SIC – 15p5	=	Standing Interpretations Committee [number], paragraph number.
DV	=	Disclose Voluntary. Disclosure is encouraged but not required and therefore represents best practice.
CA06 s992	=	Companies Act 2006, section number.
s 706(2)(a)	=	Companies Act 1985, section number.
7 Sch 6	=	Schedule [number] to the Companies Act 1985, paragraph number.

SI 1996/189   =   Statutory Instrument [year/number].

LR 9.8.6R(1)   =   The Listing Rules of the Financial Services Authority, paragraph number.

RS (OFR) p19   =   Reporting Statement: Operating and Financial Review, paragraph number.

CC A.2.1   =   Combined Code, paragraph number.

TR 35   =   Internal Control Guidance for Directors on the Combined Code, paragraph number (also known as the Turnbull Report).

APB 2002/2   =   Auditing Practices Board Bulletin, number.

APB DB 2005/4 =   Auditing Practices Board, Draft Bulletin, number.

GC 45   =   Going concern and financial reporting, paragraph number.

ISA 720p20   =   International Standard on Auditing (UK & Ireland) [number], paragraph number.

SI 2008/410 8   =   Statutory Instrument [year/number], schedule number, paragraph
Sch 4   number.

Certain items may not apply to a particular reporting entity. For example, if the reporting entity does not have material operating leases, disclosure of the accounting policy for operating leases does not need to be included (IAS1p108, 110).

Certain items that apply to an entity may have been excluded in these illustrative financial statements. Additional accounting policies have been included in appendix II. Additional critical accounting estimates and judgements have been included in appendix III. Readers should refer to other PricewaterhouseCoopers publications where necessary.

IFRS GAAP plc

Example annual report

for the year ended 31 December 2008

IFRS GAAP plc

Contents

Abbreviations
Contents

IFRS GAAP plc

1

Operating and financial review

DV, 1p9	Entities are encouraged to present, outside the financial statements, a financial review by management which describes and explains the main features of the entity's financial performance and financial position and the principal uncertainties it faces.
RS (OFR) DV	The ASB has published 'Reporting statement: Operating and financial review' ('RS (OFR)'), which is a statement of best practice on the OFR. It is written with quoted companies in mind but is also applicable to any other entities that produce an OFR. Where an entity includes an operating and financial review in the financial statements, it is recommended that it complies with the RS (OFR).

Group operating and financial review for the year ended 31 December 2008

Principles

CC C.1 RS (OFR) p15	The board should present a balanced and understandable assessment of the group's position and prospects. Note that where non-GAAP historical numbers are disclosed, they should be clearly identified as such and should be reconciled to the statutory numbers with sufficient prominence being given to the statutory numbers and to the reconciliation. The operating and financial review should give a balanced picture of performance and non-statutory numbers should be presented in a manner that achieves this objective. They should supplement and not replace statutory numbers and their purpose should be clearly stated. The descriptions of non-GAAP historical numbers should not imply any representation about future performance. For example, terms such as 'normalised', 'sustainable' or 'maintainable' earnings could be taken to imply an element of forecasting. Instead, 'adjusted' or more specific terms (such as 'profit before tax and exceptionals') can be used.
RS (OFR) p4	The OFR should set out an analysis of the business through the eyes of the board of directors.
RS (OFR) p5	The OFR should reflect the directors' view of the business. Accordingly, the entity shall disclose appropriate elements of information used in managing the entity, including its subsidiary undertakings. Where appropriate, the review may give greater emphasis to those matters which are significant to the entity and its subsidiary undertakings taken as a whole. Such matters may include issues specific to business segments where relevant to the understanding of the business as a whole. The presentation of the OFR should complement the format of the annual report as a whole.
RS (OFR) p6	The OFR should focus on matters that are relevant to the interests of members.
RS (OFR) p7	Members' needs are paramount when directors consider what information should be contained in the OFR. Information in the OFR will also be of interest to users other than members, for example other investors, potential investors, creditors, customers, suppliers, employees and general society. The directors should consider the extent to which they should report on issues relevant to the other users where, because of the influence on the performance of the business and its value, they are also of significance to members. The OFR should not, however, be seen as a replacement for other forms of reporting addressed to a wider stakeholder group.
RS (OFR) p8	The OFR should have a forward-looking orientation, identifying those trends and factors relevant to the members' assessment of the current and future performance of the business and the progress towards the achievement of long-term business objectives.
RS (OFR) p9	The particular factors discussed should be those that have affected development, performance, and position during the financial year and those which are likely to affect the entity's future development, performance and position.
RS (OFR) p10	Given the nature of some forward-looking information, in particular elements that cannot be objectively verified but have been made in good faith, directors may want to include a statement in the OFR to treat such elements with caution, explaining the uncertainties underpinning such information.
RS (OFR) p11	The OFR should comment on the impact on future performance of significant events after the balance sheet date.

IFRS GAAP plc

2

RS (OFR) p12   The OFR should discuss predictive comments, both positive and negative, made in previous reviews whether or not these have been borne out by events.

RS (OFR) p13   The OFR should complement as well as supplement the financial statements, in order to enhance the overall corporate disclosure.

RS (OFR) p14   In complementing the financial statements, the OFR should provide useful financial and non-financial information about the business and its performance that is not reported in financial statements but which the directors' judge might be relevant to the members' evaluation of past results and assessment of future prospects.

RS (OFR) p15   In supplementing the financial statements, the OFR should where relevant:

- Provide additional explanations of amounts recorded in the financial statements.
- Explain the conditions and events that shaped the information contained in the financial statements.

Where amounts from the financial statements have been adjusted for inclusion in the OFR, that fact should be highlighted and a reconciliation provided.

RS (OFR) p16   The OFR should be comprehensive and understandable.

RS (OFR) p17   Directors should consider whether the omission of information might reasonably be expected to influence significantly the assessment made by members.

RS (OFR) p18   The recommendation for the OFR to be comprehensive does not mean that the OFR should cover all possible matters: the objective is quality, not quantity of content. It is neither possible nor desirable for a reporting statement to list all the elements that might need to be included, since these will vary depending on the nature and circumstances of the particular business and how the business is run.

RS (OFR) p19   Directors should consider the evidence underpinning the information to be included in the OFR. Where relevant, directors should explain the source of the information and the degree to which the information is objectively supportable, to allow members to assess the reliability of the information presented for themselves.

RS (OFR) p20   Directors should consider the key issues to include in the OFR that will provide members with focused and relevant information. The inclusion of too much information may obscure judgements and will not promote understanding. Where additional information is discussed elsewhere in the annual report, or in other reports, cross-referencing to those sources will assist members.

RS (OFR) p21   The OFR should be written in a clear and readily understandable style.

RS (OFR) p22   The OFR should be balanced and neutral, dealing even-handedly with both good and bad aspects.

RS (OFR) p23   The directors should ensure that the OFR retains balance and that members are not misled as a result of the omission of any information on unfavourable aspects.

RS (OFR) p24   The OFR should be comparable over time.

RS (OFR) p25   Disclosure should be sufficient for the members to be able to compare the information presented with similar information about the entity for previous financial years. Comparability enables identification of the main trends and factors, and their analysis, over successive financial years. Directors may wish to consider the extent to which the OFR is comparable with reviews prepared by other entities in the same industry or sector.

RS (OFR) p79   However, no disclosure of information should be made about impending developments or about matters in the course of negotiation that would, in the opinion of the directors, be seriously prejudicial to the interests of the entity.

Disclosure framework

RS (OFR) p27   The OFR should provide information to assist members to assess the strategies adopted by the entity and the potential for those strategies to succeed. The key elements of the disclosure framework necessary to achieve this are:

IFRS GAAP plc   3

- the nature of the business, including a description of the market, competitive and regulatory environment in which the entity operates, and the entity's objectives and strategies;
- the development and performance of the business, both in the financial year under review and in the future;
- the resources, principal risks and uncertainties and relationships that may affect the entity's long-term value; and
- the position of the business including a description of the capital structure, treasury policies and objectives and liquidity of the entity, both in the financial year under review and the future.

Details of particular matters

RS (OFR) p28   To the extent necessary to meet the requirements set out in paragraph above, the OFR should include information about:

- environmental matters (including the impact of the business of the entity on the environment);
- the entity's employees;
- social and community issues;
- persons with whom the entity has contractual or other arrangements which are essential to the business of the entity;
- receipts from, and returns to, members of the entity in respect of shares held by them; and
- all other matters the directors consider to be relevant.

RS (OFR) p29   The OFR should, in particular, include:

- the entity's policies on environmental matters, the entity's employees and social and community issues; and
- the extent to which those policies have been successfully implemented

If it does not contain information and analysis of each kind mentioned in paragraphs above, it should state which of those kinds of information and analysis it does not contain.

The nature, objectives and strategies of the business

1p9(a)
RS (OFR)
p30, 31
The OFR should include a description of the business and the external environment in which it operates as context for the directors' discussion and analysis of performance and financial position. This description is recommended in order to provide members with an understanding of the industry/industries in which the entity operates, its main products, services, customers, business processes and distribution methods, the structure of the business, and its economic model, including an overview of the main operating facilities and their location.

RS (OFR) p32   Every entity is affected by its external environment. Depending on the nature of the business, the OFR should include discussion of matters such as the entity's major markets and competitive position within those markets and the significant features of the legal, regulatory, macro-economic and social environment that influence the business.

RS (OFR) p33-35 The OFR should discuss the objectives of the business to generate or preserve value over the longer-term. Objectives will often be defined in terms of financial performance; however, objectives in non-financial areas should also be discussed where appropriate. The nature of the industry will affect the directors' determination of an appropriate time perspective for reporting in the OFR.

RS (OFR) p36   The OFR should set out the directors' strategies for achieving the objectives of the business.

RS (OFR) p38-40 It should include the key performance indicators, both financial and, where appropriate, non-financial, used by the directors to assess progress against their stated objectives. The KPIs disclosed should be those that the directors judge are effective in measuring the delivery of their strategies and managing their business. Regular measurement using KPIs should enable an entity to set and communicate its performance targets and to measure whether it is achieving them. Comparability will be enhanced if the KPIs disclosed are accepted and widely used, either within the industry sector or more generally.

IFRS GAAP plc

RS (OFR) p41-42   Directors should also consider the extent to which other performance indicators and evidence should be included in the OFR. These could be narrative evidence describing how the directors manage the business or quantified measures used to monitor the entity's external environment and/ or progress towards the achievement of its objectives.

Current and future development and performance

RS (OFR) p44-46   Trends and factors in development and performance suggested by an analysis of the current and previous financial years should be highlighted. Development and performance should be described in the context of the strategic objectives of the business. The OFR should cover significant aspects of the statements of financial performance and where appropriate should be linked to other aspects of performance. It should set out the directors' analysis of the effect on current development and performance of changes during the financial year in the industry or the external environment in which the business operates and of developments within the business.

RS (OFR) p43, 47-49   The OFR should describe the significant features of the development and performance of the business in the financial year covered by the financial statements, focusing on those business segments that are relevant to an understanding of the development and performance as a whole. It should analyse the main trends and factors that directors consider likely to impact future prospects. The main trends and factors likely to affect the future development and performance will vary according to the nature of the business, but could include the development of known new products and services or the benefits expected from capital investment. The OFR should discuss the current level of investment expenditure together with planned future expenditure and should explain how that investment is directed to assist the achievement of business objectives. Any assumptions underlying the main trends and factors should be disclosed. Directors should consider the potential future significance of issues in deciding whether or not to include an analysis of them in the OFR.

Resources

IAS 1p9(c)   RS (OFR) p50-51   The OFR should include a description of the resources available to the entity and how they are managed. It should set out the key strengths and resources, tangible and intangible, available to the business, which will assist it in the pursuit of its objectives and, in particular, those items that are not reflected in the balance sheet. Depending on the nature of the business, these may include: corporate reputation and brand strength; natural resources; employees; research and development; intellectual capital; licences, patents, copyright and trademarks; and market position.

Principal risks and uncertainties

RS (OFR) p52-56   The OFR should include a description of the principal risks and uncertainties facing the entity, together with a commentary on the directors' approach to them. While different industries and entities use different risk models or approaches for identifying and managing risk, all entities face and should disclose strategic, commercial, operational and financial risks where these may significantly affect the entity's strategies and development of the entity's value. The principal risks and uncertainties facing entities will vary according to the nature of the business, although it is expected that some risks, such as the risk to reputation, will be common to all.

RS (OFR) p55-56   The description of the principal risks and uncertainties should cover both the exposure to negative consequences as well as potential opportunities. The directors' policy for managing principal risks should be disclosed. The OFR should cover the principal risks and uncertainties necessary for an understanding of the objectives and strategies of the business, both where they constitute a significant external risk to the entity, and where the entity's impact on other parties through its activities, products or services, affects its performance. Directors should consider the full range of business risks.

Relationships

RS (OFR) p57-58   The OFR should include information about significant relationships with stakeholders other than members, which are likely, directly or indirectly, to influence the performance of the business and its value. Directors, in deciding what should be included in the OFR, should take a broad view in considering the extent to which the actions of stakeholders other than members can affect an entity's performance and thus its value.

RS (OFR) p59   Where necessary for an understanding of the business, the OFR should describe receipts from, and returns to, shareholders in relation to shares held by them. This should include a description of any distributions, capital raising and share repurchases.

IFRS GAAP plc — Year ended 31 December 2008

IFRS GAAP plc

Financial position

RS (OFR) p60-62
IAS 1p9(b)
The OFR should contain an analysis of the financial position and a discussion of the capital structure of the entity. This should include the sources of funding and the targeted ratio of liabilities to equity. The analysis, whilst based upon the financial statements, should comment on the events that have impacted the financial position of the entity during the financial year, and future factors that are likely to affect the financial position going forward. The analysis should supplement the disclosures required in accounting standards, in particular those required by IFRS 7, 'Financial instruments: Disclosures'. The OFR should highlight accounting policies set out in the notes to the financial statements and discuss those accounting policies that are critical to an understanding of the performance and financial position of the entity, focusing on those which have required the particular exercise of judgement in their application and to which the results are most sensitive. In addition, it should draw attention to the accounting policies which have changed during the financial year under review.

RS (OFR) p65-67
The OFR should set out the entity's treasury policies and objectives. The OFR should also discuss the implementation of these policies in the financial year under review. The purpose and effect of major financing transactions undertaken up to the date of approval of the financial statements should be explained. The effect of interest costs on profits and the potential impact of interest rate changes should also be discussed.

RS (OFR) p63-64
The OFR should contain a discussion of the capital structure of the entity, This could include the balance between equity and debt, the maturity profile of debt, the type of capital instrument used, currency, regulatory capital and interest rate structure. The discussion should include comments on short and longer-term funding plans to support the directors' strategies to achieve the entity's objectives. In addition, the discussion should comment on why the entity has adopted its particular capital structure.

Cash flows

RS (OFR) p68
The OFR should discuss the cash inflows and outflows during the financial year, along with the entity's ability to generate cash, to meet known or probable cash requirements and to fund growth.

RS (OFR) p69-70
Any discussion should supplement the information provided in the financial statements by, for example, commenting on any special factors that have influenced cash flows in the financial year and those that may have a significant effect on future cash flows. Where entities have cash that is surplus to future operating requirements and current levels of distribution, the discussion should include future plans for making use of the excess cash. Although segmental analysis of profit may be indicative of the cash flow generated by each segment, this will not always be so, for example, because of fluctuations in capital expenditure and depreciation. Where segmental cash flows are significantly out of line with segmental revenues or profits, this should be indicated and explained.

Liquidity

RS (OFR) p71
The OFR should discuss the entity's current and prospective liquidity. Where relevant, this should include commentary on the level of borrowings, the seasonality of borrowing requirements (indicated by the peak level of borrowings during that period) and the maturity profile of both borrowings and un-drawn committed borrowing facilities.

RS (OFR) p72-74
The discussion on liquidity should discuss the ability of the entity to fund its current and future operations and stated strategies. It should cover internal sources of liquidity, referring to any restrictions on the ability to transfer funds from one part of the group to meet the obligations of another part of the group, where these represent, or might foreseeably come to represent, a significant restraint on the group. Such constraints would include exchange controls and taxation consequences of transfers. Where the entity has entered into covenants in financing contracts which could have the effect of restricting the use of financing arrangements or credit facilities, and negotiations with the lenders on the operation of these covenants are taking place or are expected to take place, this fact should be indicated in the OFR. Where a breach of a covenant has occurred or is expected to occur, the OFR should give details of the measures taken or proposed to remedy the situation.

Key performance indicators

RS (OFR) p75
The entity should provide information that enables members to understand each KPI disclosed in the OFR.

IFRS GAAP plc   6

RS (OFR) p76   For each KPI disclosed in the OFR:

- the definition and its calculation method should be explained;
- its purpose should be explained;
- the source of underlying data should be disclosed and, where relevant, assumptions explained;
- quantification or commentary on future targets should be provided;
- where information from the financial statements has been adjusted for inclusion in the OFR, that fact should be highlighted and a reconciliation provided;
- where available, corresponding amount for the financial year immediately preceding the current year should be disclosed; and
- any changes to KPIs should be disclosed and the calculation method used compared to previous financial years, including significant changes in the underlying accounting policies adopted in the financial statements, should be identified and explained.

RS (OFR) p77   Quantification or commentary on future targets is about communicating the direction the entity is taking by, for example, setting out future strategies and goals.

Other performance indicators

RS (OFR) p78   Where a quantified measure, other than a KPI, is included, the OFR should disclose:

- the definition and its calculation method; and
- where available, the corresponding amount for the financial year immediately preceding the current year.

RS (OFR) p80
DV   Entities are encouraged to include a statement as to whether the OFR is prepared in accordance with this Reporting Statement and contain particulars of, and reasons for any departure.

By order of the Board

AB Smith
Company Secretary   31 March 2009

IFRS GAAP plc

7

Directors' report

Group directors' report for the year ended 31 December 2008

s 234(1) CA06 s415(1)	The directors present their report and the audited financial statements for the year ended 31 December 2008.

General requirements

s 234ZZA(1),(2) CA06 s416(1), (3)	(1) The directors' report for the financial year must state:

    (a) the names of the persons who, at any time during the financial year were directors of the company;

    (b) the principal activities of the company and its subsidiary undertakings included in the consolidation in the course of the year; and

    (c) the amount (if any) that the directors recommend should be paid by way of a dividend.

s 234ZZA(3) CA06 s416(4)	The directors' report must also comply with the relevant requirements of Schedule 7.

Principal activities

s 234ZZA(1)(b) 7 Sch 6(d) s 698(2) 1p126(b) CA06 s416(1)(b)	The narrative should cover the principal activities of the entity and its subsidiary undertakings included in the consolidation.

1p126(a)	In addition there should be disclosure of the:

- Domicile and legal form of entity.
- Country of incorporation.
- Address of the registered office or principal place of business, if different.[1]

Review of business[2]

s 234(1)(a) CA06 s417(3)(a)	The report must contain a fair review of the development and performance of the group's business during the year and of its position at the year end.

DV	Where non-statutory numbers are disclosed, it should be clear that these differ from the statutory numbers, the equivalent statutory number should be disclosed and there should be a reconciliation between the statutory and non-statutory numbers.

The review of the business should include:

s 234ZZB(1) CA06 s417(3)	(a) a fair review of the business of the company; and

    (b) a description of the principal risks and uncertainties facing the company.

s 234ZZB(2) CA06 s417(4)	The review is required to give a balanced and comprehensive analysis of:

    (a) the development and performance of the business of the company during the financial year; and

    (b) the position of the company at the end of the year,

consistent with the size and complexity of the business.

s 234ZZB(3) CA06 s417(6)	The review must to the extent necessary for an understanding of the development, performance or position of the business of the company include:

---

[1] This disclosure can be given in the note to the accounts and not in the directors' report

[2] Often the information that is required to be included in the business review section of the directors' report is included in the OFR or other document published together with the directors' report. This is permitted, provided that specific cross-references are included in the directors' report to where the information is disclosed.

IFRS GAAP plc   8

(a) analysis using the financial key performance indicators and

(b) where appropriate, analysis using other key performance indicators, including information relating to environmental matters and employee matters.

CA06 s417(5) For quoted companies for periods beginning on or after 6 April 2008, the review must, to the extent necessary for an understanding of the development, performance or position of the business of the company include:

(a) the main trends and factors likely to affect the future development, performance and position of the business;

(b) information about:

  (i) environmental matters (including the impact of the company's business on the environment);

  (ii) the company's employees; and

  (iii) social and community issues.

  including information about any policies of the company in relation to these matters and their effectiveness.

(c) Information about contractual and other arrangements that are essential to the business of the company, although nothing need be disclosed about a person if, in the opinion of the directors, such disclosure would be seriously prejudicial to that person or contrary to the public interest.

s 234ZZB(4) The review must, where appropriate, include references to, and additional explanations of, CA06 s417(8) amounts included in the financial statements of the company.

Branches outside the UK

7 Sch 6(d) The directors' report should disclose the existence of any branches that operate outside of the SI 2008/410 7 UK.
Sch 7(1)(d)

Future developments

7 Sch 6(1)(b) The directors' report shall contain an indication should be given of the likely future SI 2008/410 7 developments in the group's business.
Sch 7(1)(b)

Results and dividends

s 234ZZB(3),(4) Details of the results should be provided (where not included in the business review above).
CA06 s417(3),(4)

s 234ZZA(1)(c) Details of the recommended dividend should be provided.
CA06 s416(3)

Research and development

7 Sch 6(1) (c) ▪ The directors' report should provide an indication of the group's research and SI 2008/410 7 Sch development activities.
7(1)(c)

DV ▪ It is recommended that a statement is included with regard to the charge to the income statement for the year (which should be separately disclosed in the notes to financial statements).

Political donations and political expenditure

7 Sch 3 If the company, or any of its subsidiaries made any donations to a registered political party in SI2008/410 7Sch the EU (including the UK) or incurred EU political expenditure exceeding €200 (for periods 3(2) commencing on or after 6 April 2008, £2,000) in the financial year, the directors' report should disclose:

  ▪ EU donations – name of political party and total amount given per party, by the entity and each subsidiary that has donated or incurred such expenditure individually.

IFRS GAAP plc

9

- EU political expenditure – total amount incurred in the financial year by the company and each subsidiary that has donated or incurred such expenditure individually.

7 Sch 4
SI2008/410 7
Sch 4

Total contributions to non-EU political organisations should be disclosed, for the group as a whole in aggregate. (There is no threshold for this disclosure.)

Charitable donations

7 Sch 5 SI2008/
410 7 Sch 5

If the company, or any of its subsidiaries, has given money in excess of €200 (for periods beginning on or after 6 April 2008, £2,000) in aggregate for charitable purposes during the year, disclose the total amount given for each such purpose.

Land

7 Sch 1(2)
SI2008/410 7
Sch 2

If significant, the directors' report should indicate the difference between market value and book value of land for the company or any of its subsidiary undertakings.

Post balance sheet events

7 Sch 6 (1)(a)
SI2008/410 7 Sch
7(1)(a)

The directors' report must include particulars of any important events affecting the company or group since the year end.

Directors' interests

s 234ZZA(1)(a)
CA06 s416(1)(a)

Provide the names of all persons who were directors during any part of the period.

DV

Include changes in directors since the end of the financial year and the dates of any appointments and/ or resignations of directors occurring during the financial year.

DV

Include information regarding the retirement of the directors at the AGM and whether they offer themselves for election.

LR9.8.6R(1)

Disclose all interests in respect of which transactions are notifiable to the company under DTR 3.1.2 R[1], including spouse and children's interests for individuals who are directors at the end of the period under review.

LR 9.8.6R(1)(a)
(b)

All changes in directors' interests that have occurred between the end of the period under review and a date not more than one month prior to the date of the notice of the annual general meeting must be disclosed. If there is not change a statement to that effect is required. Further information about the directors' interests is provided in the remuneration report.

Directors third party indemnity provisions

s 309C
CA06 s236(2)

The directors' report needs to include a statement if a qualifying third party indemnity provision (whether made by the company or otherwise) has been in place for one or more directors of the company or of an associated company at any time during the financial year.

Employees[2]

7 Sch 11(3)
SI2008/410 7 Sch
11(3)

A statement is required describing the action that has been taken during the period to introduce, maintain or develop arrangements aimed at involving UK employees in the entity's affairs. This statement should discuss the group's policy on:

- systematic provision of relevant information to employees;
- regular consultation with employees or their representatives so that the employees' views may be taken into account in making decisions that are likely to affect their interests;

[1] In accordance with DTR 3.1.2 R interests includes shares of the issuer, or derivatives or any other financial instruments relating to those shares. Refer to DTR 3.1.23 R for a definition of financial instruments.
[2] The requirements below only apply if the company employed on average 250 or more employees in the UK each week during the financial year (7Sch11(1); SI2008/410 7 Sch 11(1)).

IFRS GAAP plc

- encouragement of employees' participation in the group's performance by employee share schemes or other means; and
- achieving awareness on the part of all employees of the financial and economic factors affecting the group's performance.

7 Sch 9(3)
SI2008/410 7
Sch 10(3)

A statement should be included as to the policy for giving full and fair consideration to applications for employment that disabled people make to the company, the policy for employment, training, career development and promotion of disabled people and for the continuing employment and training of employees who have become disabled while employed by the company.

Policy and practice on payment of creditors[1]

7 Sch 12(2), (3)
SI2008/410 7 Sch
12(2),(3)

The company's policy and practice on payment of creditors should be disclosed, which should include a policy statement for the following financial year and the number of days (calculated in the prescribed manner) taken to pay bills in the current financial year. The statement must include whether:

7 Sch 12(2)(a)
SI2008/410 7 Sch
12(2)(a)

- in respect of some or all of its suppliers, it is the company's policy to follow any code or standard on payment practice and, if so, give the name of the code or standard and the place where information about the code or standard can be obtained; and/or

7 Sch 12(2)(b)
SI2008/410 7
Sch 12(2)(b)

- in respect of some or all of its suppliers, it is the company's policy:
  i) to settle the terms of payment with those suppliers when agreeing the terms of each transaction;
  ii) to ensure that the suppliers are made aware of the terms of payment; and
  iii) to abide by the terms of payment.

7 Sch 12(2)(c)
SI2008/410 7
Sch 12(2)(c)

Where the statement does not cover all suppliers, the policy for the other suppliers needs to be disclosed.

Financial instruments

7 Sch 5A(1)
7 Sch (1A)
SI2008/410 7 Sch 6

- Where material for the assessment of the assets, liabilities, financial position and profit or loss of the group, the directors' report must contain an indication of:

  - the financial risk management objectives and policies of the entity, including the policy for hedging each major type of forecasted transaction for which hedge accounting is used, and
  - the exposure of the entity to price risk, credit risk, liquidity risk and cash flow risk,

Purchase of own shares and sale of treasury shares

7 Sch 7,8
SI2008/410 7
Sch 8, 9

Where a company purchases or places a charge on its own shares, there are specific disclosures to be made. These disclosures are:

- the number and nominal value of the shares purchased, the aggregate amount of the consideration paid by the company for such shares and the reasons for their purchase;
- the number and nominal value of the shares acquired by the company, acquired by another person in such circumstances and charged during the financial year;
- the maximum number and nominal value of shares which, having been acquired by the company, acquired by another person in such circumstances or charged (whether or not during that year) are held at any time by the company or that other person during that year;
- the number and nominal value of the shares acquired by the company, acquired by another person in such circumstances or charged (whether or not during that year) which are disposed of by the company or that other person or cancelled by the company during that year;
- where the number and nominal value of the shares of any particular description are stated in pursuance of any of the preceding sub-paragraphs, the percentage of the called-up share capital which shares of that description represent;
- where any of the shares have been charged the amount of the charge in each case; and

[1] An additional statement regarding the group's policy and practice and number of days for the company and its UK subsidiaries, whilst not mandatory, is considered best practice.

IFRS GAAP plc   11

■ where any of the shares have been disposed of by the company or the person who acquired them in such circumstances for money or money's worth the amount or value of the consideration in each case.

LR 9.8.6R(4)(a), (b), (c), (d) Details of any shareholders' authority for the purchase, by the company, of its own shares still valid at the end of the period under review. Where any such purchases are made, or proposed to be made, otherwise than through the market, or by tender to all shareholders, details must be given of the names of the sellers of such shares purchased in the period. In respect of purchases, made otherwise than through the market or by tender to all shareholders, or options or contracts to make such purchases entered into since the year end, information listed above, should be given. Details should be given of the names of the purchasers of treasury shares sold or proposed to be sold for cash, (otherwise than through the market or in connection with an employees' share scheme, or where sales are not pursuant to an opportunity available to all holders of the company's securities on the same terms), during the period under review.

Substantial shareholdings

LR 9.8.6(2) (a), (b) Particulars, as at a date not more than a month prior to the date of the notice of the general meeting, should be given of substantial shareholdings (material interests of three per cent or more and non-material interests of ten per cent or more) disclosed to the company, in any part of the company's share capital. Where there have been no such disclosures, this fact should be stated.

Placing of shares

LR 9.8.4R(9) Where a listed company is a subsidiary and an undertaking of another company, particulars should be given of the participation by its parent company in any placing made during the period under review.

Waiver of dividends

LR 9.8.4R (12) (13)
LR 9.8.5R Details should be disclosed of any arrangement under which a shareholder has waived or agreed to waive any dividends or future dividends. Where a shareholder has agreed to waive future dividends, details of the waiver together with those relating to dividends which are payable during the period under review should be given. Waivers of less than one per cent of the total value of any dividend are not required to be disclosed provided that some payment has been made on each share of the relevant class clearing the relevant calendar year.

Contracts of significance

LR 9.8.4R(10)(b)
LR 9.8.4R(11) Particulars should be given of any contract of significance (including contracts for the provision of services) between the company (including subsidiary undertakings) and controlling shareholder subsisting in the period. 'Significance' is defined as more than one per cent of the relevant transactions for the group.

LR 9.8.4R(10)(a) Disclosure is required of the particulars of any contract of significance to which the company, or one of its subsidiaries, is a party and in which a director of the company is or was materially interested.

LR9.8.4R (3)
LR 11.1.10R (2)(c) Details should be disclosed of small related party transactions notified to the Financial Services Authority.

Health and safety

DV This includes areas such as:

■ Policy on health and safety.
■ Risks faced by employees and controls in place.
■ Health and safety goals and progress towards their achievement.
■ The total cost of occupational injuries and illnesses suffered by staff in the reporting period.

IFRS GAAP plc 12

Corporate social responsibility

DV — This includes areas such as:

- Whether the board takes regular account of the significance of social, environmental and ethical (SEE) matters to the group.
- Whether the board has identified and assessed the significant risks to the group's short and long-term value arising from SEE matters, as well as the opportunities to enhance value that may arise from an appropriate response.
- Whether the board has received adequate training and information to make this assessment.
- Information on the SEE-related risks and opportunities identified and how they may impact the business.
- Whether the group has effective systems for managing significant risks which, where relevant, incorporate performance management systems and appropriate remuneration incentives.
- A description of the policies and procedures in place for managing short-term and long-term risks arising from SEE matters (or, if there are none, that this is the case and the reason for this) and information about the group's level of compliance with these policies and procedures.
- A description of how the disclosures in respect of SEE matters are verified.

Requirements from the Takeover Directive

DTR 7.2.6
7 Sch13(2)(a)
SI2008/410 7
Sch 13(2)(a)

The following information should be disclosed:
The structure of the company's capital including:

(a) The rights and obligations attached to each class of shares
(b) Where there are two or more classes, the percentage of the total share capital represented by each class

A company's capital includes any shares or debentures in the company that are not admitted to trading on a regulated market.

7 Sch 13(2)(b)
SI2008/410 7
Sch 13(2)(b)

Details of any restrictions on the transfer of securities (shares or debentures) in the company including limitations on the holding of securities and requirements to obtain the approval of the company or of other holders prior to a transfer of securities.

7 Sch 13(2)(c)
SI2008/410 7
Sch 13(2)(c)

In respect of each person with a significant direct or indirect holding of securities in the company, the identity of the person, the size of the holding and the nature of the holding.

7 Sch 13(2)(d)
SI2008/410 7
Sch 13(2)(d)

In the case of each person who holds securities carrying special rights with regard to control of the company, the identity of the person and the nature of the rights.

7 Sch 13(2)(e)
SI2008/410 7
Sch 13(2)(e)

Where the company has an employees' share scheme and shares to which the scheme relates have rights with regard to control of the company that are not exercisable directly by the employees, details of how these rights are exercisable.

7 Sch 13(2)(f)
SI2008/410 7
Sch 13(2)(f)

Details of any restrictions on voting rights including limitations on voting rights of holders of a given percentage or number of votes; deadlines for exercising voting rights; and arrangements by which, with the company's cooperation, financial rights carried by securities are held by a person other than the holder of the securities.

7 Sch 13(2)(g)
SI2008/410 7
Sch 13(2)(g)

Details of any agreements between holders of securities that are known to the company and may result in restrictions on the transfer of securities or on voting rights.

7 Sch 13(2)(h)
SI2008/410 7
Sch 13(2)(h)

Details of any rules that the company has about appointment and replacement of directors and details of any rules about the amendment of the company's articles of association.

7 Sch 13(2)(i)
SI2008/410 7
Sch 13(2)(i)

Details of the powers of the company's directors, including, in particular, any powers in relation to the issuing or buying back by the company of its shares.

IFRS GAAP plc 13

7 Sch 13(2)(j) SI2008/410 7 Sch 13(2)(j)	Details of any significant arrangements to which the company is a party that take effect, alter or terminate upon a change of control of the company following a takeover bid, and the effects of any such agreements. This does not apply if disclosure would be seriously prejudicial to the company and the company is not under any other obligation to disclose it.
7 Sch 13(2)(k) SI2008/410 7 Sch 13(2)(k)	Details of any agreements between the company and its directors or employees providing for compensation for loss of office or employment (through resignation, purported redundancy or otherwise) that occurs because of a takeover bid.
s234ZZA(5) SI2008/410 7 Sch 14	Details of any other information and explanations required in respect of the details included above.

AGM Notice

LR13.8.10	Where the shareholders of a listed company are sent a notice of a meeting (which includes any business other than routine business at an AGM) and an explanatory circular does not accompany the notice, an explanation of the business to be conducted at the AGM must be included in the directors' report.

Auditors and disclosure of information to auditors[1]

s 234ZA CA06 s 418	The report must contain a statement to the effect that, in the case of each of the persons who are directors at the time when the report is approved, the following applies:

- so far as the director is aware, there is no relevant audit information of which the company's auditors are unaware, and
- he has taken all the steps that he ought to have taken as a director in order to make himself aware of any relevant audit information and to establish that the company's auditors are aware of that information.

DV s 384(1) CA06 s489(1)	The auditors, PricewaterhouseCoopers LLP, have indicated their willingness to continue in office, and a resolution that they be re-appointed will be proposed at the annual general meeting.

DTR 7.2.1, 7.2.9	**Corporate Governance**
	The company's statement on Corporate Governance is included in the Corporate Governance report on pages 25-30 of these financial statements.

s 234A(1) CA06 s419(1)	By order of the board

s 234A(2) CA06 s419(1)	AB Smith

Company Secretary[2] 28 March 2009

---

[1] This section is applicable unless the directors have taken advantage of the exemption conferred by s249A(1) or 249AA(1) (CA06 s 477, s480).

[2] The directors' report has to be signed by the company secretary or a director after it has been approved by the board of directors. The copy of the directors' report which is delivered to the Registrar of Companies must be manually signed by the company secretary or a director.

IFRS GAAP plc   14

Remuneration report

s234(B)
CA06 s420-421

Requirements for the directors' remuneration report – policy section of the remuneration report (unaudited).

The remuneration report should include the following:

Remuneration committee

7A Sch 2(1)(a)
SI 2008/410 8
Sch 2(1)(a)

Names of the members of the remuneration committee (at any time during the year)[1]

Advice to the remuneration committee

7A Sch 2(1)(b)
SI 2008/410 8
Sch 2(1)(b)

The names of any person(s) providing advice to the remuneration committee that has materially assisted the committee with their decisions.

7A Sch 2(1)(c)
SI 2008/410 8
Sch 2(1)(c)

For any advisor to the remuneration committee who is not a director, disclosure of the nature of any other services performed by the advisor to the company during the year and whether the advisor was appointed by the remuneration committee.

Remuneration policy

7A Sch 3(1)
SI 2008/410 8
Sch 3(1)
LR 9.8.8(1)
LR9.8.8(10)

A statement of the company's policy on executive directors' remuneration for the year following the financial year under review and future years.

Explanations and justifications of any departure from the policy in the period under review and any changes in the policy from the preceding year.

7A Sch 3(3)
SI 2008/410 8
Sch 3(3)

For each director, an explanation of the relative importance of those elements that are related to performance and those elements that are not related to performance.

Share options/long-term incentive schemes

7A Sch 3(2)(a)
SI 2008/410 8
Sch 3(2)(a)

Summary of the performance conditions attaching to share option or long-term incentive entitlements (including matching awards under deferred annual bonus schemes) by director.

7A Sch 3(2)(b)
SI 2008/410 8
Sch 3(2)(b)

An explanation for the choice of performance conditions.

7A Sch 3(2)(f)
SI 2008/410 8
Sch 3(2)(f)

If share options or long-term incentive awards are not subject to performance conditions, an explanation of why that is the case.

7A Sch 3(2)(c)
SI 2008/410 8
Sch 3(2)(c)

A summary of the methods for assessing whether performance conditions have been met and the reasons for choosing these.

7A Sch 3(2)(d)
SI 2008/410 8
Sch 3(2)(d)

For comparative performance conditions, a summary of the external factors used for comparison.

7A Sch 3(2)(d)
SI 2008/410 8
Sch 3(2)(d)

For comparative performance conditions, the identity of the companies in the comparator group or index.

7A Sch 3(2)(e)
SI 2008/410 8
Sch 3(2)(e)

Description and explanation of any proposed amendments to the terms and conditions of outstanding share options or LTIS awards.

Statement of consideration of conditions elsewhere in the company and group[2]

SI 2008/410 8
Sch 4

A statement of how the pay and employment conditions of employees of the company and elsewhere in the group were taken into account when determining directors' remuneration for the relevant financial year.

CC B.2.1-2.4

[1] The board should establish a remuneration committee of at least three (smaller companies – two) independent, non-executive directors. The chairman may also be a member of, but not chair, the committee if he/she is considered to be independent. The committee should make available its terms of reference. The committee should be responsible for setting remuneration for all executive directors and the chairman and also monitoring the remuneration for senior management. The board should determine the remuneration of non-executive directors. Shareholders should be invited to approve all new long-term incentive schemes.
[2] Effective for accounting periods commencing on or after 6 April 2009.

IFRS GAAP plc 15

Performance graph

7A Sch 4(1)(a)(b)
SI 2008/410 8
Sch 5(1)(a)(b)

A performance graph showing the company's total shareholder return compared with a broad equity market index chosen by the company over the five preceding financial years (including the financial year covered by the report) and the name of and the reasons for the choice of broad equity market index.

Directors contracts

7A Sch 3(4)
SI 2008/410 8
Sch 3(4)

The company's policy on the duration of service contracts for directors and notice periods and termination payments under such contracts.

7A Sch 5(1)
SI 2008/410 8
Sch 6(1)

In relation to individual directors' service contracts:

  (i) the date of the contract;
  (ii) the unexpired term;
  (iii) the contractual notice period;
  (iv) any provision for compensation payable upon early termination of the contract; and
  (v) details of any other arrangements which are necessary to enable investors to estimate the possible liability of the company upon early termination of the contract.

LR 9.8.8(8)-(9)

Details of any director's service contract that has notice period in excess of one year, or with provisions for pre-determined compensation on termination that exceeds one year's salary and benefits in kind, including the reasons for such a notice period.

LR 9.8.8(8)-(9)

Details of the unexpired term of any director's service contract for a director proposed for election or re-election at the forthcoming annual general meeting.

LR 9.8.8(8)-(9)

If any director proposed for election or re-election at the forthcoming annual general meeting does not have a director's service contract, a statement to that effect.

Awards to past/former directors

7A Sch 5(2)
SI 2008/410 8
Sch 6(2)

An explanation of any significant award made to past directors during the year.

7A Sch 14
SI 2008/410 8
Sch 15
LR 9.8.8(2)(c)

Details of any significant award made in the year to any person who was not a director of the company at the time the award was made but had previously been a director of the company.

External appointments

CC B.1.4

Where a company releases an executive director to serve as a non-executive director elsewhere, a statement is required as to whether or not the director will retain such earnings, and if so, what the remuneration is.

7A Sch 15
SI 2008/410 8
Sch 16

For each director who served as a director at any time during the year, the aggregate amount of consideration paid to or receivable by third parties for making available the services of the director.

APB bull 2002/2
p 12-16

Where the remuneration report does not clarify which parts of the report have been audited, such clarification should be included in the audit report.

Corporate governance requirements

The details of compliance and policy will usually be set out as a remuneration committee report. Section 234C(1) of the Companies Act 1985 (section 422(1) of the Companies Act 2006) requires that this must be approved by the board as it is the board's responsibility to report to shareholders. Schedule 7A of the Companies Act 1985 (Schedule 8 to SI 2008/410) and paragraph 9.8.8R of the Listing Rules contain information to be included in the report.

s241A
CA06 s439(1)

The board should put an ordinary resolution to shareholders for approval of the remuneration report.

CC B.1
CC B.1.1

A significant proportion of executive directors' remuneration should be structured so as to link rewards to corporate and individual performance and should be designed to align their interests with those of shareholders. In designing schemes of performance-related remuneration, remuneration committees should follow the provisions of Schedule A to the Combined Code.

IFRS GAAP plc
16

CC.B.1.3 The remuneration of all non-executive directors should reflect the time commitment and responsibilities of the role. Their remuneration should not include share options.

CC B.1.5 The remuneration committee should carefully consider what compensation commitments (including pension contributions and all other elements) their directors' terms of appointment would entail in the event of early termination. The aim should be to avoid rewarding poor performance. They should take a robust line on reducing compensation to reflect departing directors' obligations to mitigate loss.

CC B.2.1
CC B.2.2 To avoid potential conflicts of interest, boards of directors should set up remuneration committees of independent non-executive directors to make recommendations to the board, within agreed terms of reference, on the company's framework of executive remuneration and its cost; and to determine on their behalf the level and structure of remuneration for senior management, including pension rights and any compensation payments. The remuneration committee's terms of reference should be publicly available (that is, available on request and on the company's web site).

CC B.2.2 The definition of senior management is determined by the board but would normally include the first layer of management below board level.

CC B.2 The chairman of the board should ensure that the company maintains contact as required with its principal shareholders about remuneration in the same way as for other matters.

Remuneration report for the year ended 31 December 2008[1]

(Amounts in C thousands unless otherwise stated).

This part of the remuneration report is unaudited.

Remuneration committee
The members of the remuneration committee during the year were:
R Graham (Chairman)
Lord Callender
N Chamois
A Cartwright

All the members of the remuneration committee are non-executive directors and are considered to be independent.

The remuneration committee is responsible for setting all aspects of executive directors' remuneration and for monitoring the remuneration of senior management. The terms of reference of the remuneration committee are available on the group's website at www.IFRSGAAPplc.com. The remuneration of non-executive directors is determined by the board within the limits set by the company's Articles of Association.

Advice to the remuneration committee
During the year, the following parties were appointed by the remuneration committee to provide advice that materially assisted the remuneration committee:
Accounting Services Limited
E F Logan (HR Director)
NS Watkins (Group senior payroll manager)
Accounting Services Limited also provided advice on personal tax issues to the group.

Remuneration policy
CC B.1 The company's policy on remuneration of directors is to attract, retain and motivate the best people, recognising the input they have to the ongoing success of the business.

7A Sch3(1)
SI 2008/410 8
Sch 3(1)
CC B.1.1
LR 9.8.8(1) Consistent with this policy, the benefit packages awarded by IFRS GAAP plc to directors are intended to be competitive and comprise a mix of performance-related and non-performance-related remuneration designed to incentivise directors and align their interests with those of shareholders.

---

[1] Please note that the content of the remuneration report is not intended to illustrate good practice in executive pay arrangements.

IFRS GAAP plc   17

The remuneration consists of the following elements:

Base pay

7A Sch3(1)
SI 2008/410 8
Sch 3(1)
LR 9.8.8(1)

Executive directors base pay is designed to reflect individual's capabilities and role within the business. Salary levels are reviewed annually and targeted at the median position against similar industries and the FTSE 100.

Annual Bonus and deferred shares

7A Sch3(1)
SI 2008/410 8
Sch 3(1)
LR 9.8.8(1)
LR 9.8.8(10)

All executive directors participate in the company's annual bonus scheme. Subject to the achievement of individual and company performance targets, the remuneration committee may award bonuses of up to 50% of the director's basic salary. Financial targets represent 75% of the bonus award and include EPS, turnover and operating profit measures, each given equal weighting; the remaining 25% of the bonus is awarded on the satisfaction of individual targets. Half of each director's bonus is awarded in cash with the remainder taking the form of deferred shares in IFRS GAAP plc, which are held in trust for a period of three years before they are released to the director. In the event that the director leaves the company, these shares may be immediately released to the director at the discretion of the remuneration committee. Dividends accrue to the directors from the date the bonus is awarded.

There have been no changes to the policy from the preceding year and no departures from this policy in the current year. The current policy is expected to continue in place through the next financial year, during which a detailed review of the remuneration policy is to be undertaken for the year 2010.

Long-term incentive scheme

7ASch3(1), (2)
SI 2008/410 8
Sch 3(1), (2)
LR 9.8.8 (10)

The long-term incentive scheme rewards future performance of the directors by linking the size of the award to the increase in shareholder return. Share options under the LTIS are granted at the discretion of the remuneration committee, up to a maximum value of 100% of salary. For the current year, shares were awarded under the long-term incentive scheme at the maximum level.

Shares vest after three years, subject to the achievement of the performance conditions attached to the share options. The vesting condition is dependent on the company's 'total shareholder return' (TSR) compared with the Total Shareholder Return of all companies in the FTSE 100 over the three year period from the date of grant. If the company's cumulative TSR over the three year period is in the upper quartile of the comparator group, the options will vest in full. If the company's TSR over that period is in the second quartile, 50% of the options will vest. If the company is in the third or fourth quartiles, the options will lapse. Share options that vest must be exercised within five years of the vesting date, otherwise the shares will lapse. The committee has selected the TSR performance condition as the committee believes that this best aligns the interests of the directors with those of the shareholders.

In the event that a director resigns, any options that have not vested or have not been exercised will lapse.

Share option scheme

It is the board's intention to continue to award shares to all executive directors under the group's share option scheme. The shares awarded will vest after a period of three years if the performance condition attached to the share options is met and the director is still in employment. Vesting will be dependent on an average annual increase in earnings per share (as reported in the financial statements) of at least the growth in the UK retail price index plus 4%. The committee feels that this scheme rewards the directors for their contribution towards the long-term profitability of the group. In the event that a director resigns as a director, the awards will lapse. In any year the value of shares notionally awarded to a director under this scheme will not exceed that director's salary.

DV – p2.1 of
ABI guidelines
Dec 2006

The remuneration committee has reviewed the current policy on both the long-term incentive scheme and the share option scheme as regards to their operation, including how discretion has been exercised and including grant levels, performance criteria and vesting schedules during the year. The committee feels the current policy remains appropriate to the company's current circumstances and prospects.

There have been no changes to the policy from the preceding year and no departures from this policy in the current year. The current policy is expected to continue in place through the next financial year, during which a detailed review of the remuneration policy is to be undertaken for the year 2010.

IFRS GAAP plc

7A Sch3(3)
SI 2008/410 8
Sch 3(3)
CC B.1.1

If the TSR growth under the long-term incentive scheme is on target, such that 50% of the LTIS options will vest and also assuming that 100% of the share options under the group's share option scheme will vest, the composition of each executive director's remuneration will be as follows:

	Non-performance related Basic salary	Performance related Bonus	Performance related LTIS and Share option scheme
C D Suede	36%	11%	53%
G Wallace	36%	11%	53%
F Leather	37%	8%	55%
E F Logan	36%	10%	54%

SI 2008/410 8
Sch 4

Statement of consideration of conditions elsewhere in the group[1]

In determining remuneration, consideration will be given to reward levels throughout the organisation as well as in the external employment market. The remuneration committee aim to reward all employees fairly based on their role, their performance and salary levels in the wider market.

In the year under review, the average base salary increase for the executive directors was 5% and for all other staff was 2%.

Director pension schemes

All executive directors are members of the final salary defined benefit pension arrangements. In addition, Mr Suede and Mr Wallace also participate in the US defined contribution pension arrangement.

Non-executive directors remuneration

CC B.1.3

Non-executive directors receive a fee of C10,000 per year. In addition, Mr R Graham receives an additional fee of C2,000 per year for chairing the remuneration committee, reflecting the additional responsibilities of that role. Non-executive directors do not participate in the company's share option scheme, long-term incentive scheme or pension schemes.[2]

External appointments

CC B.1.4

During the year, Mr E F Logan has served as a non-executive director with E Group plc. He has retained his earnings in respect of this service of C15,000 (2007: C12,500).

Directors' service contracts

CC B.1.6
7ASch3(4)
SI 2008/410 8
Sch 3(4)

It is IFRS GAAP plc's policy that executive directors' service contracts have a notice period of not more than one year. There are no contractual termination payments.

Non-executive directors are appointed for an initial period of three years. Their service contracts are terminable by either the company or the directors themselves with six months' notice. It is IFRS GAAP plc's policy that non-executive directors may serve a maximum of a three-year term. Thereafter, they are reappointed annually.

---

[1] Effective for accounting periods commencing on or after 6 April 2009.

[2] If exceptionally, options are granted to non-executive directors, shareholder approval should be sought in advance and any shares acquired by the exercise of options should be held for at least one year after the non-executive leaves the board. Holding of share options could be relevant in determining a non-executive director's independence.

IFRS GAAP plc

The details of the service contracts of those who served as directors during the year are:

	Contract date	Notice period
Executive Directors		
C D Suede	27 May 04	1 year
G Wallace	15 Sep 04	1 year
F Leather	07 Jan 03	1 year
E F Logan	26 Feb 03	9 months
D Scott[a]	02 Oct 03	6 months
Non-Executive Directors		
R Graham[b]	08 Sep 08	6 months
Lord Callender	24 Jun 06	6 months
N Chamois[b]	03 Dec 08	6 months
A Cartwright	13 Oct 07	6 months

7ASch5
SI 2008/410
8 Sch 6
LR 9.8.8R (9)

[a] Mr D Scott resigned on 29 March 2008 and, consequently, his contract was terminated.

LR 9.8.8R (8)

[b] Mr R Graham and Mr N Chamois will retire by rotation and seek re-election at the AGM. As non-executive directors both R Graham and N Chamois have service contracts with the company. The agreements require that the company give them 6 months notice of termination. Biographical details of the directors standing for re-election are given in the corporate governance report.

Performance graph

7A Sch 4(1)
SI 2008/410 8
Sch 5(1)

The graph provided below shows the group's TSR performance against the FTSE 100 over the past five years. In the opinion of the directors, the FTSE 100 is the most appropriate index against which the total shareholder return of IFRS GAAP plc should be measured because it is an index of similar-sized companies to IFRS GAAP plc. The calculations assume the reinvestment of dividends.

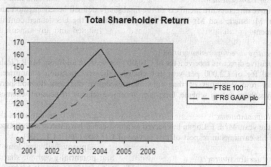

Total Shareholder Return

Source: Date Limited

Requirements for the directors' remuneration report – remuneration package (audited)

LR 9.8.8 (2) (a),
(b)

Amounts of each element of the remuneration package for each director (executive and non-executive) by name from all sources, and in total for both current and prior years, including but not restricted to:

7A Sch 6(1)
SI 2008/410 8
Sch 7(1)

- Basic salary and fees.
- Estimated money value of benefits in kind other than those disclosed in other bullet point headings.
- Bonuses.
- Total amount of expense allowances that are (or would be if the director was an individual) chargeable to UK income tax.
- Compensation for loss of office/payments for breach of contract/other termination payments.

7A Sch 6(2)
SI 2008/410 8
Sch 7(2)

- Total remuneration for each director for current and corresponding accounting period.

7A Sch 6 (3)-(4)
SI 2008/410 8
Sch 7(3)-(4)
LR 9.8.4R (5),(6)

Such details should be in tabular form and the nature of any non-cash element of a remuneration package must be stated. Disclosure should be made of any arrangements to waive any emoluments (both current and future).

IFRS GAAP plc   20

LR 9.8.8R(7) CC Sch A (6),(7)	In general, only basic salary should be pensionable. There must be explanations and justifications given for any elements of remuneration except basic salary which are pensionable. The remuneration committee should consider the pension consequences and associated costs of basic salary increases and any other changes in pensionable remuneration, especially for directors nearing retirement.
7A Sch 14 SI 2008/410 8 Sch 15 LR 9.8.8R(2)(a)	Significant payments to former directors made during the current accounting period that have not been included in the table should be disclosed separately.
LR 9.8.8R(1), (2)(d) 7A Sch 7 SI 2008/410 8 Sch 8	Information on share options including SAYE options should be given for each director, by name. Such details should be in tabular form and explanations should be given where necessary.
CC Sch A (5)	There should be an explanation and justification where share options are awarded in large blocks rather than phased.
LR 9.8.8R(3)	Details of long-term incentive schemes, including the following, for each director, by name:

- Interests at the start (or date of appointment, if late) and end of the period (or date of cessation, if earlier).
- Details of entitlements/awards granted and commitments made to each director during the period, showing which crystallised in the same period or later periods.
- Number of shares, with award date and market price on that date and on vesting date, performance conditions, cash payments and value of other assets receivable by each director under such schemes during the period.
- Dates when qualifying conditions have to be fulfilled and any variation in terms and conditions of scheme interests.

Notes:

LR 9.4.3R	(a) Additional disclosures are required in the first annual report published following the date on which the relevant director becomes eligible to participate in an arrangement in which that director is the only participant and the arrangement is established specifically to facilitate, in unusual circumstances, the recruitment or retention of that director.
CC Sch A(5)	(b) There should be an explanation and justification where incentives are awarded in large blocks rather than phased.
CC B.2.4	(c) Shareholders should be invited specifically to approve all new long-term incentive schemes (including share option schemes) that potentially commit shareholders' funds over more than one year or dilute the equity, save as permitted by LR 9.4.2R and significant changes to existing schemes.
CC B.1.2	Executive share options should not be offered at a discount save as permitted by LR 9.4.6.

The remuneration report should include the following for defined benefit pension schemes for each director by name:

LR 9.8.8(12)	• Amount of the increase in accrued benefit during the year (excluding inflation). • The accrued benefit as at the year end. • The transfer value of the relevant increase in accrued benefit as at the year end or specific information to enable this value to be calculated.
7ASch12 SI 2008/410 8 Sch 13	• The change in accrued benefits during the year under the scheme.

- The accrued benefit at the end of the year.
- The transfer value at the end of the year of the accrued benefits.
- The transfer value of accrued benefits at the previous year end in respect of qualifying services.
- The increase in the transfer value in respect of qualifying services in the year less the director's contributions.

IFRS GAAP plc

Notes:

(a) It should be made clear that the transfer value represents a liability of the company, but not a sum paid or due to the individual; and that it cannot meaningfully be added to annual remuneration.

(b) Where the group makes provisions in respect of unfunded pensions of a defined benefit type, it should take the related benefits provided to directors into account when determining the amounts to be disclosed in respect of directors' pension entitlements under defined benefit schemes

7A Sch 12(3) SI 2008/410 8 Sch 13(3) LR 9.8.8R(11)	The details of the contribution or allowance payable or made by the company for money purchase (that is, defined contribution) schemes should be disclosed for each director by name. Disclosure includes provisions for unfunded money purchase benefits as well as actual contributions paid or payable to a scheme.
LR 9.8.8R(12)(c)	No disclosure of voluntary contributions and benefits for defined benefit schemes is required.
LR 9.8.4(5)(6)	■ Give details of any arrangement under which a director has waived or agreed to waive any emoluments from the company or any subsidiary. ■ Where a director has agreed to waive future emoluments, give details of such waiver together with those relating to emoluments which were waived in the year. ■ Where an executive director is released to serve as non-executive director elsewhere, state whether remuneration is retained.

Continuation of the Remuneration report for the year ended 31 December 2008

(Amounts in C thousands unless otherwise stated).

This part of the remuneration report is audited.

Directors' detailed emoluments

LR 9.8.8R(2)(a)

7A Sch 6
(1),(2),(4)
SI 2008/410 8
Sch 7(1), (2), (4)

						2008	2007
Executive	Salary and fees	Benefits in kinds	Expense allowance	Annual bonus	Compensation for loss of office	Total	Total
C D Suede	132	29	–	41	–	**202**	140
G Wallace	107	24	–	33	–	**164**	118
F Leather	161	13	5	34	-	**213**	174
E F Logan	63	13	–	18	–	**94**	24
D Scott	31	3	–	8	103	**145**	73
J Rush	–	–	–	–	–	**–**	92
Non-executive							
R Graham (chairman)	12	–	–	–	–	**12**	10
Lord Callender	10	–	–	–	–	**10**	10
N Chamois	10	–	–	–	–	**10**	10
A Cartwright	10	–	–	–	–	**10**	10
	536	82	5	134	103	**860**	661

7A Sch 6(3) SI 2008/410 8 Sch 7(3)	Benefits in kind include the provision of a company car, fuel, financial counselling and medical and life insurance for every executive director. In addition, C D Suede and E Wallace have the use of a driver.
CC Sch A (2)	Half of each executive director's annual bonus comprises shares in IFRS GAAP plc. Shares awarded in this way are required to be held for three years.
7A Sch 15 (1) SI 2008/410 8 Sch 16(1) LR 9.8.8R(2)(a)	Salary and fees include an amount of C54,000 (2007: C63,000) paid to third parties in respect of making available the services of Mr F Leather to the company.
7A Sch 6(1)(d), 6(3) SI 2008/410 8 Sch 7(1)(d), 7(3)	The compensation for loss of office payment to Mr D Scott who resigned on 29 March 2008 includes the monetary value of a car retained by the director, a contribution to his personal money purchase pension plan and a cash bonus. The discretionary elements of this compensation were approved by the remuneration committee and were paid in respect of his past service to the company.

IFRS GAAP plc   22

<table>
<tr><td>7A Sch 5(2), 14
SI 2008/410 8
Sch 6 (2)
LR 9.8.8R2(c)</td><td>In addition to the payments included in the table above, C100,000 (2007: Cnil) was paid to Mr K W Grommitt, who resigned as a director in 2003. This sum was in respect of a claim by Mr Grommitt for unfair dismissal and represents the contractual entitlement under his then service contract, plus interest thereon, which was withheld by the company pending the outcome of the litigation.</td></tr>
<tr><td>LR 9.8.4R(5),(6)</td><td>No director waived emoluments in respect of the years ended 31 December 2008 or 31 December 2007.</td></tr>
<tr><td>7A Sch 13 (1)
SI 2008/410 8
Sch 14(1)
LR 9.8.8R(2)(a)</td><td>In addition to the amounts included in the table above an additional pension of C11,376 (2007: Cnil) was paid to Mr J Rush in the year in connection with his retirement in 2007. The payment is in excess of Mr Rush's normal entitlement under the group's defined benefit pension scheme arrangements.</td></tr>
<tr><td>DV</td><td>In the year ended 31 December 2007, C87,000 was paid in respect of compensation for loss of office to Mr J Rush, former director. This amount is included in the amount disclosed for Mr Rush in the table above.</td></tr>
</table>

Share schemes

Date of grant	Earliest exercise date	Expiry date	Exercise price (C)	Number at 1 January 2008 (C1 shares)	Granted in year	Exercised in year	Lapsed in year	Number at 31 December 2008 (C1 shares)*
CD Suede								
01 Jul 00	01 Jul 03	30 Jun 08	1.10	500	–	500	–	–
01 Jul 01	01 Jul 04	30 Jun 09	1.20	55,000	–	55,000	–	–
01 Jul 04	01 Jul 07	30 Jun 12	1.35	300,000	–	55,000	–	245,000
01 Jul 06	01 Jul 09	30 Jun 14	2.00	100,000	–	–	–	100,000
01 Jul 07	01 Jul 10	30 Jun 15	2.38	500,000	–	–	–	500,000
01 Jul 08	01 Jul 11	30 Jun 16	2.95		300,000	–	–	300,000
				955,500	300,000	110,500	–	1,145,000
G Wallace								
01 Jul 06	01 Jul 09	30 Jun 14	2.00	75,000	–	–	–	75,000
01 Jul 07	01 Jul 10	30 Jun 15	2.38	120,000	–	–	–	120,000
01 Jul 08	01 Jul 11	30 Jun 16	2.95	–	80,000	–	–	80,000
				195,000	80,000	–	–	275,000
D Scott								
01 Jul 06	01 Jul 09	30 Jun 14	2.00	25,000	–	–	25,000	–
01 Jul 07	01 Jul 10	30 Jun 15	2.38	100,000	–	–	100,000	–
				125,000	–	–	125,000	–
F Leather								
01 Jul 01	01 Jul 04	30 Jun 09	1.20	50,000	–	50,000	–	–
01 Jul 04	01 Jul 07	30 Jun 12	1.35	50,000	–	50,000	–	–
01 Jul 06	01 Jul 09	30 Jun 14	2.00	300,000	–	–	–	300,000
01 Jul 07	01 Jul 10	30 Jun 15	2.38	400,000	–	–	–	400,000
01 Jul 08	01 Jul 11	30 Jun 16	2.95	–	250,000	–	–	250,000
				800,000	250,000	100,000	–	950,000
E F Logan								
01 Jul 07	01 Jul 10	30 Jun 15	2.38	200,000	–	–	–	200,000
01 Jul 08	01 Jul 11	30 Jun 16	2.95	–	95,000	–	–	95,000
				200,000	95,000	–	–	295,000

* Or date of resignation, if earlier.

<table>
<tr><td>7A Sch 8(d)
SI 2008/410 8
Sch 9(d)</td><td>No other directors have been granted share options in the shares in the company or other group entities. None of the terms and conditions of the share options was varied during the year. All options were granted in respect of qualifying services.</td></tr>
</table>

IFRS GAAP plc

7A Sch 8(c)(i), 8(e) The options were granted at nil cost to the directors and were in respect of past performance.
SI 2008/410 8 The performance criteria for all the above share options were consistent with the remuneration
Sch 9(c)(i), 9(e) policy. Once the award has vested, the exercise of the share options is unconditional.

7A Sch 8(g) The market price of the company's shares at the end of the financial year was 290p and the range
SI 2008/410 8 of market prices during the year was between 210p and 293p.
Sch 9(g)

7A Sch 8(f) The market price when Mr C D Suede and Mr F Leather exercised their share options was 275p.
SI 2008/410 8
Sch 9(f)

Long-term incentive scheme

LR 9.8.8R(3), **Directors' interests in the long-term incentive plan**
(4), (5), (6)

7A Sch 10, 11 Shares awarded to executive directors and former directors under the long-term incentive plan
SI 2008/410 8 are as follows:
Sch 11, 12

	Cycle ending	Award date	At 1 January 2008 Number	Shares awarded Number	Shares vested Number	Shares lapsed	At 31 Dec 2008* Number	Value vested C'000	Vesting date
C D Suede	2007	01 Jul 04	30,000	–	(15,000)	(15,000)	0	40	01 Jul 07
	2008	01 Jul 05	25,000	–	–	–	25,000	–	01 Jul 08
	2009	01 Jul 06	33,000	–	–	–	33,000	–	01 Jul 09
	2010	01 Jul 07	–	20,000	–	–	20,000	–	01 Jul 10
G Wallace	2008	01 Jul 05	10,000	–	–	–	10,000	–	01 Jul 08
	2009	01 Jul 06	8,000	–	–	–	8,000	–	01 Jul 09
	2010	01 Jul 07	–	7,000	–	–	7,000	–	01 Jul 10
D Scott	2007	01 Jul 04	22,000	–	–	(22,000)	–	–	01 Jul 07
	2008	01 Jul 05	15,000	–	–	(15,000)	–	–	01 Jul 08
	2009	01 Jul 06	17,000	–	–	(17,000)	–	–	01 Jul 09
	2010	01 Jul 07	–	7,000	–	(7,000)	–	–	01 Jul 10
F Leather	2007	01 Jul 04	27,500	–	(13,750)	(13,750)	–	36	01 Jul 07
	2008	01 Jul 05	25,000	–	–	–	25,000	–	01 Jul 08
	2009	01 Jul 06	33,000	–	–	–	33,000	–	01 Jul 09
	2010	01 Jul 07	–	28,750	–	–	20,000	–	01 Jul 10
Totals of awards vested in 2008				**28,750**				**76**	

* or if earlier on date of retirement Mr D Scott retired on 29 March 2008 and all his share options under the
long-term incentive scheme lapsed on this date.

7A Sch11(3)(c) The market price on 1 July 2005 was 155p, on 1 July 2006 was 230p, on 1 July 2007 was 274p
SI 2008/410 8 and on 1 July 2008 was 339p.
Sch 12(3)(c)

IFRS GAAP plc

7A Sch11(3)(e) SI 2008/410 8 Sch 12(3)(e)	The performance criteria attached to the awards that vested on 1 July 2008 and those awarded on the same date was TSR versus companies in the FTSE 100. If the company's cumulative TSR over the three year period is in the upper quartile of the comparator group, the options will vest in full. If the company's TSR over that period is in the second quartile, 50% of the options will vest. If the company is in the third or fourth quartiles, the options will lapse. For the options that vested on 1 July 2008, the TSR was in the second quartile, therefore 50% of the award vested.
7A Sch11(1)(d) SI 2008/410 8 Sch 12(1)(d)	There have been no variations in the terms and conditions of scheme interests during the year.
7A Sch11(1)(e) SI 2008/410 8 Sch 12(1)(e)	The shares awarded in July 2005 vested on 1 July 2008; based on the performance of the company over the three year period ended on that date the shares vested as to 50 per cent. The gain attributable to each director will be disclosed as remuneration in 2008.
DV	Any shares issued arising from meeting the requisite performance criteria on the conditional shares awarded in July 2006, July 2007 and July 2008 will vest in July 2009, July 2010 and July 2011 respectively. At 31 December 2008 the performance percentage reflecting performance to date, was 50% for the shares awarded in July 2006 and July 2007 and 100% for the shares awarded in July 2008.

Pensions

Directors' pension entitlement

7A Sch 12(2) SI 2008/410 8 Sch 13(2)	Set out below are details of the pension benefits to which each of the executive directors is entitled:

	Additional accrued benefits earned in the year C'000	Accrued entitlement C'000	Transfer value at 31 December 2008 C'000	Transfer value at 31 December 2007 C'000	Increase in transfer value less directors' contributions C'000
C D Suede	28	181	1,719	1,472	236
G Wallace	31	98	962	684	269
F Leather	18	103	984	820	153
E F Logan	26	94	907	687	215
D Scott*	7	27	243	194	41

	Additional accrued benefits earned in the year (excluding inflation) C'000	Transfer value of increase in accrued benefits less directors' contributions C'000
C D Suede	26	173
G Wallace	28	184
F James	16	113
F Leather	25	164
D Scott*	7	36

* Mr D Scott retired from the company on 29 March 2008.

7A Sch 12 2(a)(ii) SI 2008/410 8 Sch 13(2)(a)(ii) LR 9.8.8R(12)(a)	The accrued pension entitlement is the amount that the director would receive if he retired at the end of the year.
	The increase in the accrued entitlement is the difference between the accrued benefit at the year end and that at the previous year end. The Listing Rules require this to be disclosed excluding inflation.

IFRS GAAP plc 25

7A Sch 12(2)(b)
SI 2008/410 8
Sch 13(2)(b)
LR 9.8.8R(12)(b)
All transfer values have been calculated on the basis of actuarial advice in accordance with Actuarial Guidance Note GN 11. The transfer values of the accrued entitlement represent the value of assets that the pension scheme would need to transfer to another pension provider on transferring the scheme's liability in respect of the directors' pension benefits. They do not represent sums payable to individual directors and, therefore, cannot be added meaningfully to annual remuneration.

7A Sch 12(2)(d)
SI 2008/410 8
Sch 13(2)(d)
The increase in the transfer value less directors' contributions is the increase in the transfer value of the accrued benefits during the year after deducting the director's personal contributions to the scheme.

The transfer value of the increase in accrued benefits, required by the Listing Rules, discloses the current value of the increase in accrued benefits that the director has earned in the period, whereas the change in his transfer value, required by the Companies Act discloses the absolute increase or decrease in his/her transfer value and includes the change in value of the accrued benefits that results from market volatility affecting the transfer value at the beginning of the period, as well as the additional value earned in the year.

7A Sch 12(3)
SI 2008/410 8
Sch 13(3)
Mr C D Suede and Mr G Wallace also participate in a US defined contribution pension arrangement. During the year the group contributed C54,000 (2007: Cnil) and C18,000 (2007: Cnil) respectively.

Gains made by directors on share options

The table below shows gains made by individual directors from the exercise of share options during 2008. The gains are calculated as at the exercise date, although the shares may have been retained.

	2008 C'000	2007 C'000
C D Suede	163	99
F Leather	148	58
Total gains on share options	**311**	157

This part of the remuneration report is unaudited.

Interests in shares (and derivatives or any other financial instrument relating to those shares)[1]

LR 9.8.6R(1)
The interests of the directors and their connected persons in the shares of the company and other group members were:

	1 January 2008	31 December 2008
The company – ordinary shares 1p		
Executive directors		
C D Suede	1,000,000	1,110,500
G Wallace	110,000	110,000
F Leather	–	27,500
EF Logan	–	1,500
Non-executive directors		
R Graham	80,000	80,000
Lord Callender	25,000	25,000
Executive directors		
A Limited – ordinary shares C1		
F Leather	10,000	10,000
Non-executive directors		
T Limited – preference shares 50c		
A Cartwright	5,000	5,000

[1] This disclosure is only required by the Listing Rules.

IFRS GAAP plc 26

LR 9.8.6R(1) There has been no change in the interests set out above between 31 December 2008 and 28 March 2009.

On behalf of the board
R Graham
Chairman of the remuneration committee[1] 28 March 2009

---

[1] The remuneration report should be approved by the board and signed on its behalf by a director or the company secretary. The remuneration report includes the requirements of Schedule 7A to the Companies Act 1985 (Schedule 8 to SI 2008/410). In addition, Schedule 6 to the Companies Act 1985 (Schedule 5 to SI 2008/410) requires certain aggregate information on emoluments to be included by quoted companies in the notes to the financial statements.

IFRS GAAP plc 27

Corporate governance

Application of the Combined Code

The Combined Code on corporate governance issued in June 2008 (Combined Code (2008)) contains only a limited number of modifications to the Combined Code (2006). The Combined Code (2008) takes effect for reporting periods commencing on or after 29 June 2008.

DTR 7.2.2, 7.2.3(1)(a)   The corporate governance statement must state which Combined Code the company is subject to and where a copy of that code is publicly available (www.frc.org).

Compliance

LR 9.8.6(5)   A statement should be made of how the company has applied the principles in section 1 of the Combined Code that enables shareholders to evaluate how the principles have been applied. (For periods beginning on or after 29 June 2008, companies need comment on how the main principles only have been applied.) It is noted that the form and content of this part of the statement are not prescribed, with the intention being that companies can explain their governance policies in light of the Combined Code principles, although the Preamble to the Combined Code 2008 does contain some guidance in this area.

LR 9.8.6(6)
DTR 7.2.3 (1)(b), (2), (3)   A statement as to whether the company has complied throughout the accounting period with all relevant Combined Code provisions set out in section 1 should be made. Where the company has not complied with all of the provisions, or has complied for only part of the accounting period, then a statement to that effect should be made specifying the provisions that have not been complied with and where details of the company's corporate governance practices can be found. Reasons should also be given for any non-compliance and where relevant the period of non-compliance should be stated.

The board

CC A.1.1
DTR 7.2.7   A statement should be made about how the board operates, including a high level statement of which types of decisions are taken by the board and which are delegated to management.

CC A.1.1   *Note: The board should meet sufficiently regularly to discharge its duties effectively. There should be a formal schedule of matters specifically reserved for its decision.*

CC A.1.2   The annual report should identify:

- The chairman.
- The deputy chairman (where applicable).
- The chief executive.
- The senior independent director.
- The chairman and members of each of the nomination, audit and remuneration committees.

CC A.1.2   It should also set out the number of meetings of the board and each committee and individual attendance by directors.

Notes:

CC A.2.1   *(a) The roles of chairman and chief executive should not be exercised by the same individual. Division of responsibilities should be clearly established, set out in writing and agreed by the board.*

CC A.1.5   *(b) The company should arrange appropriate insurance cover in respect of legal action against its directors.*

CC A.1.4   *(c) Directors' concerns about the running of the company or a proposed action which cannot be resolved should be recorded in the board minutes. On resignation, non-executive directors should provide a written statement to the chairman, for circulation to the board, if they have any such concerns.*

CC A.4.1, B.2.1, C.3.3   *(d) The terms of reference of the nomination, audit and remuneration committees, including each committee's role and authority delegated to it by the board, should be made publicly available. The recommendation can be met by making the information available on the company's web site.*

IFRS GAAP plc

28

Re-election of directors

CC A.7.1 The names of directors submitted for election or re-election should be accompanied by sufficient biographical details to enable shareholders to make an informed decision on their election.

Notes:

CC A.4.1 *(a) A nomination committee should be established to make recommendations to the board on all new board appointments.*

CC A.7.2 *(b) Non-executive directors should be appointed for specified terms subject to re-election and to Companies Act provisions relating to the removal of a director. Any term beyond six years should be subject to rigorous review. For terms in excess of nine years, non-executive directors should be subject to annual re-election. Re-appointment should not be automatic.*

CC A.7.1 *(c) All directors should be subject to election by shareholders at the first AGM after their appointment and to re-election thereafter at intervals of no more than three years.*

Notes:

(a) The details above that are referenced to the Combined Code may be provided in other suitable positions within the annual report, such as the remuneration report, the corporate governance report or the list of directors and advisers.

CC C.3.1, CC B.2.1 *(b) The audit committee and remuneration committee should each comprise a minimum of three members, or in the case of smaller companies (that is, those below the FTSE 350 throughout the year immediately prior to the reporting year) two members, confined to independent non-executive directors.*

CC B.2.1 *(c) The company chairman may also be a member of, but not chair, the remuneration committee if he or she was considered independent on appointment. This is in addition to the three (or two, for smaller companies) independent non-executive directors.*

CC C.3.1 *(d) For smaller companies, for periods commencing on or after 29 June 2008, the company chairman may also be a member of, but not chair, the audit committee if he or she was considered independent on appointment. This is in addition to the two independent non-executive directors.*

CC A.4.1 *(e) The nomination committee should have a majority of independent non-executive directors and the chairman should be either the chairman of the board (but the chairman should not chair the nomination committee when it is dealing with the appointment of a successor to the chairmanship) or an independent non-executive director.*

CC A.6.1 The report should state how performance evaluations of the board, its committees and its individual directors have been conducted.

Notes:

CC A.1.3, CC A.6.1 *(a) The chairman should hold meetings with the non-executive directors (without the executive directors present). At least annually the non-executives should meet, without the chairman present, to appraise the chairman's performance, and on such other occasions as appropriate, such meetings being led by the senior independent non-executive director.*

CC A.2.2 *(b) A chief executive should not go on to be chairman of a company. If, exceptionally, the board decides that a chief executive should become chairman, the reasons for that appointment should be set out in the annual report.*

CC A.2.2 *(c) On appointment, the chairman should meet the independence criteria set out below.*

CC A.3.1 The annual report should identify the non-executive directors that are considered to be independent. If the board considers a director to be independent, but circumstances or relationships exist that may appear relevant to that decision, disclosure should be made of the reasons for determining that director to be independent.

IFRS GAAP plc

Notes:

CC A.3.1   *(a) Circumstances that could appear to affect a director's independence will include:*

- *Employment with the company or group within the last five years.*
- *A material business relationship within the last three years between the company and the director, or a body of which he/she is a partner, shareholder, director or senior employee.*
- *Any entitlement to remuneration from the company other than a director's fee or participation in the share option or performance-related pay scheme or membership of the company's pension scheme.*
- *Close family ties between the director and any of the company's advisers, directors or senior employees.*
- *A cross-directorship or significant links with other directors through involvement in other companies or bodies.*
- *Representing a significant shareholder.*
- *More than nine years' service on the board.*

CC A.3.2   *(b) At least half the board, excluding the chairman, should comprise independent non-executive directors. A smaller company (that is, companies that were below the FTSE 350 throughout the year immediately prior to the reporting year) should have at least two independent non-executive directors.*

CC A.3.3   *(c) An independent non-executive director should be appointed by the board as the senior independent director. This director should be available to shareholders if they have concerns which contact through the normal channels of chairman, chief executive or finance director has failed to resolve or for which such contact is inappropriate.*

CC A4.3   Disclosure should be made of the chairman's other significant commitments and any changes to these during the year.

Notes:

CC A.4.3   *(a) The nomination committee should prepare a job specification for the appointment of a chairman, including an assessment of the time commitment expected, recognising the need for availability in the event of crises.*

CC A.4.4   *(b) The terms and conditions of appointment of non-executive directors should be made available for inspection (at the company's registered office during business hours and at the AGM (for 15 minutes before the meeting and during the meeting).*

CC A.4.4   *(c) Letters of appointment should set out the expected time commitment. Non-executive directors should undertake that they will have sufficient time to meet what is expected of them. Their other significant commitments should be disclosed to the board before appointment, and upon subsequent changes.*

CC A.4.5   *(d) The board should not agree to a full time executive director taking on more than one non-executive directorship in a FTSE 100 company nor the chairmanship of such a company.*

CC B.1.4   *(e) Where a company releases an executive director to serve as a non-executive director elsewhere, the remuneration report should include a statement as to whether or not the director will retain such earnings and, if so, what the remuneration is.*

CC A.5.2   *(f) All directors should have access to independent professional advice, at the expense of the company, where they judge it necessary to discharge their responsibilities as directors.*

CC A.5.3   *(g) All directors should have access to the advice and services of the company secretary who is responsible to the board for ensuring that board procedures are complied with. The appointment and removal of the company secretary should be a matter for the board as a whole.*

IFRS GAAP plc

Report of the nomination committee

Notes:

CC A.4.1   *(a) The nomination committee should lead the process for board appointments and make recommendations to the board. The majority of the committee should be independent non-executive directors.*

CC A.4.2   *(b) The nomination committee should evaluate the balance of skills, knowledge and experience on the board and, in the light of this evaluation, prepare a description of the role for new appointments.*

CC A.4.6   A separate section describing the work of the nomination committees should be given in the annual report. This should include the process used in relation to board appointments and an explanation if neither external search consultancy nor open advertising has been used in the appointment of a chairman or non-executive director.

CC A.5.1   *Note: The chairman should ensure that new directors receive full, formal and tailored induction on joining the board, part of which should be an opportunity for major shareholders to meet new non-executive directors.*

Report of the audit committee

Notes:

CC C.3.1
DTR 7.1.1, 7.1.2   *(a) The audit committee should consist of at least three (or for smaller companies, two) members, all of whom are independent non-executive directors and at least one of whom has recent and relevant financial experience.*

CC C.3.2
DTR 7.1 3   *(b) The audit committee should have written terms of reference setting out its responsibilities that should include:*

- *Monitoring the integrity of the company's financial statements and announcements relating to financial performance and reviewing significant financial reporting judgements contained in them.*
- *Reviewing the company's financial and non-financial internal controls and risk management systems (to the extent that these are not delegated to another committee made up of independent non-executive directors).*
- *Monitoring and reviewing the effectiveness of the group's internal audit function.*
- *Making recommendations to the board relating to the appointment, reappointment and removal of the external auditor and approving the remuneration and terms of engagement of the external auditor.*
- *Reviewing and monitoring the external auditor's independence and effectiveness of the audit processes.*
- *Developing and implementing a policy on the engagement of the external auditor to supply non-audit services and reporting to the board, identifying matters where action or improvement is needed.*

CC C.3.3   A separate section of the annual report should describe the work of the audit committee in discharging its responsibilities.

CC C.3.5   Where there is no internal audit function, the reasons for its absence should be explained.

Notes:

CC C.3.5   *(a) The audit committee should monitor and review the effectiveness of the internal audit activities. Where there is no internal audit function, the audit committee should consider annually whether there is a need for one and make a recommendation to the board.*

CC C.3.4   *(b) The audit committee should ensure that arrangements are in place, and review such arrangements, for staff to raise concerns (over matters of financial reporting or other matters) in confidence. It should ensure the proportionate and independent investigation of such matters and follow up actions.*

CC C.3.6
DTR 7.1.4   The audit committee should have primary responsibility for making a recommendation to the board on the appointment, reappointment and removal of the external auditors. If the board does not accept the audit committee's recommendation, the annual report should include a

IFRS GAAP plc

statement from the audit committee explaining its recommendation and the reasons why the board has taken a different position.

CC C.3.7 If the auditor provides non-audit services, it should be explained how auditor objectivity and independence is safeguarded.

Remuneration committee

CC B.1.4 The report should include a description of the work of the remuneration committee, including, where an executive director serves as a non-executive director elsewhere, whether or not the director will retain such earnings and, if so, what the remuneration is.

Internal controls

DTR 7.2.5 The corporate governance must include a description of the main features of the company's internal control and risk management systems insofar as they relate to the financial reporting process.

CC C.2.1 The directors should at least annually conduct a review of the effectiveness of the group's system of internal control and should report to shareholders that they have done so.

The review should cover all material controls, including financial, operational and compliance controls and risk management systems.

Reporting under the Turnbull guidance (2005)

TG 34 ■ The board should, as a minimum, disclose that there is an ongoing process for identifying, evaluating and managing the significant risks faced by the company, that it has been in place for the year under review and up to the date of approval of the annual report, that it is regularly reviewed by the board and accords with the Turnbull guidance (2005).

TG 33 ■ The annual report should include such meaningful, high-level information as the board considers necessary to assist shareholders' understanding of the main features of the company's risk management processes and system of internal control, and should not give a misleading impression.

TG 35 ■ The board should acknowledge that it is responsible for the company's system of internal control and for reviewing its effectiveness. It should also explain that such a system is designed to manage rather than eliminate the risk of failure to achieve business objectives and can provide reasonable, but not absolute assurance against material misstatement or loss.

TG 36 ■ The board should summarise the process it (where applicable, through its committees) has applied in reviewing the effectiveness of the system of internal control and confirm that necessary actions have been or are being taken to remedy any significant failings or weaknesses identified from that review. It should also disclose the process it has applied to deal with material internal control aspects of any significant problems disclosed in the annual report.

TG 37 ■ Where a board cannot make one or more of the disclosures in paragraphs 34 and 36 described above, it should state this fact and provide an explanation. The Listing Rules require the board to disclose if it has failed to conduct a review of the effectiveness of the company's system of internal control.

TG 38 ■ Where material joint ventures and associates have not been dealt with as part of the group for the purposes of applying this guidance, this should be disclosed.

Note: For the purpose of making its public statement on internal control the board should undertake an annual assessment. The assessment should consider issues dealt with in reports reviewed by it during the year together with any additional information necessary to ensure that the board has taken account of all significant aspects of internal control for the company for the year under review and up to the date of approval of the annual report.

IFRS GAAP plc   32

TG 31   *The board's annual assessment should, in particular, consider:*

- *The changes since the last annual assessment in the nature and extent of significant risks and the company's ability to respond to changes in its business and the external environment.*

- *The scope and quality of management's ongoing monitoring of risks and of the system of internal control and, where applicable, the work of its internal audit function and other providers of assurance.*

- *The extent and frequency of the communication of the results of the monitoring to the board (or board committee(s)) that enables it to build up a cumulative assessment of the state of control in the company and the effectiveness with which risk is being managed.*

- *The incidence of significant control failings or weaknesses that have been identified at any time during the period and the extent to which they have resulted in unforeseen outcomes or contingencies that have had, could have had, or may in the future have, a material impact on the company's financial performance or condition.*

- *The effectiveness of the company's public reporting processes.*

Requirements from the Takeover Directive

DTR 7.2.6,   Where the corporate governance statement is excluded from the directors' report but included
7.2.9(1)   elsewhere in the annual report, a cross-reference to the directors' report, where this information
              is disclosed as required by company law, must be given.

Going concern

LR 9.8.6(3),   There should be a statement by the directors that the business is a going concern, with
CC C.1.2,   supporting assumptions or qualifications as necessary. This statement should cover both the
GC 47-55   parent company and the group as a whole.

GC 56   *Note: The statement by the directors should be made in accordance with what is known to them at the date on which they approve the financial statements; in practice directors will need to perform their work to a date before the approval of the financial statements and update their work as appropriate.*

Dialogue with institutional shareholders and constructive use of the AGM

CC D.1.2   Disclosure should be made of the steps that the board have taken to ensure that the members of the board, and in particular the non-executive directors, develop an understanding of the views of the major shareholders (for example through direct face-to-face contact, analysts' or brokers' briefings and surveys of shareholder opinion) about their company.

Notes:

CC D.1.1   *(a) The chairman should ensure that the views of shareholders are communicated to the board as a whole.*

CC D.1.1   *(b) The chairman should discuss governance and strategy with major shareholders. Non-executive directors should be offered the opportunity to attend meetings with major shareholders and should expect to attend if requested by major shareholders. The senior independent director should also attend sufficient meetings with a range of major shareholders to listen to their views.*

CC D.2.3   *(c) The chairman should arrange for the chairmen of the audit, remuneration and nomination committees should attend the AGM to answer questions.*

CC D.2.1   *(d) The company should propose a separate resolution on each substantially separate issue and should in particular propose a resolution at the AGM relating to the report and accounts. For each resolution, proxy appointments form should provide shareholders with the option to direct their proxy to vote either for or against the resolution or to withhold their vote. The proxy form and any announcement of the results of a vote should make clear that a vote withheld is not a vote in law and will not be counted in the calculation of the proportion of votes for and against the resolution.*

IFRS GAAP plc 33

CC D.2.2   *(e) The company should ensure that all proxy votes received for general meetings are properly recorded and counted. For each resolution, after a vote has been taken, except where taken on a poll, the company should ensure that the following information is given at the general meeting and made available as soon as reasonably practicable on the company's web site:*

- *the number of shares in respect of which proxy appointments have been validly made; and*
- *the number of votes (i) for, and (ii) against the resolution, and (iii) the number of shares in respect of which the vote was directed to be withheld.*

CC D.2.4   *(f) The company should arrange for the Notice of the AGM and related papers to be sent to shareholders at least 20 days before the meeting.*

IFRS GAAP plc 34

Statement of directors' responsibilities

CC C.1.1
APB2007/01 ISA
(UK and Ireland)
700 p9-1

The directors are responsible for preparing the annual report, the directors' remuneration report and the financial statements in accordance with applicable law and regulations.

Company law requires the directors to prepare financial statements for each financial year. Under that law the directors have prepared the group and parent company financial statements in accordance with International Financial Reporting Standards (IFRSs) as adopted by the European Union. In preparing these financial statements, the directors have also elected to comply with IFRSs, issued by the International Accounting Standards Board (IASB). The financial statements are required by law to give a true and fair view of the state of affairs of the company and the group and of the profit or loss of the group for that period.

In preparing those financial statements the directors are required to:

- Select suitable accounting policies and then apply them consistently.
- Make judgements and estimates that are reasonable and prudent[1].
- State that the financial statements comply with IFRSs as adopted by the European Union[2].
- Prepare the financial statements on the going concern basis, unless it is inappropriate to presume that the group will continue in business[3], in which case there should be supporting assumptions or qualifications as necessary. *This statement should cover both the parent company and the group as a whole.*

The directors are also required by the Disclosure and Transparency Rules of the Financial Services Authority to include a management report containing a fair review of the business and a description of the principal risks and uncertainties facing the group and company.

The directors are responsible for keeping proper accounting records that disclose with reasonable accuracy at any time the financial position of the company and the group and to enable them to ensure that the financial statements and the Directors' Remuneration Report comply with the Companies Act 1985 (for periods commencing on or after 6 April 2008, the Companies Act 2006) and, as regards the group financial statements, Article 4 of the IAS Regulation. They are also responsible for safeguarding the assets of the company and the group and hence for taking reasonable steps for the prevention and detection of fraud and other irregularities.

The directors are responsible for the maintenance and integrity of the company's website and legislation in the United Kingdom governing the preparation and dissemination of financial statements may differ from legislation in other jurisdictions.

Directors' statement pursuant to the Disclosure and Transparency Rules

Each of the directors, whose names and functions are listed in [refer to section of annual report containing details of directors] confirm that, to the best of each person's knowledge and belief:

- the financial statements, prepared in accordance with IFRSs as adopted by the EU, give a true and fair view of the assets, liabilities, financial position and profit [loss] of the group and company; and
- the directors report contained in the Annual Report includes a fair review of the development and performance of the business and the position of the company and group, together with a description of the principal risks and uncertainties that they face.

The directors are responsible for the maintenance and integrity of the group web site, www.IFRSGAAPplc.com. Legislation in the UK governing the preparation and dissemination of financial statements may differ from legislation in other jurisdictions.

By order of the board
AB Smith
Company Secretary **28 March 2009**

---

[1] Paragraph 12 of Part II of Schedule 4 to CA 1985 (paragraph 29 of Part 2 of Schedule 1 to SI 2008/410) requires that the amount of any item 'shall be determined on a prudent basis'.
[2] This bullet does not apply to small and medium-sized companies as defined by CA85 or CA06.
[3] This bullet can be omitted if the directors have voluntarily given a separate statement about going concern.

IFRS GAAP plc

Notes:

(a) *There is no requirement for the corporate governance report to be signed. However, it is good practice for the company secretary or the senior non-executive director to sign it.*

(b) *The statement by the directors should be made in accordance with what is known to them at the date on which they approve the financial statements; in practice directors will need to perform their work to a date before the approval of the financial statements and update their work as appropriate.*

LR 9.8.10R	*The Listing Rules require that the auditors should review the following aspects of the company's 'statement of compliance' with the Combined Code of corporate governance:*
CC C.1.1	■ *Directors' responsibility statement for preparing the financial statements and auditors' reporting responsibilities.*
CC C.2.1	■ *Directors' report to shareholders on the company's system of internal controls.*
CC C.3.1-7	■ *Disclosure relating to the audit committee and auditors.*
LR 9.8.8R	■ *Detailed disclosure in the directors' remuneration report relating to total remuneration, share options, long-term incentive schemes and pension entitlements.*
LR 9.8.6(3)	*In addition, the Listing Rules require that the auditors should review the directors' statement on going concern.*

Independent auditors' report to the members of IFRS GAAP plc

APB 2006/06   *This audit report is included for illustrative purposes only and is not intended for use as a template.*

We have audited the group and company financial statements (the 'financial statements') of IFRS GAAP plc for the year ended 31 December 2008 which comprise the consolidated income statement, the consolidated and company balance sheets, the consolidated and company cash flow statements, the consolidated statement of recognised income and expense and the related notes. These financial statements have been prepared under the accounting policies set out therein. We have also audited the information in the remuneration report that is described as having been audited.

Respective responsibilities of directors and auditors

The directors' responsibilities for preparing the annual report, the remuneration report and the financial statements in accordance with applicable law and International Financial Reporting Standards (IFRSs) as adopted by the European Union are set out in the statement of directors' responsibilities.

Our responsibility is to audit the financial statements and the part of the remuneration report to be audited in accordance with relevant legal and regulatory requirements and International Standards on Auditing (UK and Ireland). This report, including the opinion, has been prepared for and only for the company's members as a body in accordance with Section 235 of the Companies Act 1985 and for no other purpose. We do not, in giving this opinion, accept or assume responsibility for any other purpose or to any other person to whom this report is shown or into whose hands it may come save where expressly agreed by our prior consent in writing.

We report to you our opinion as to whether the financial statements give a true and fair view and whether the financial statements and the part of the Remuneration report to be audited have been properly prepared in accordance with the Companies Act 1985 and Article 4 of the IAS Regulation. We also report to you whether in our opinion the information given in the directors' report is consistent with the financial statements. The information given in the directors' report includes that specific information presented in the operating and financial review that is cross referenced from the review of business section of the directors' report.

In addition we report to you if, in our opinion, the company has not kept proper accounting records, if we have not received all the information and explanations we require for our audit, or if information specified by law regarding directors' remuneration and other transactions is not disclosed.

We review whether the corporate governance statement reflects the company's compliance with the nine provisions of the Combined Code 2006 specified for our review by the Listing Rules of the Financial Services Authority, and we report if it does not. We are not required to consider whether the board's statements on internal control cover all risks and controls, or form an opinion on the effectiveness of the group's corporate governance procedures or its risk and control procedures.

We read other information contained in the annual report and consider whether it is consistent with the audited financial statements. The other information comprises only the directors' report, the unaudited part of the remuneration report, the operating and financial review, the corporate governance statement and all of the other information listed on the contents page. We consider the implications for our report if we become aware of any apparent misstatements or material inconsistencies with the financial statements. Our responsibilities do not extend to any other information.

Basis of audit opinion

We conducted our audit in accordance with International Standards on Auditing (UK and Ireland) issued by the Auditing Practices Board. An audit includes examination, on a test basis, of evidence relevant to the amounts and disclosures in the financial statements and the part of the remuneration report to be audited. It also includes an assessment of the significant estimates and judgments made by the directors in the preparation of the financial statements, and of whether the accounting policies are appropriate to the group's and company's circumstances, consistently applied and adequately disclosed.

IFRS GAAP plc

We planned and performed our audit so as to obtain all the information and explanations which we considered necessary in order to provide us with sufficient evidence to give reasonable assurance that the financial statements and the part of the remuneration report to be audited are free from material misstatement, whether caused by fraud or other irregularity or error. In forming our opinion we also evaluated the overall adequacy of the presentation of information in the financial statements and the part of the directors' remuneration report to be audited.

Opinion

In our opinion:

- the group financial statements give a true and fair view, in accordance with IFRSs as adopted by the European Union, of the state of the group's and the company's affairs as at 31 December 2008 and of its profit and cash flows for the year then ended;
- the company financial statements give a true and fair view, in accordance with IFRSs as adopted by the European Union as applied in accordance with the provisions of the Companies Act 1985, of the state of the company's affairs as at 31 December 2008 and cash flows for the year then ended;
- the financial statements and the part of the remuneration report to be audited have been properly prepared in accordance with the Companies Act 1985 and Article 4 of the IAS Regulation; and
- the information given in the directors' report is consistent with the financial statements.

PricewaterhouseCoopers LLP
Chartered Accountants and Registered Auditors
London
28 March 2009

Notes:

Where the report is included on the client's web site, include these notes (on the web site version of the audit report, but not on the hard copy version) unless the statement of directors' responsibilities clearly:

- *states the directors' responsibility for the maintenance and integrity of the web site; and*
- *refers to the fact that uncertainty regarding legal requirements is compounded as information published on the internet is accessible in many countries with different legal requirements relating to the preparation and dissemination of financial statements.*

(a) The maintenance and integrity of the [name of entity] web site is the responsibility of the directors; the work carried out by the auditors does not involve consideration of these matters and, accordingly, the auditors accept no responsibility for any changes that may have occurred to the financial statements since they were initially presented on the web site.

(b) Legislation in the United Kingdom governing the preparation and dissemination of financial statements may differ from legislation in other jurisdictions.

IFRS GAAP plc 38

(Amounts in C thousands unless otherwise stated)

Consolidated balance sheet

		Note	Group As at 31 December 2008	Group As at 31 December 2007	Company As at 31 December 2008	Company As at 31 December 2007
1p68, 1p104, 1p36						
1p51	**Assets**					
	Non-current assets					
1p68(a)	Property, plant and equipment	6	**155,341**	100,233	–	–
1p68(c)	Intangible assets	7	**26,272**	20,700	–	–
27p37	Investment in subsidiaries	8a	–	–	**36,592**	22,170
1p68(e)	Investments in associates	8b	**13,373**	13,244		
1p68(n), 1p70	Deferred income tax assets	22	**3,520**	3,321	–	–
1p68(d), IFRS7p8(d)	Available-for-sale financial assets	10	**17,420**	14,910	–	–
1p68(d), IFRS7p8(a)	Derivative financial instruments	11	**395**	245		
1p68(h), IFRS7p8(c)	Trade and other receivables	12	**2,322**	1,352		–
			218,643	154,005	**36,592**	22,170
1p51, 1p57	**Current assets**					
1p68(g)	Inventories	13	**24,700**	18,182	–	–
1p68(h), IFRS7p8(c)	Trade and other receivables	12	**19,765**	18,330	**41,147**	31,296
1p68(d), IFRS7p8(d)	Available-for-sale financial assets	10	**1,950**	–	–	–
1p68(d), IFRS7p8(a)	Derivative financial instruments	11	**1,069**	951		
1p68(d), IFRS7p8(a)	Financial assets at fair value through profit or loss	14	**11,820**	7,972		
1p68(i), IFRS7p8	Cash and cash equivalents	15	**17,928**	34,062	**3,261**	6,234
			77,232	79,497	**44,408**	37,530
IFRS5p38	Assets of disposal group classified as held-for-sale	16	**3,333**	–	**81,000**	59,700
			80,565	79,497	**44,408**	37,530
	Total assets		**299,208**	233,502	**81,000**	59,700
	Equity					
1p68(p)	**Capital and reserves attributable to equity holders of the company**					
1p75(e)	Ordinary shares	17	**25,300**	21,000	**25,300**	21,000
1p75(e)	Share premium	17	**17,144**	10,494	**17,144**	10,494
1p75(e)	Other reserves	19	**15,549**	7,005	–	–
1p75(e)	Retained earnings	18	**66,592**	48,681	**8,735**	11,613
			124,585	87,180	**51,179**	43,107
1p68(o)	**Minority interest in equity**		**7,188**	1,766	–	–
	Total equity		**131,773**	88,946	**51,179**	43,107
1p51	**Liabilities**					
	Non-current liabilities					
1p68(l), IFRS7p8(f)	Borrowings	21	**115,121**	96,346	–	–
1p68(l), IFRS7p8(e)	Derivative financial instruments	11	**135**	129	–	–
1p68(n), 1p70	Deferred income tax liabilities	22	**12,370**	9,053	–	–
1p68(k), 1p75(d)	Retirement benefit obligations	23	**4,635**	2,233	–	–
1p68(k), 1p75(d)	Provisions for other liabilities and charges	24	**320**	274	–	–
			133,581	108,035	–	–

IFRS GAAP plc

39

(Amounts in C thousands unless otherwise stated)

Current liabilities					
1p51, 1p60 1p68(j), IFRS7p8(f)	Trade and other payables	20	**16,670**	12,478	**29,821** 16,593
1p68(m)	Current income tax liabilities		**2,566**	2,771	– –
1p68(l), IFRS7p8(f)	Borrowings	21	**11,716**	18,258	– –
1p68(l), IFRS7p8(e)	Derivative financial instruments	11	**460**	618	– –
1p68(k)	Provisions for other liabilities and charges	24	**2,222**	2,396	– –
			33,634	36,521	– –
IFRS5p38	Liabilities of disposal group classified as held-for-sale	16	**220**	–	– –
			33,854	36,521	– –
	Total liabilities		**167,435**	144,556	**29,821** 16,593
	Total equity and liabilities		**299,208**	233,502	**81,000** 59,700

10p17   The notes on pages 43 to 111 are an integral part of these consolidated financial statements.

The financial statements on pages 40 to 111 were authorised for issue by the board of directors on 28 March 2009 and were signed on its behalf.

CD Suede   G Wallace
Chief Executive   **Finance Director**

IFRS GAAP plc

40

(Amounts in C thousands unless otherwise stated)

Consolidated income statement — by function of expense

| | | | Group | |
| | | | Year ended 31 December | |
		Note	2008	2007
1p81-83, 1p92,1p36 1p104				
	Continuing operations			
1p81(a)	Revenue	5	**211,034**	112,360
1p92	Cost of sales		**(77,366)**	(46,682)
1p92	**Gross profit**		**133,668**	65,678
1p81(a), 92	Distribution costs		**(52,140)**	(21,213)
1p92	Administrative expenses		**(28,778)**	(10,426)
1p92	Other income	26	**1,900**	1,259
1p83	Other (losses)/gains – net	25	**(90)**	63
1p83	Loss on expropriated land	27	**(1,117)**	–
1p83	**Operating profit[1]**		**53,443**	35,361
1p83	Finance income	30	**1,730**	1,609
1p81(b)	Finance costs	30	**(8,173)**	(12,197)
1p83	Finance costs – net	30	**(6,443)**	(10,588)
1p81(c)	Share of (loss)/profit of associates	8	**(174)**	145
1p92	**Profit before income tax**		**46,826**	24,918
1p81(d), 12p77	Income tax expense	31	**(14,611)**	(8,670)
1p81(f)	**Profit for the year from continuing operations**		**32,215**	16,248
IFRS5p33(a)	**Discontinued operations**			
	Profit for the year from discontinued operations	16	**100**	120
1p81(f)	**Profit for the year**		**32,315**	16,368
1p82	**Attributable to:**			
1p82(b)	Equity holders of the company		**29,767**	15,512
1p82(a)	Minority interest		**2,548**	856
			32,315	16,368

		Note	2008	2007
	Earnings per share for profit and profit from discontinued operations attributable to the equity holders of the company during the year (expressed in C per share)			
	Basic earnings per share			
33p66	From continuing operations	33	**1.26**	0.75
33p68	From discontinuing operations		**0.01**	0.01
			1.27	0.76
	Diluted earnings per share[2]			
33p66	From continuing operations	33	**1.15**	0.71
33p68	From discontinuing operations		**0.01**	0.01
			1.16	0.72

[1] The disclosure of operating profit on the face of the income statement is not prescribed by IAS 1. There is, however, no prohibition from disclosing this or a similar line item.

[2] EPS for discontinued operations may be given in the notes to the accounts instead of the face of the income statement.

The notes on pages 43 to 111 are an integral part of these consolidated financial statements.

S 230   The company has elected to take the exemption under section 230 of the Companies Act 1985 to not present the parent company profit and loss account.

The profit for the parent company for the year was C9,098 (2006: C10,491).

IFRS GAAP plc 41

(Amounts in C thousands unless otherwise stated)

Consolidated statement of recognised income and expense

| | | | Group | |
| | | | Year ended 31 December | |
		Note	2008	2007
1p96(b)	**Items net of tax**			
16p77(f)	Gains on revaluation of land and buildings	19	–	759
IFRS7p20(a)(ii)	Available-for-sale financial assets	19	**362**	62
IAS28p39	Share of available-for-sale financial asset reserve of associates	19	**(12)**	(14)
19p93A	Actuarial loss on post employment benefit obligations	23	–	(494)
12p80(d)	Impact of change in UK tax rate on deferred tax[1]	22	**(10)**	–
1p96(b), IFRS7p23(c)	Cash flow hedges	19	**64**	(3)
1p96(b)	Net investment hedge	19	**(45)**	40
1p96(b)	Currency translation differences	19	**2,244**	(156)
IFRS3p59	Increase in fair values of proportionate holding of Your Shoes Group (note 38)	19	**850**	–
1p96(b)	**Net income recognised directly in equity**		**3,453**	194
1p96(a)	Profit for the year		**32,315**	16,368
1p96(c)	**Total recognised income for the year**		**35,768**	16,562
	Attributable to:			
1p96(c)	– Equity holders of the company		**32,968**	15,746
1p96(c)	– Minority interest		**2,800**	816
			35,768	16,562

[1] Solely for illustrative purposes, a change in tax rates has been assumed to have taken place in 2008. UK companies with 31 December 2008 year ends will have reflected an actual change in tax rates in 2007.

The notes on pages 43 to 111 are an integral part of these consolidated financial statements.

There are no movements to be recognised through the parent company statement of recognised income and expense in 2008 or 2007.

IFRS GAAP plc

42

(Amounts in C thousands unless otherwise stated)

Consolidated cash flow statement

			Group Year ended 31 December		Company Year ended 31 December	
7p10, 18(b), 1p36		Note	**2008**	2007	**2008**	2007
1p104						
	Cash flows from operating activities					
	Cash generated from operations	35	**56,234**	41,776	**(4,693)**	(4,315)
7p31	Interest paid		**(7,835)**	(14,773)	**–**	–
7p35	Income tax paid		**(14,317)**	(10,526)	**–**	–
	Net cash generated from operating activities		**34,082**	16,477	**(4,693)**	(4,315)
7p21, 7p10	**Cash flows from investing activities**					
7p39	Acquisition of subsidiary, net of cash acquired	38	**(3,950)**	–	**(4,250)**	–
7p16(a)	Purchases of property, plant and equipment (PPE)	6	**(9,755)**	(6,042)	**–**	–
7p16(b)	Proceeds from sale of PPE	35	**6,354**	2,979	**–**	–
7p16(a)	Purchases of intangible assets	7	**(3,050)**	(700)	**–**	–
'7p16(c)	Purchases of available-for-sale financial assets	10	**(2,781)**	(1,126)	**–**	–
7p16(e)	Loans granted to associates	39	**(1,000)**	(50)		
7p16(f)	Loan repayments received from associates	39	**14**	64	**–**	–
7p17(c)	Loans granted to subsidiary undertakings		**–**	–	**(9,851)**	–
7p17(f)	Loan repayments received from subsidiary undertakings					1,126
7p31	Interest received		**1,254**	1,193	**–**	–
7p31	Dividends received		**1,180**	1,120	**13,809**	14,806
	Net cash used in investing activities		**(11,734)**	(2,562)	**(292)**	15,932
7p21, 7p10	**Cash flows from financing activities**					
7p17(a)	Proceeds from issuance of ordinary shares	17	**950**	1,070	**950**	1,070
7p17(b)	Purchase of treasury shares	18	**(2,564)**	–	**(2,564)**	–
7p17(c)	Proceeds from issuance of convertible bonds	21	**50,000**	–	**–**	–
7p17(c)	Proceeds from issuance of redeemable preference shares	21	**–**	30,000	**–**	–
7p17(c)	Proceeds from borrowings		**8,500**	18,000	**–**	–
7p17(d)	Repayments of borrowings		**(78,117)**	(34,674)	**–**	–
7p17(c)	Proceeds from loan from subsidiary undertaking				**13,210**	7,209
7p31	Dividends paid to company's shareholders		**(10,102)**	(15,736)	**(10,102)**	(15,736)
7p31	Dividends paid to holders of redeemable preferences shares		**(1,950)**	(1,950)		
7p31	Dividends paid to minority interests		**(1,920)**	(550)	**–**	–
	Net cash used in financing activities		**(35,203)**	(3,840)	**(1,170)**	(10,685)
	Net (decrease)/increase in cash, cash equivalents and bank overdrafts		**(12,855)**	10,075	**(2,973)**	4,160
	Cash, cash equivalents and bank overdrafts at beginning of year	15	**27,598**	17,587	**6,234**	2,074
	Exchange gains/(losses) on cash and bank overdrafts		**535**	(64)	**–**	–
	Cash, cash equivalents and bank overdrafts at end of year	15	**15,278**	27,598	**3,261**	6,234

The notes on pages 43 to 111 are an integral part of these consolidated financial statements.

IFRS GAAP plc   43

(Amounts in C thousands unless otherwise stated)

Notes to the consolidated financial statements

1 General information

<table>
<tr><td>1p126(b), (c)
1p46(a)(b)</td><td>IFRS GAAP plc ('the company') and its subsidiaries (together 'the group') manufacture, distribute and sell shoes through a network of independent retailers. The group has manufacturing plants around the world and sells mainly in countries within the UK, the US and Europe. During the year, the group acquired control of 'Your Shoes Group', a shoe and leather goods retailer operating in the US and most western European countries.</td></tr>
<tr><td>1p126(a)</td><td>The company is a public limited company which is listed on the London Stock Exchange and is incorporated and domiciled in the UK. The address of its registered office is Nice Walk Way, London.</td></tr>
</table>

2 Summary of significant accounting policies

<table>
<tr><td>1p103(a)
1p108(b) 1p110</td><td>The principal accounting policies applied in the preparation of these consolidated financial statements are set out below. These policies have been consistently applied to all the years presented, unless otherwise stated.</td></tr>
</table>

2.1 Basis of preparation

<table>
<tr><td>1p14
1p108(a)</td><td>The consolidated financial statements of IFRS GAAP plc have been prepared in accordance with International Financial Reporting Standards as adopted by the European Union (IFRSs as adopted by the EU), IFRIC Interpretations and the Companies Act 1985/2006 applicable to companies reporting under IFRS. The consolidated financial statements have been prepared under the historical cost convention, as modified by the revaluation of land and buildings, available-for-sale financial assets, and financial assets and financial liabilities (including derivative instruments) at fair value through profit or loss.</td></tr>
</table>

The preparation of financial statements in conformity with IFRS requires the use of certain critical accounting estimates. It also requires management to exercise its judgement in the process of applying the group's accounting policies. The areas involving a higher degree of judgement or complexity, or areas where assumptions and estimates are significant to the consolidated financial statements, are disclosed in note 4.

(a) Interpretations effective in 2008

<table>
<tr><td>8p28</td><td>IFRIC 14, 'IAS 19 – The limit on a defined benefit asset, minimum funding requirements and their interaction', provides guidance on assessing the limit in IAS 19 on the amount of the surplus that can be recognised as an asset. It also explains how the pension asset or liability may be affected by a statutory or contractual minimum funding requirement. This interpretation does not have any impact on the group's financial statements, as the group has a pension deficit and is not subject to any minimum funding requirements. The interpretation does not have an impact on the companys financial statements as it does not operate a defined benefit pension schemes.</td></tr>
<tr><td>8p28</td><td>IFRIC 11, 'IFRS 2 – Group and treasury share transactions', provides guidance on whether share-based transactions involving treasury shares or involving group entities (for example, options over a parent's shares) should be accounted for as equity-settled or cash-settled share-based payment transactions in the stand-alone accounts of the parent and group companies. This interpretation does not have an impact on the group's financial statements. The company's accounting policy for share based compensation arrangements is already in compliance with the interpretation.</td></tr>
</table>

(b) Standards and amendments early adopted by the group

<table>
<tr><td>8p28</td><td>IFRS 8, 'Operating segments', was early adopted in 2008. IFRS 8 replaces IAS 14, 'Segment reporting', and aligns segment reporting with the requirements of the US standard SFAS 131, 'Disclosures about segments of an enterprise and related information'. The new standard requires a 'management approach', under which segment information is presented on the same basis as that used for internal reporting purposes. This has resulted in an increase in the number of reportable segments presented. In addition, the segments are reported in a manner that is more consistent with the internal reporting provided to the chief operating decision-maker. As goodwill is allocated by management to groups of cash-generating units on a segment level, the change in reportable segments has required a reallocation of goodwill of C146 and C4,750 from</td></tr>
</table>

IFRS GAAP plc
44

(Amounts in C thousands unless otherwise stated)

the 'other countries' operating segment to the newly identified operating segments, China and Russia respectively. The reallocation has not resulted in any additional impairment of goodwill. Comparatives for 2007 have been restated.

(c) Interpretations effective in 2008 but not relevant
The following interpretation to published standards is mandatory for accounting periods beginning on or after 1 January 2008 but is not relevant to the group's operations:

- IFRIC 12, 'Service concession arrangements'; and
- IFRIC 13, 'Customer loyalty programmes'.

8p30 *(d) Standards, amendments and interpretations to existing standards that are not yet effective and have not been early adopted by the group*
The following standards and amendments to existing standards have been published and are mandatory for the group's accounting periods beginning on or after 1 January 2009 or later periods, but the group has not early adopted them:

- IAS 23 (amendment), 'Borrowing costs' (effective from 1 January 2009). The amendment to the standard is still subject to endorsement by the EU. It requires an entity to capitalise borrowing costs directly attributable to the acquisition, construction or production of a qualifying asset (one that takes a substantial period of time to get ready for use or sale) as part of the cost of that asset. The option of immediately expensing those borrowing costs will be removed. The group and company will apply IAS 23 (amendment) retrospectively from 1 January 2009, subject to endorsement by the EU, but is currently not applicable to the group or company as there are no qualifying assets.
- IAS 1 (revised), 'Presentation of financial statements' (effective from 1 January 2009). The standard is still subject to endorsement by the EU. The revised standard will prohibit the presentation of items of income and expenses (that is, 'non-owner changes in equity') in the statement of changes in equity, requiring 'non-owner changes in equity' to be presented separately from owner changes in equity. All non-owner changes in equity will be required to be shown in a performance statement, but entities can choose whether to present one performance statement (the statement of comprehensive income) or two statements (the income statement and statement of comprehensive income). Where entities restate or reclassify comparative information, they will be required to present a restated balance sheet as at the beginning comparative period in addition to the current requirement to present balance sheets at the end of the current period and comparative period. The group and company will apply IAS 1 (revised) from 1 January 2009, subject to endorsement by the EU. It is likely that both the income statement and statement of comprehensive income will be presented as performance statements.
- IFRS 2 (amendment), 'Share-based payment' (effective from 1 January 2009). The amendment to the standard is still subject to endorsement by the EU. It deals with vesting conditions and cancellations. It clarifies that vesting conditions are service conditions and performance conditions only. Other features of a share-based payment are not vesting conditions. These features would need to be included in the grant date fair value for transactions with emloyees and others providing similiar services; they would not impact the number of awards expected to vest or valuation there of subsequent to grant date. All cancellations, whether by the entity or by other parties, should receive the same accounting treatment. The group and company will apply IFRS 2 (amendment) from 1 January 2009, subject to endorsement by the EU. It is not expected to have a material impact on the group or company's financial statements.
- IAS 32 (amendment), 'Financial instruments: Presentation', and IAS 1 (amendment), 'Presentation of financial statements' – 'Puttable financial instruments and obligations arising on liquidation' (effective from 1 January 2009). The amendment to the standard is still subject to endorsement by the EU. It require entities to classify puttable financial instruments and instruments, or components of instruments that impose on the entity an obligation to deliver to another party a pro rata share of the net assets of the entity only on liquidation as equity, provided the financial instruments have particular features and meet specific conditions. The group will apply the IAS 32 and IAS 1(amendment) from 1 January 2009, subject to endorsement by the EU. It is not expected to have any impact on the group or company's financial statements.
- IFRS 1 (amendment), 'First time adoption of IFRS', and IAS 27, 'Consolidated and separate financial statements', (effective from 1 January 2009). The revised standard is still subject to endorsement by the EU. The amended standard allows first-time adopters to use a deemed cost of either fair value or the carrying amount under previous accounting practice to measure the initial cost of investments in subsidiaries, jointly controlled entities and associates in the separate financial statements. The amendment also removes the definition of the cost method from IAS 27 and replaces it with a

IFRS GAAP plc 45

(Amounts in C thousands unless otherwise stated)

requirement to present dividends as income in the separate financial statements of the investor. The group will apply IFRS 1 (amendment) from 1 January 2009, subject to endorsement by the EU and company, as all subsidiaries of the group will transition to IFRS. The amendment will not have any impact on the group's financial statements. The IFRS 1 amendment will not have an impact on the company's financial statements which are already prepared under IFRS.

- IAS 27 (revised), 'Consolidated and separate financial statements', (effective from 1 July 2009). The amendment to the standard is still subject to endorsement by the EU. The revised standard requires the effects of all transactions with non-controlling interests to be recorded in equity if there is no change in control and these transactions will no longer result in goodwill or gains and losses. The standard also specifies the accounting when control is lost. Any remaining interest in the entity is re-measured to fair value, and a gain or loss is recognised in profit or loss. The group will apply IAS 27 (revised) prospectively to transactions with non-controlling interests from 1 January 2010, subject to endorsement by the EU.

- IFRS 3 (revised), 'Business combinations' (effective from 1 July 2009). The revised standard is still subject to endorsement by the EU. The revised standard continues to apply the acquisition method to business combinations, with some significant changes. For example, all payments to purchase a business are to be recorded at fair value at the acquisition date, with contingent payments classified as debt subsequently re-measured through the income statement. There is a choice on an acquisition-by-acquisition basis to measure the non-controlling interest in the acquiree either at fair vale or at the non-controlling interest's proportionate share of the acquiree's net assets. All acquisition-related costs should be expensed. The group will apply IFRS 3 (revised) prospectively to all business combinations from 1 January 2010, subject to endorsement by the EU.

- IFRS 5 (amendment), 'Non-current assets held-for-sale and discontinued operations', (and consequential amendment to IFRS 1, 'First-time adoption') (effective from 1 July 2009). The amendment is part of the IASB's annual improvements project published in May 2008. The amendment to the standard is still subject to endorsement by the EU. The amendment clarifies that all of a subsidiary's assets and liabilities are classified as held for sale if a partial disposal sale plan results in loss of control. Relevant disclosure should be made for this subsidiary if the definition of a discontinued operation is met. A consequential amendment to IFRS 1 states that these amendments are applied prospectively from the date of transition to IFRSs. The group will apply the IFRS 5 (amendment) prospectively to all partial disposals of subsidiaries from 1 January 2010, subject to endorsement by the EU.

- IAS 23 (amendment), 'Borrowing costs' (effective from 1 January 2009). The amendment is part of the IASB's annual improvements project published in May 2008. The amendment to the standard is still subject to endorsement by the EU. The definition of borrowing costs has been amended so that interest expense is calculated using the effective interest method defined in IAS 39 'Financial instruments: Recognition and measurement'. This eliminates the inconsistency of terms between IAS 39 and IAS 23. The group and company will apply the IAS 23 (amendment) prospectively to the capitalisation of borrowing costs on qualifying assets from 1 January 2009, subject to endorsement by the EU, but is currently not applicable to the group or company as there are no qualifying assets.

- IAS 28 (amendment), 'Investments in associates' (and consequential amendments to IAS 32, 'Financial Instruments: Presentation', and IFRS 7, 'Financial instruments: Disclosures') (effective from 1 January 2009). The amendment is part of the IASB's annual improvements project published in May 2008. The amendment to the standard is still subject to endorsement by the EU. An investment in associate is treated as a single asset for the purposes of impairment testing. Any impairment loss is not allocated to specific assets included within the investment, for example, goodwill. Reversals of impairment are recorded as an adjustment to the investment balance to the extent that the recoverable amount of the associate increases. The group will apply the IAS 28 (amendment) to impairment tests related to investments in associates and any related impairment losses from 1 January 2009, subject to endorsement by the EU.

- IAS 36 (amendment), 'Impairment of assets', (effective from 1 January 2009). The amendment is part of the IASB's annual improvements project published in May 2008. The amendment to the standard is still subject to endorsement by the EU. Where fair value less costs to sell is calculated on the basis of discounted cash flows, disclosures equivalent to those for value-in-use calculation should be made. The group and company will apply the IAS 36 (amendment) and provide the required disclosure where applicable for impairment tests from 1 January 2009, subject to endorsement by the EU.

- IAS 38 (amendment), 'Intangible assets', (effective from 1 January 2009). The amendment is part of the IASB's annual improvements project published in May 2008. The amendment to the standard is still subject to endorsement by the EU. A

IFRS GAAP plc

(Amounts in C thousands unless otherwise stated)

prepayment may only be recognised in the event that payment has been made in advance of obtaining right of access to goods or receipt of services. This means that an expense will be recognised for shoe mail order catalogues when the group has access to the catalogues and not when the catalogues are distributed to customers, as is the group's current accounting policy. The group will apply the IAS 38 (amendment) from 1 January 2009, subject to endorsement by the EU, with an expected write-off of prepayments of C500 to retained earnings. The amendment is not currently applicable to the company.

- IAS 19 (amendment), 'Employee benefits', (effective from 1 January 2009). The amendment is part of the IASB's annual improvements project published in May 2008. The amendment to the standard is still subject to endorsement by the EU.

    - The amendment clarifies that a plan amendment that results in a change in the extent to which benefit promises are affected by future salary increases is a curtailment, while an amendment that changes benefits attributable to past service gives rise to a negative past service cost if it results in a reduction in the present value of the defined benefit obligation.

    - The definition of return on plan assets has been amended to state that plan administration costs are deducted in the calculation of return on plan assets only to the extent that such costs have been excluded from measurement of the defined benefit obligation.

    - The distinction between short term and long term employee benefits will be based on whether benefits are due to be settled within or after 12 months of employee service being rendered.

    - IAS 37, 'Provisions, contingent liabilities and contingent assets', requires contingent liabilities to be disclosed, not recognised. IAS 19 has been amended to be consistent.

The group will apply the IAS 19 (amendment) from 1 January 2009, subject to endorsement by the EU. The amendment will not have an impact on the company's financial statements as it does not operate a defined benefit obligation.

- IAS 39 (amendment), 'Financial instruments: Recognition and measurement' (effective from 1 January 2009). The amendment is part of the IASB's annual improvements project published in May 2008. The amendment to the standard is still subject to endorsement by the EU.

    - This amendment clarifies that it is possible for there to be movements into and out of the fair value through profit or loss category where a derivative commences or ceases to qualify as a hedging instrument in cash flow or net investment hedge.

    - The definition of financial asset or financial liability at fair value through profit or loss as it relates to items that are held for trading is also amended. This clarifies that a financial asset or liability that is part of a portfolio of financial instruments managed together with evidence of an actual recent pattern of short-term profit-taking is included in such a portfolio on initial recognition.

    - The current guidance on designating and documenting hedges states that a hedging instrument needs to involve a party external to the reporting entity and cites a segment as an example of a reporting entity. This means that in order for hedge accounting to be applied at segment level, the requirements for hedge accounting are currently required to be met by the applicable segment. The amendment removes the example of a segment so that the guidance is consistent with IFRS 8, 'Operating segments', which requires disclosure for segments to be based on information reported to the chief operating decision-maker. Currently, for segment reporting purposes, each subsidiary designates contracts with group treasury as fair value or cash flow hedges so that the hedges are reported in the segment to which the hedged items relate. This is consistent with the information viewed by the chief operating decision-maker. See note 3.1 for further details. After the amendment is effective, the hedge will continue to be reflected in the segment to which the hedged items relate (and information provided to the chief operating decision-maker), but the group will not formally document and test this relationship.

    - When remeasuring the carrying amount of a debt instrument on cessation of fair value hedge accounting, the amendment clarifies that a revised effective interest rate (calculated at the date fair value hedge accounting ceases) are used.

The group any company will apply the IAS 39 (amendment) from 1 January 2009, subject to endorsement by the EU. It is not expected to have an impact on the group or company's income statement.

- IAS 1 (amendment), 'Presentation of financial statements', (effective from 1 January 2009). The amendment is part of the IASB's annual improvements project published in May 2008. The amendment to the standard is still subject to endorsement by the EU. The amendment clarifies that some rather than all financial assets and liabilities classified as held for trading in accordance with IAS 39, 'Financial instruments: Recognition and measurement' are examples of current assets and liabilities respectively. The group and

1051

IFRS GAAP plc 47

(Amounts in C thousands unless otherwise stated)

company will apply the IAS 39 (amendment) from 1 January 2009, subject to endorsement by the EU. It is not expected to have an impact on the group or company's financial statements.

- There are a number of minor amendments to IFRS 7, 'Financial instruments: Disclosures', IAS 8, 'Accounting policies, changes in accounting estimates and errors', IAS 10, 'Events after the reporting period', IAS 18, 'Revenue', and IAS 34, 'Interim financial reporting', which are part of the IASB's annual improvements project published in May 2008 (not addressed above). The amendments to the standards are still subject to endorsement by the EU. These amendments, subject to endorsement by the EU, are unlikely to have an impact on the group or company's accounts and have, therefore, not been analysed in detail.

- IFRIC 16, 'Hedges of a net investment in a foreign operation' (effective from 1 October 2008). The amendment to the interpretation is still subject to endorsement by the European Union. IFRIC 16 clarifies the accounting treatment in respect of net investment hedging. This includes the fact that net investment hedging relates to differences in functional currency not presentation currency, and hedging instruments may be held anywhere in the group. The requirements of IAS 21, 'The effects of changes in foreign exchange rates', do apply to the hedged item. The group will apply IFRIC 16 from 1 January 2009. It is not expected to have a material impact on the group or company's financial statements.

DV *(e) Interpretations and amendments to existing standards that are not yet effective and not relevant for the group's operations*

The following interpretations and amendments to existing standards have been published and are mandatory for the group's accounting periods beginning on or after 1 January 2009 or later periods but are not relevant for the group's operations:

- IFRIC 13, 'Customer loyalty programmes' (effective from 1 July 2008). IFRIC 13 clarifies that where goods or services are sold together with a customer loyalty incentive (for example, loyalty points or free products), the arrangement is a multiple-element arrangement, and the consideration receivable from the customer is allocated between the components of the arrangement using fair values. IFRIC 13 is not relevant to the group or company's operations because none of the group's companies operate any loyalty programmes.

- IAS 16 (amendment), 'Property, plant and equipment' (and consequential amendment to IAS 7, 'Statement of cash flows') (effective from 1 January 2009). The amendment is part of the IASB's annual improvements project published in May 2008. Entities whose ordinary activities comprise renting and subsequently selling assets present proceeds from the sale of those assets as revenue and should transfer the carrying amount of the asset to inventories when the asset becomes held for sale. A consequential amendment to IAS 7 states that cash flows arising from purchase, rental and sale of those assets are classified as cash flows from operating activities. The amendment will not have an impact on the group or company's operations because none of the group's companies ordinary activities comprise renting and subsequently selling assets.

- IAS 27 (amendment), 'Consolidated and separate financial statements' (effective from 1 January 2009). The amendment is part of the IASB's annual improvements project published in May 2008. Where an investment in a subsidiary that is accounted for under IAS 39, 'Financial instruments: recognition and measurement', is classified as held for sale under IFRS 5, 'Non-current assets held for sale and discontinued operations', IAS 39 would continue to be applied. The amendment will not have an impact on the group or company's operations because it is the group's policy for an investment in subsidiary to be recorded at cost in the standalone accounts of each entity.

- IAS 28 (amendment), 'Investments in associates' (and consequential amendments to IAS 32, 'Financial Instruments: Presentation' and IFRS 7, 'Financial instruments: Disclosures') (effective from 1 January 2009). The amendment is part of the IASB's annual improvements project published in May 2008. Where an investment in associate is accounted for in accordance with IAS 39 'Financial instruments: recognition and measurement', only certain, rather than all disclosure requirements in IAS 28 need to be made in addition to disclosures required by IAS 32, 'Financial Instruments: Presentation' and IFRS 7 'Financial Instruments: Disclosures'. The amendment will not have an impact on the group's operations because it is the group's policy for an investment in an associate to be equity accounted in the group's consolidated accounts.

- IAS 29 (amendment), 'Financial reporting in hyperinflationary economies' (effective from 1 January 2009). The amendment is part of the IASB's annual improvements project published in May 2008. The guidance has been amended to reflect the fact that a number of assets and liabilities are measured at fair value rather than historical cost. The

IFRS GAAP plc

48

(Amounts in C thousands unless otherwise stated)

amendment will not have an impact on the group or company's operations, as none of the group's subsidiaries or associates or company operate in hyperinflationary economies.

- IAS 31 (amendment), 'Interests in joint ventures', (and consequential amendments to IAS 32 and IFRS 7) (effective from 1 January 2009). The amendment is part of the IASB's annual improvements project published in May 2008. Where an investment in joint venture is accounted for in accordance with IAS 39, only certain rather than all disclosure requirements in IAS 31 need to be made in addition to disclosures required by IAS 32, 'Financial instruments: Presentation', and IFRS 7 'Financial instruments: Disclosures'. The amendment will not have an impact on the group's operations as there are no interests held in joint ventures.

- IAS 38 (amendment), 'Intangible assets' (effective from 1 January 2009). The amendment is part of the IASB's annual improvements project published in May 2008. The amendment deletes the wording that states that there is 'rarely, if ever' support for use of a method that results in a lower rate of amortisation than the straight-line method. The amendment will not have an impact on the group's operations, as all intangible assets are amortised using the straight-line method. The company does not have any intangible assets.

- IAS 40 (amendment), 'Investment property' (and consequential amendments to IAS 16) (effective from 1 January 2009). The amendment is part of the IASB's annual improvements project published in May 2008. Property that is under construction or development for future use as investment property is within the scope of IAS 40. Where the fair value model is applied, such property is, therefore, measured at fair value. However, where fair value of investment property under construction is not reliably measurable, the property is measured at cost until the earlier of the date construction is completed and the date at which fair value becomes reliably measurable. The amendment will not have an impact on the group or company's operations, as there are no investment properties are held by the group or company.

- IAS 41 (amendment), 'Agriculture' (effective from 1 January 2009). The amendment is part of the IASB's annual improvements project published in May 2008. It requires the use of a market-based discount rate where fair value calculations are based on discounted cash flows and the removal of the prohibition on taking into account biological transformation when calculating fair value. The amendment will not have an impact on the group or company's operations as no agricultural activities are undertaken.

- IAS 20 (amendment), 'Accounting for government grants and disclosure of government assistance' (effective from 1 January 2009). The benefit of a below-market rate government loan is measured as the difference between the carrying amount in accordance with IAS 39, 'Financial instruments: Recognition and measurement', and the proceeds received with the benefit accounted for in accordance with IAS 20. The amendment will not have an impact on the group or company's operations as there are no loans received or other grants from the government.

- The minor amendments to IAS 20 'Accounting for government grants and disclosure of government assistance', and IAS 29, 'Financial reporting in hyperinflationary economies', IAS 40, 'Investment property', and IAS 41, 'Agriculture', which are part of the IASB's annual improvements project published in May 2008 (not addressed above). These amendments will not have an impact on the group or company's operations as described above.

- IFRIC 15, 'Agreements for construction of real estates' (effective from 1 January 2009). The interpretation clarifies whether IAS 18, 'Revenue', or IAS 11, 'Construction contracts', should be applied to particular transactions. It is likely to result in IAS 18 being applied to a wider range of transactions. IFRIC 15 is not relevant to the group or company's operations as all revenue transactions are accounted for under IAS 18 and not IAS 11.

1p110 **2.2 Consolidation**

27p12 *(a) Subsidiaries*
27p14 Subsidiaries are all entities (including special purpose entities) over which the group has the
27p30 power to govern the financial and operating policies generally accompanying a shareholding of more than one half of the voting rights. The existence and effect of potential voting rights that are currently exercisable or convertible are considered when assessing whether the group controls another entity. Subsidiaries are fully consolidated from the date on which control is transferred to the group. They are de-consolidated from the date that control ceases.

IFRS3p14 The purchase method of accounting is used to account for the acquisition of subsidiaries by the
IFRS3p24 group. The cost of an acquisition is measured as the fair value of the assets given, equity

IFRS GAAP plc 49

(Amounts in C thousands unless otherwise stated)

IFRS3p28 / IFRS3p36, 37 / IFRS3p51 instruments issued and liabilities incurred or assumed at the date of exchange, plus costs directly attributable to the acquisition. Identifiable assets acquired and liabilities and contingent liabilities assumed in a business combination are measured initially at their fair values at the acquisition date, irrespective of the extent of any minority interest. The excess of the cost of acquisition over the fair value of the group's share of the identifiable net assets acquired is recorded as goodwill. If the cost of acquisition is less than the fair value of the net assets of the subsidiary acquired, the difference is recognised directly in the income statement (note 2.6). **(IFRS3p56)**

27p24 / 27p28 Inter-company transactions, balances and unrealised gains on transactions between group companies are eliminated. Unrealised losses are also eliminated. Accounting policies of subsidiaries have been changed where necessary to ensure consistency with the policies adopted by the group.

(b) Transactions and minority interests
The group applies a policy of treating transactions with minority interests as transactions with parties external to the group. Disposals to minority interests result in gains and losses for the group and are recorded in the income statement. Purchases from minority interests result in goodwill, being the difference between any consideration paid and the relevant share acquired of the carrying value of net assets of the subsidiary[1].

(c) Associates
1p110 / 28p13 / 28p11 Associates are all entities over which the group has significant influence but not control, generally accompanying a shareholding of between 20% and 50% of the voting rights. Investments in associates are accounted for using the equity method of accounting and are initially recognised at cost. The group's investment in associates includes goodwill identified on acquisition, net of any accumulated impairment loss. See note 2.7 for the impairment of non-financial assets including goodwill.

28p29 / 28p30 The group's share of its associates' post-acquisition profits or losses is recognised in the income statement, and its share of post-acquisition movements in reserves is recognised in reserves. The cumulative post-acquisition movements are adjusted against the carrying amount of the investment. When the group's share of losses in an associate equals or exceeds its interest in the associate, including any other unsecured receivables, the group does not recognise further losses, unless it has incurred obligations or made payments on behalf of the associate.

28p22 / 28p26 Unrealised gains on transactions between the group and its associates are eliminated to the extent of the group's interest in the associates. Unrealised losses are also eliminated unless the transaction provides evidence of an impairment of the asset transferred. Accounting policies of associates have been changed where necessary to ensure consistency with the policies adopted by the group.

Dilution gains and losses arising in investments in associates are recognised in the income statement[2].

2.3 Segment reporting
1p110

IFRS8p5(b) Operating segments are reported in a manner consistent with the internal reporting provided to the chief operating decision-maker. The chief operating decision-maker, who is responsible for allocating resources and assessing performance of the operating segments, has been identified as the steering committee that makes strategic decisions.

2.4 Foreign currency translation
1p110

(a) Functional and presentation currency
1p110 / 21p17 / 21p9, 18 / 1p46(d) Items included in the financial statements of each of the group's entities are measured using the currency of the primary economic environment in which the entity operates ('the functional currency'). The consolidated financial statements are presented in 'currency' (C), which is the company's functional and the group's presentation currency.

(b) Transactions and balances
1p110 / 21p21, 28 / 21p32 Foreign currency transactions are translated into the functional currency using the exchange rates prevailing at the dates of the transactions or valuation where items are remeasured. Foreign exchange gains and losses resulting from the settlement of such transactions and from

---

[1] These consolidated financial statements are prepared on the basis of 'parent company model'. See Appendix III for accounting policy if the economic entity model is adopted.

[2] The company may alternatively adopt an accounting policy to recognise dilution gains or losses in equity.

IFRS GAAP plc

(Amounts in C thousands unless otherwise stated)

39p95(a)
39p102(a)
the translation at year-end exchange rates of monetary assets and liabilities denominated in foreign currencies are recognised in the income statement, except when deferred in equity as qualifying cash flow hedges and qualifying net investment hedges.

Foreign exchange gains and losses that relate to borrowings and cash and cash equivalents are presented in the income statement within 'finance income or cost'. All other foreign exchange gains and losses are presented in the income statement within 'other (losses)/gains – net'.

39AG83
Changes in the fair value of monetary securities denominated in foreign currency classified as available for sale are analysed between translation differences resulting from changes in the amortised cost of the security and other changes in the carrying amount of the security. Translation differences related to changes in amortised cost are recognised in profit or loss, and other changes in carrying amount are recognised in equity.

21p30
Translation differences on non-monetary financial assets and liabilities such as equities held at fair value through profit or loss are recognised in profit or loss as part of the fair value gain or loss. Translation differences on non-monetary financial assets such as equities classified as available for sale are included in the available for sale reserve in equity.

1p110
21p39
(c) Group companies
The results and financial position of all the group entities (none of which has the currency of a hyper-inflationary economy) that have a functional currency different from the presentation currency are translated into the presentation currency as follows:

21p39(a)
(a) assets and liabilities for each balance sheet presented are translated at the closing rate at the date of that balance sheet;

21p39(b)
21p39
(b) income and expenses for each income statement are translated at average exchange rates (unless this average is not a reasonable approximation of the cumulative effect of the rates prevailing on the transaction dates, in which case income and expenses are translated at the rate on the dates of the transactions); and

1p76(b)
(c) all resulting exchange differences are recognised as a separate component of equity.

1p76(b)
21p39(c)
1p76(b)
39p102
On consolidation, exchange differences arising from the translation of the net investment in foreign operations, and of borrowings and other currency instruments designated as hedges of such investments, are taken to shareholders' equity. When a foreign operation is partially disposed of or sold, exchange differences that were recorded in equity are recognised in the income statement as part of the gain or loss on sale.

21p47
Goodwill and fair value adjustments arising on the acquisition of a foreign entity are treated as assets and liabilities of the foreign entity and translated at the closing rate.

1p110
2.5 Property, plant and equipment

16p73(a)
Land and buildings comprise mainly factories, retail outlets and offices. Land and buildings are shown at fair value, based on periodic, but at least triennial, valuations by external independent valuers, less subsequent depreciation for buildings. Any accumulated depreciation at the date of revaluation is eliminated against the gross carrying amount of the asset, and the net amount is restated to the revalued amount of the asset. All other property, plant and equipment is stated at historical cost less depreciation. Historical cost includes expenditure that is directly attributable to the acquisition of the items. Cost may also include transfers from equity of any gains/losses on qualifying cash flow hedges of foreign currency purchases of property, plant and equipment[1].

16p35(b)
16p15
16p17

16p12
39p98(b)
Subsequent costs are included in the asset's carrying amount or recognised as a separate asset, as appropriate, only when it is probable that future economic benefits associated with the item will flow to the group and the cost of the item can be measured reliably. The carrying amount of the replaced part is derecognised. All other repairs and maintenance are charged to the income statement during the financial period in which they are incurred.

16p39, 1p76(b)
1p76(b)
Increases in the carrying amount arising on revaluation of land and buildings are credited to other reserves in shareholders' equity. Decreases that offset previous increases of the same asset are charged against other reserves directly in equity; all other decreases are charged to the income statement. Each year the difference between depreciation based on the revalued carrying amount of the asset charged to the income statement and depreciation based on the asset's original cost is transferred from 'other reserves' to 'retained earnings'.

16p40
16p41

---

[1] Management may choose to keep these gains/(losses) in equity until the acquired asset affects profit or loss. At this time, management should reclassify the gains/(losses) into profit or loss.

IFRS GAAP plc

51

(Amounts in C thousands unless otherwise stated)

16p73(b), 50 16p73(c)	Land is not depreciated. Depreciation on other assets is calculated using the straight-line method to allocate their cost or revalued amounts to their residual values over their estimated useful lives, as follows:

– Buildings	25-40 years
– Machinery	10-15 years
– Vehicles	3-5 years
– Furniture, fittings and equipment	3-8 years

16p51	The assets' residual values and useful lives are reviewed, and adjusted if appropriate, at each balance sheet date.
36p59	An asset's carrying amount is written down immediately to its recoverable amount if the asset's carrying amount is greater than its estimated recoverable amount (note 2.7).
16p68, 71	Gains and losses on disposals are determined by comparing the proceeds with the carrying amount and are recognised within 'Other (losses)/gains – net' in the income statement.
16p41, 1p76(b)	When revalued assets are sold, the amounts included in other reserves are transferred to retained earnings.

1p110   2.6 Intangible assets

1p110	*(a) Goodwill*
1p110 IFRS3p51 38p118(a) IFRS3p54 36p124	Goodwill represents the excess of the cost of an acquisition over the fair value of the group's share of the net identifiable assets of the acquired subsidiary at the date of acquisition. Goodwill on acquisitions of subsidiaries is included in 'intangible assets'. Goodwill is tested annually for impairment and carried at cost less accumulated impairment losses. Impairment losses on goodwill are not reversed. Gains and losses on the disposal of an entity include the carrying amount of goodwill relating to the entity sold.
36p80	Goodwill is allocated to cash-generating units for the purpose of impairment testing. The allocation is made to those cash-generating units or groups of cash-generating units that are expected to benefit from the business combination in which the goodwill arose identified according to operating segment.
1p110 38p74 38p97 38p118(a)(b)	*(b) Trademarks and licences* Separately acquired trademarks and licences are shown at historical cost. Trademarks and licences acquired in a business combination are recognised at fair value at the acquisition date. Trademarks and licences have a finite useful life and are carried at cost less accumulated amortisation. Amortisation is calculated using the straight-line method to allocate the cost of trademarks and licences over their estimated useful lives of 15 to 20 years.
38p4 38p118(a)(b)	Acquired computer software licences are capitalised on the basis of the costs incurred to acquire and bring to use the specific software. These costs are amortised over their estimated useful lives of three to five years.
	(c) Contractual customer relationships Contractual customer relationships acquired in a business combination are recognised at fair value at the acquisition date. The contractual customer relations have a finite useful life and are carried at cost less accumulated amortisation. Amortisation is calculated using the straight-line method over the expected life of the customer relationship.
1p110 38p57	*(d) Computer software* Costs associated with maintaining computer software programmes are recognised as an expense as incurred. Development costs that are directly attributable to the design and testing of identifiable and unique software products controlled by the group are recognised as intangible assets when the following criteria are met:

- it is technically feasible to complete the software product so that it will be available for use;
- management intends to complete the software product and use or sell it;
- there is an ability to use or sell the software product;
- it can be demonstrated how the software product will generate probable future economic benefits;
- adequate technical, financial and other resources to complete the development and to use or sell the software product are available; and

IFRS GAAP plc

52

(Amounts in C thousands unless otherwise stated)

    – the expenditure attributable to the software product during its development can be reliably measured.

38p66	Directly attributable costs that are capitalised as part of the software product include the software development employee costs and an appropriate portion of relevant overheads.
38p68,71	Other development expenditures that do not meet these criteria are recognised as an expense as incurred. Development costs previously recognised as an expense are not recognised as an asset in a subsequent period
38p97 38p118(a)(b)	Computer software development costs recognised as assets are amortised over their estimated useful lives, which does not exceed three years.

2.7 Impairment of non-financial assets

1p110

36p9
36p10

Assets that have an indefinite useful life, for example goodwill, are not subject to amortisation and are tested annually for impairment. Assets that are subject to amortisation are reviewed for impairment whenever events or changes in circumstances indicate that the carrying amount may not be recoverable. An impairment loss is recognised for the amount by which the asset's carrying amount exceeds its recoverable amount. The recoverable amount is the higher of an asset's fair value less costs to sell and value in use. For the purposes of assessing impairment, assets are grouped at the lowest levels for which there are separately identifiable cash flows (cash-generating units). Non-financial assets other than goodwill that suffered an impairment are reviewed for possible reversal of the impairment at each reporting date.

2.8 Non-current assets (or disposal groups) held for sale

1p110

IFRS5p6, 15

Non-current assets (or disposal groups) are classified as assets held for sale when their carrying amount is to be recovered principally through a sale transaction and a sale is considered highly probable. They are stated at the lower of carrying amount and fair value less costs to sell if their carrying amount is to be recovered principally through a sale transaction rather than through continuing use.

2.9 Financial assets

1p110

2.9.1 Classification

IFRS7p21
39p9

The group classifies its financial assets in the following categories: at fair value through profit or loss, loans and receivables, and available for sale. The classification depends on the purpose for which the financial assets were acquired. Management determines the classification of its financial assets at initial recognition.

(a) Financial assets at fair value through profit or loss

39p9

41p57, 59

Financial assets at fair value through profit or loss are financial assets held for trading. A financial asset is classified in this category if acquired principally for the purpose of selling in the short-term. Derivatives are also categorised as held for trading unless they are designated as hedges. Assets in this category are classified as current assets.

(b) Loans and receivables

39p9
1p57, 59

Loans and receivables are non-derivative financial assets with fixed or determinable payments that are not quoted in an active market. They are included in current assets, except for maturities greater than 12 months after the balance sheet date. These are classified as non-current assets. The group's loans and receivables comprise 'trade and other receivables' and cash and cash equivalents in the balance sheet (notes 2.11 and 2.12).

(c) Available-for-sale financial assets

39p9
1p57, 59
IFRS7 AppxB5(b)

Available-for-sale financial assets are non-derivatives that are either designated in this category or not classified in any of the other categories. They are included in non-current assets unless management intends to dispose of the investment within 12 months of the balance sheet date.

2.9.2 Recognition and measurement

39p38
IFRS7
AppxBp5(c)
39p43
39p16
39p46

Regular purchases and sales of financial assets are recognised on the trade-date – the date on which the group commits to purchase or sell the asset. Investments are initially recognised at fair value plus transaction costs for all financial assets not carried at fair value through profit or loss. Financial assets carried at fair value through profit or loss are initially recognised at fair value, and transaction costs are expensed in the income statement. Financial assets are derecognised when the rights to receive cash flows from the investments have expired or have been transferred

IFRS GAAP plc 53

(Amounts in C thousands unless otherwise stated)

and the group has transferred substantially all risks and rewards of ownership. Available-for-sale financial assets and financial assets at fair value through profit or loss are subsequently carried at fair value. Loans and receivables are carried at amortised cost using the effective interest method.

39p55(a)
IFRS7Appx
Bp5(e)

Gains or losses arising from changes in the fair value of the 'financial assets at fair value through profit or loss' category are presented in the income statement within 'other (losses)/gains – net' in the period in which they arise. Dividend income from financial assets at fair value through profit or loss is recognised in the income statement as part of other income when the group's right to receive payments is established.

39p55(b)
IFRS7Appx
Bp5(e)
39AG83
1p76(b)

Changes in the fair value of monetary securities denominated in a foreign currency and classified as available for sale are analysed between translation differences resulting from changes in amortised cost of the security and other changes in the carrying amount of the security. The translation differences on monetary securities are recognised in profit or loss; translation differences on non-monetary securities are recognised in equity. Changes in the fair value of monetary and non-monetary securities classified as available for sale are recognised in equity.

When securities classified as available for sale are sold or impaired, the accumulated fair value adjustments recognised in equity are included in the income statement as 'gains and losses from investment securities'.

39p67

Interest on available-for-sale securities calculated using the effective interest method is recognised in the income statement as part of other income. Dividends on available-for-sale equity instruments are recognised in the income statement as part of other income when the group's right to receive payments is established.

IFRS7p27(a)
39AG72,
73
39AG74

The fair values of quoted investments are based on current bid prices. If the market for a financial asset is not active (and for unlisted securities), the group establishes fair value by using valuation techniques. These include the use of recent arm's length transactions, reference to other instruments that are substantially the same, discounted cash flow analysis, and option pricing models, making maximum use of market inputs and relying as little as possible on entity-specific inputs.

39p58
39p67
39p68
IFRS7
Appx
Bp5(f)
39p69

The group assesses at each balance sheet date whether there is objective evidence that a financial asset or a group of financial assets is impaired. In the case of equity securities classified as available for sale, a significant or prolonged decline in the fair value of the security below its cost is considered as an indicator that the securities are impaired. If any such evidence exists for available-for-sale financial assets, the cumulative loss – measured as the difference between the acquisition cost and the current fair value, less any impairment loss on that financial asset previously recognised in profit or loss – is removed from equity and recognised in the income statement. Impairment losses recognised in the income statement on equity instruments are not reversed through the income statement. Impairment testing of trade receivables is described in note 2.12.

1p110

2.10 Derivative financial instruments and hedging activities

IFRS7p21
IFRS7p22

Derivatives are initially recognised at fair value on the date a derivative contract is entered into and are subsequently remeasured at their fair value. The method of recognising the resulting gain or loss depends on whether the derivative is designated as a hedging instrument, and if so, the nature of the item being hedged. The group designates certain derivatives as either:

(a) hedges of the fair value of recognised assets or liabilities or a firm commitment (fair value hedge);
(b) hedges of a particular risk associated with a recognised asset or liability or a highly probable forecast transaction (cash flow hedge); or
(c) hedges of a net investment in a foreign operation (net investment hedge).

39p88

The group documents at the inception of the transaction the relationship between hedging instruments and hedged items, as well as its risk management objectives and strategy for undertaking various hedging transactions. The group also documents its assessment, both at hedge inception and on an ongoing basis, of whether the derivatives that are used in hedging transactions are highly effective in offsetting changes in fair values or cash flows of hedged items.

IFRS7p23, 24

The fair values of various derivative instruments used for hedging purposes are disclosed in note 11. Movements on the hedging reserve in shareholders' equity are shown in note 19. The full fair value of a hedging derivative is classified as a non-current asset or liability when the remaining

IFRS GAAP plc

54

(Amounts in C thousands unless otherwise stated)

hedged item is more than 12 months, and as a current asset or liability when the remaining maturity of the hedged item is less than 12 months. Trading derivatives are classified as a current asset or liability.

39p89   *(a) Fair value hedge*

Changes in the fair value of derivatives that are designated and qualify as fair value hedges are recorded in the income statement, together with any changes in the fair value of the hedged asset or liability that are attributable to the hedged risk. The group only applies fair value hedge accounting for hedging fixed interest risk on borrowings. The gain or loss relating to the effective portion of interest rate swaps hedging fixed rate borrowings is recognised in the income statement within 'finance costs'. The gain or loss relating to the ineffective portion is recognised in the income statement within 'other gains/(losses) – net'. Changes in the fair value of the hedge fixed rate borrowings attributable to interest rate risk are recognised in the income statement within 'finance costs'.

39p92   If the hedge no longer meets the criteria for hedge accounting, the adjustment to the carrying amount of a hedged item for which the effective interest method is used is amortised to profit or loss over the period to maturity.

39p95
1p76(b)   *(b) Cash flow hedge*

The effective portion of changes in the fair value of derivatives that are designated and qualify as cash flow hedges is recognised in equity. The gain or loss relating to the ineffective portion is recognised immediately in the income statement within 'other gains/(losses) – net'.

39p99, 100   Amounts accumulated in equity are recycled in the income statement in the periods when the hedged item affects profit or loss (for example, when the forecast sale that is hedged takes place). The gain or loss relating to the effective portion of interest rate swaps hedging variable rate
39p98(b)   borrowings is recognised in the income statement within 'finance costs'. The gain or loss relating to the ineffective portion is recognised in the income statement within 'other gains/(losses) – net'. However, when the forecast transaction that is hedged results in the recognition of a non-financial asset (for example, inventory or fixed assets), the gains and losses previously deferred in equity are transferred from equity and included in the initial measurement of the cost of the asset. The deferred amounts are ultimately recognised in cost of goods sold in the case of inventory or in depreciation in the case of fixed assets.

39p101   When a hedging instrument expires or is sold, or when a hedge no longer meets the criteria for hedge accounting, any cumulative gain or loss existing in equity at that time remains in equity and is recognised when the forecast transaction is ultimately recognised in the income statement. When a forecast transaction is no longer expected to occur, the cumulative gain or loss that was reported in equity is immediately transferred to the income statement within 'other gains/(losses) – net'.

39p102(a)(b)   *(c) Net investment hedge*

Hedges of net investments in foreign operations are accounted for similarly to cash flow hedges.

1p76(b)   Any gain or loss on the hedging instrument relating to the effective portion of the hedge is recognised in equity. The gain or loss relating to the ineffective portion is recognised immediately in the income statement within 'other gains/(losses) – net'.

Gains and losses accumulated in equity are included in the income statement when the foreign operation is partially disposed of or sold.

39p55(a)   *(d) Derivatives at fair value through profit or loss and accounted for at fair value through profit or loss*

Certain derivative instruments do not qualify for hedge accounting. Changes in the fair value of any these derivative instruments are recognised immediately in the income statement within 'other gains/(losses) – net'.

1p110   **2.11 Inventories**

2p36(a), 9
2p10, 25   Inventories are stated at the lower of cost and net realisable value. Cost is determined using the first-in, first-out (FIFO) method. The cost of finished goods and work in progress comprises
23p6, 7   design costs, raw materials, direct labour, other direct costs and related production overheads (based on normal operating capacity). It excludes borrowing costs. Net realisable value is the

   1059

IFRS GAAP plc   55

(Amounts in C thousands unless otherwise stated)

2p28, 30
39p98(b)

estimated selling price in the ordinary course of business, less applicable variable selling expenses. Costs of inventories include the transfer from equity of any gains/losses on qualifying cash flow hedges purchases of raw materials[1].

1p110
IFRS7p21

2.12 Trade receivables

39p43
39p46(a)
39p59
IFRS7
Appx Bp5(f)
IFRS7
Appx Bp5(d)

Trade receivables are recognised initially at fair value and subsequently measured at amortised cost using the effective interest method, less provision for impairment. A provision for impairment of trade receivables is established when there is objective evidence that the group will not be able to collect all amounts due according to the original terms of the receivables. Significant financial difficulties of the debtor, probability that the debtor will enter bankruptcy or financial reorganisation, and default or delinquency in payments (more than 30 days overdue) are considered indicators that the trade receivable is impaired. The amount of the provision is the difference between the asset's carrying amount and the present value of estimated future cash flows, discounted at the original effective interest rate. The carrying amount of the asset is reduced through the use of an allowance account, and the amount of the loss is recognised in the income statement within 'selling and marketing costs'. When a trade receivable is uncollectible, it is written off against the allowance account for trade receivables. Subsequent recoveries of amounts previously written off are credited against 'selling and marketing costs' in the income statement.

1p110
IFRS7p21

2.13 Cash and cash equivalents

7p45

Cash and cash equivalents includes cash in hand, deposits held at call with banks, other short-term highly liquid investments with original maturities of three months or less, and bank overdrafts. Bank overdrafts are shown within borrowings in current liabilities on the balance sheet.

1p110
IFRS7p21

2.14 Share capital

32p18(a)

Ordinary shares are classified as equity. Mandatorily redeemable preference shares are classified as liabilities (note 2.16).

32p37

Incremental costs directly attributable to the issue of new shares or options are shown in equity as a deduction, net of tax, from the proceeds.

32p33

Where any group company purchases the company's equity share capital (treasury shares), the consideration paid, including any directly attributable incremental costs (net of income taxes) is deducted from equity attributable to the company's equity holders until the shares are cancelled or reissued. Where such shares are subsequently reissued, any consideration received, net of any directly attributable incremental transaction costs and the related income tax effects, is included in equity attributable to the company's equity holders.

1p110

2.15 Trade payables

IFRS7p21
39p43, 39p47

Trade payables are recognised initially at fair value and subsequently measured at amortised cost using the effective interest method.

1p110
IFRS7p21

2.16 Borrowings

39p43
39p47

Borrowings are recognised initially at fair value, net of transaction costs incurred. Borrowings are subsequently stated at amortised cost; any difference between the proceeds (net of transaction costs) and the redemption value is recognised in the income statement over the period of the borrowings using the effective interest method.

Fees paid on the establishment of loan facilities are recognised as transaction costs of the loan to the extent that it is probable that some or all of the facility will be drawn down. In this case, the fee is deferred until the draw-down occurs. To the extent there is no evidence that it is probable that some or all of the facility will be drawn down, the fee is capitalised as a pre-payment for liquidity services and amortised over the period of the facility to which it relates.

32p18(a)
32p33

Preference shares, which are mandatorily redeemable on a specific date, are classified as liabilities. The dividends on these preference shares are recognised in the income statement as interest expense.

---

[1] Management may choose to keep these gains in equity until the acquired asset affects profit or loss. At this time, management should re-classify the gains to profit or loss.

IFRS GAAP plc 56
(Amounts in C thousands unless otherwise stated)

IFRS7p27(a)
32p18, 28
32AG31 — The fair value of the liability portion of a convertible bond is determined using a market interest rate for an equivalent non-convertible bond. This amount is recorded as a liability on an amortised cost basis until extinguished on conversion or maturity of the bonds. The remainder of the proceeds is allocated to the conversion option. This is recognised and included in shareholders' equity, net of income tax effects.

1p60 — Borrowings are classified as current liabilities unless the group has an unconditional right to defer settlement of the liability for at least 12 months after the balance sheet date.

1p110 **2.17 Current and deferred income tax**

12p58
12p61 — The tax expense for the period comprises current and deferred tax. Tax is recognised in the income statement, except to the extent that it relates to items recognised directly in equity. In this case the tax is also recognised in equity.

12p12
12p46 — The current income tax charge is calculated on the basis of the tax laws enacted or substantively enacted at the balance sheet date in the countries where the company's subsidiaries and associates operate and generate taxable income. Management periodically evaluates positions taken in tax returns with respect to situations in which applicable tax regulation is subject to interpretation. It establishes provisions where appropriate on the basis of amounts expected to be paid to the tax authorities.

12p24
12p15
12p47 — Deferred income tax is recognised, using the liability method, on temporary differences arising between the tax bases of assets and liabilities and their carrying amounts in the consolidated financial statements. However, the deferred income tax is not accounted for if it arises from initial recognition of an asset or liability in a transaction other than a business combination that at the time of the transaction affects neither accounting nor taxable profit or loss. Deferred income tax is determined using tax rates (and laws) that have been enacted or substantially enacted by the balance sheet date and are expected to apply when the related deferred income tax asset is realised or the deferred income tax liability is settled.

12p24, 34 — Deferred income tax assets are recognised only to the extent that it is probable that future taxable profit will be available against which the temporary differences can be utilised.

12p39, 44 — Deferred income tax is provided on temporary differences arising on investments in subsidiaries and associates, except where the timing of the reversal of the temporary difference is controlled by the group and it is probable that the temporary difference will not reverse in the foreseeable future.

1p110 **2.18 Employee benefits**

1p110 *(a) Pension obligations*
19p27
19p25
19p7
19p120A(b) — Group companies operate various pension schemes. The schemes are generally funded through payments to insurance companies or trustee-administered funds, determined by periodic actuarial calculations. The group has both defined benefit and defined contribution plans. A defined contribution plan is a pension plan under which the group pays fixed contributions into a separate entity. The group has no legal or constructive obligations to pay further contributions if the fund does not hold sufficient assets to pay all employees the benefits relating to employee service in the current and prior periods. A defined benefit plan is a pension plan that is not a defined contribution plan. Typically defined benefit plans define an amount of pension benefit that an employee will receive on retirement, usually dependent on one or more factors such as age, years of service and compensation.

19p79, 19p80,
19p64 — The liability recognised in the balance sheet in respect of defined benefit pension plans is the present value of the defined benefit obligation at the balance sheet date less the fair value of plan assets, together with adjustments for unrecognised past-service costs. The defined benefit obligation is calculated annually by independent actuaries using the projected unit credit method. The present value of the defined benefit obligation is determined by discounting the estimated future cash outflows using interest rates of high-quality corporate bonds that are denominated in the currency in which the benefits will be paid, and that have terms to maturity approximating to the terms of the related pension liability.

19p93-93D
19p120A(a) — Actuarial gains and losses arising from experience adjustments and changes in actuarial assumptions are charged or credited to equity in the statement of recognised income and expense (SORIE) in the period in which they arise.

IFRS GAAP plc 57

(Amounts in C thousands unless otherwise stated)

19p96 Past-service costs are recognised immediately in income, unless the changes to the pension plan are conditional on the employees remaining in service for a specified period of time (the vesting period). In this case, the past-service costs are amortised on a straight-line basis over the vesting period.

19p44 For defined contribution plans, the group pays contributions to publicly or privately administered pension insurance plans on a mandatory, contractual or voluntary basis. The group has no further payment obligations once the contributions have been paid. The contributions are recognised as employee benefit expense when they are due. Prepaid contributions are recognised as an asset to the extent that a cash refund or a reduction in the future payments is available.

1p110
19p120A(a)
19p120A(b)
(b) Other post-employment obligations
Some group companies provide post-retirement healthcare benefits to their retirees. The entitlement to these benefits is usually conditional on the employee remaining in service up to retirement age and the completion of a minimum service period. The expected costs of these benefits are accrued over the period of employment using the same accounting methodology as used for defined benefit pension plans. Actuarial gains and losses arising from experience adjustments and changes in actuarial assumptions are charged or credited to equity in the SORIE in the period in which they arise. These obligations are valued annually by independent qualified actuaries.

1p110
IFRS2p15(b)
IFRS2p19
(c) Share-based compensation
The group operates a number of equity-settled, share-based compensation plans, under which the entity receives services from employees as consideration for equity instruments (options) of the group. The fair value of the employee services received in exchange for the grant of the options is recognised as an expense. The total amount to be expensed is determined by reference to the fair value of the options granted, excluding the impact of any non-market service and performance vesting conditions (for example, profitability, sales growth targets and remaining an employee of the entity over a specified time period). Non-market vesting conditions are included in assumptions about the number of options that are expected to vest. The total amount expensed is recognised over the vesting period, which is the period over which all of the specified vesting conditions are to be satisfied. At each balance sheet date, the entity revises its estimates of the number of options that are expected to vest based on the non-marketing vesting conditions. It recognises the impact of the revision to original estimates, if any, in the income statement, with a corresponding adjustment to equity.

The proceeds received net of any directly attributable transaction costs are credited to share capital (nominal value) and share premium when the options are exercised. The grant by the company of options over its equity instruments to the employees of subsidiary undertakings in the group is treated as a capital contribution. The fair value of employee services received, measured by reference to the grant date fair value, is recognised over the investing period as an increase to investment in subsidiary undertakings, with a corresponding credit to equity.

1p110
19p133
19p134
19p139
(d) Termination benefits
Termination benefits are payable when employment is terminated by the group before the normal retirement date, or whenever an employee accepts voluntary redundancy in exchange for these benefits. The group recognises termination benefits when it is demonstrably committed to either: terminating the employment of current employees according to a detailed formal plan without possibility of withdrawal; or providing termination benefits as a result of an offer made to encourage voluntary redundancy. Benefits falling due more than 12 months after the balance sheet date are discounted to their present value.

1p110
19p17
(e) Profit-sharing and bonus plans
The group recognises a liability and an expense for bonuses and profit-sharing, based on a formula that takes into consideration the profit attributable to the company's shareholders after certain adjustments. The group recognises a provision where contractually obliged or where there is a past practice that has created a constructive obligation.

1p110 **2.19 Provisions**

37p14
37p72
37p63
Provisions for environmental restoration, restructuring costs and legal claims are recognised when: the group has a present legal or constructive obligation as a result of past events; it is probable that an outflow of resources will be required to settle the obligation; and the amount has been reliably estimated. Restructuring provisions comprise lease termination penalties and employee termination payments. Provisions are not recognised for future operating losses.

IFRS GAAP plc 58

(Amounts in C thousands unless otherwise stated)

37p24 Where there are a number of similar obligations, the likelihood that an outflow will be required in settlement is determined by considering the class of obligations as a whole. A provision is recognised even if the likelihood of an outflow with respect to any one item included in the same class of obligations may be small.

37p45 Provisions are measured at the present value of the expenditures expected to be required to settle the obligation using a pre-tax rate that reflects current market assessments of the time value of money and the risks specific to the obligation. The increase in the provision due to passage of time is recognised as interest expense.

1p110 **2.20 Revenue recognition**

18p35(a) Revenue comprises the fair value of the consideration received or receivable for the sale of goods and services in the ordinary course of the group's activities. Revenue is shown net of value-added tax, returns, rebates and discounts and after eliminating sales within the group.

The group recognises revenue when the amount of revenue can be reliably measured, it is probable that future economic benefits will flow to the entity and when specific criteria have been met for each of the group's activities as described below. The amount of revenue is not considered to be reliably measurable until all contingencies relating to the sale have been resolved. The group bases its estimates on historical results, taking into consideration the type of customer, the type of transaction and the specifics of each arrangement.

18p14 *(a) Sales of goods – wholesale*
The group manufactures and sells a range of footwear products in the wholesale market. Sales of goods are recognised when a group entity has delivered products to the wholesaler, the wholesaler has full discretion over the channel and price to sell the products, and there is no unfulfilled obligation that could affect the wholesaler's acceptance of the products. Delivery does not occur until the products have been shipped to the specified location, the risks of obsolescence and loss have been transferred to the wholesaler, and either the wholesaler has accepted the products in accordance with the sales contract, the acceptance provisions have lapsed, or the group has objective evidence that all criteria for acceptance have been satisfied.

The footwear products are often sold with volume discounts; customers have a right to return faulty products in the wholesale market. Sales are recorded based on the price specified in the sales contracts, net of the estimated volume discounts and returns at the time of sale. Accumulated experience is used to estimate and provide for the discounts and returns. The volume discounts are assessed based on anticipated annual purchases. No element of financing is deemed present as the sales are made with a credit term of 60 days, which is consistent with the market practice.

18p14 *(b) Sales of goods – retail*
The group operates a chain of retail outlets for selling shoes and other leather products. Sales of goods are recognised when a group entity sells a product to the customer. Retail sales are usually in cash or by credit card.

It is the group's policy to sell its products to the retail customer with a right to return within 28 days. Accumulated experience is used to estimate and provide for such returns at the time of sale. The group does not operate any loyalty programmes.

18p20 *(c) Sales of services*
The group sells design services and transportation services to other shoe manufacturers. These services are provided on a time and material basis or as a fixed-price contract, with contract terms generally ranging from less than one year to three years.

Revenue from time and material contracts, typically from delivering design services, is recognised under the percentage-of-completion method. Revenue is generally recognised at the contractual rates. For time contracts, the stage of completion is measured on the basis of labour hours delivered as a percentage of total hours to be delivered. For material contracts, the stage of completion is measured on the basis of direct expenses incurred as a percentage of the total expenses to be incurred.

Revenue from fixed-price contracts for delivering design services is also recognised under the percentage-of-completion method. Revenue is generally recognised based on the services performed to date as a percentage of the total services to be performed.

IFRS GAAP plc 59

(Amounts in C thousands unless otherwise stated)

Revenue from fixed-price contracts for delivering transportation services is generally recognised in the period the services are provided, using a straight-line basis over the term of the contract.

If circumstances arise that may change the original estimates of revenues, costs or extent of progress toward completion, estimates are revised. These revisions may result in increases or decreases in estimated revenues or costs and are reflected in income in the period in which the circumstances that give rise to the revision become known by management.

18p30(a)
39p93

(d) Interest income

Interest income is recognised on a time-proportion basis using the effective interest method. When a receivable is impaired, the group reduces the carrying amount to its recoverable amount, being the estimated future cash flow discounted at the original effective interest rate of the instrument, and continues unwinding the discount as interest income. Interest income on impaired loans is recognised using the original effective interest rate.

18p30(b)

(e) Royalty income

Royalty income is recognised on an accruals basis in accordance with the substance of the relevant agreements.

18p30(c)

(f) Dividend income

Dividend income is recognised when the right to receive payment is established.

1p110

2.21 Leases

17p33
SIC-15p5

Leases in which a significant portion of the risks and rewards of ownership are retained by the lessor are classified as operating leases. Payments made under operating leases (net of any incentives received from the lessor) are charged to the income statement on a straight-line basis over the period of the lease.

1p110

The group leases certain property, plant and equipment. Leases of property, plant and equipment where the group has substantially all the risks and rewards of ownership are classified as finance leases. Finance leases are capitalised at the lease's commencement at the lower of the fair value of the leased property and the present value of the minimum lease payments.

17p20
17p27

Each lease payment is allocated between the liability and finance charges so as to achieve a constant rate on the finance balance outstanding. The corresponding rental obligations, net of finance charges, are included in other long-term payables. The interest element of the finance cost is charged to the income statement over the lease period so as to produce a constant periodic rate of interest on the remaining balance of the liability for each period. The property, plant and equipment acquired under finance leases is depreciated over the shorter of the useful life of the asset and the lease term.

1p110

2.22 Dividend distribution

10p12

Dividend distribution to the company's shareholders is recognised as a liability in the group's financial statements in the period in which the dividends are approved by the company's shareholders.

3 Financial risk management

Group

3.1 Financial risk factors

IFRS7p31

The group's activities expose it to a variety of financial risks: market risk (including currency risk, fair value interest rate risk, cash flow interest rate risk and price risk), credit risk and liquidity risk. The group's overall risk management programme focuses on the unpredictability of financial markets and seeks to minimise potential adverse effects on the group's financial performance. The group uses derivative financial instruments to hedge certain risk exposures.

Risk management is carried out by a central treasury department (group treasury) under policies approved by the board of directors. Group treasury identifies, evaluates and hedges financial risks in close co-operation with the group's operating units. The board provides written principles for overall risk management, as well as written policies covering specific areas, such as foreign exchange risk, interest rate risk, credit risk, use of derivative financial instruments and non-derivative financial instruments, and investment of excess liquidity.

IFRS GAAP plc

(Amounts in C thousands unless otherwise stated)

(a) Market risk

(i) Foreign exchange risk

IFRS7p33(a) The group operates internationally and is exposed to foreign exchange risk arising from various currency exposures, primarily with respect to the US dollar and the UK pound. Foreign exchange risk arises from future commercial transactions, recognised assets and liabilities and net investments in foreign operations.

IFRS7p33(b), 22(c) Management has set up a policy to require group companies to manage their foreign exchange risk against their functional currency. The group companies are required to hedge their entire foreign exchange risk exposure with the group treasury. To manage their foreign exchange risk arising from future commercial transactions and recognised assets and liabilities, entities in the group use forward contracts, transacted with group treasury. Foreign exchange risk arises when future commercial transactions or recognised assets or liabilities are denominated in a currency that is not the entity's functional currency.

IFRS7p22(c) The group treasury's risk management policy is to hedge between 75% and 100% of anticipated cash flows (mainly export sales and purchase of inventory) in each major foreign currency for the subsequent 12 months. Approximately 90% (2007: 95%) of projected sales in each major currency qualify as 'highly probable' forecast transactions for hedge accounting purposes.

39p73 For segment reporting purposes, each subsidiary designates contracts with group treasury as fair value hedges or cash flow hedges, as appropriate. External foreign exchange contracts are designated at group level as hedges of foreign exchange risk on specific assets, liabilities or future transactions on a gross basis.

IFRS7p33(a)(b) The group has certain investments in foreign operations, whose net assets are exposed to foreign
IFRS7p22(c) currency translation risk. Currency exposure arising from the net assets of the group's foreign operations is managed primarily through borrowings denominated in the relevant foreign currencies.

IFRS 7p40 At 31 December 2008, if the Currency had weakened/strengthened by 11% against the US dollar
IFRS 7IG36 with all other variables held constant, post-tax profit for the year would have been C362 (2007: C51) higher/lower, mainly as a result of foreign exchange gains/losses on translation of US dollar-denominated trade receivables, financial assets at fair value through profit or loss, debt securities classified as available for sale and foreign exchange losses/gains on translation of US dollar-denominated borrowings. Profit is more sensitive to movement in currency/US dollar exchange rates in 2008 than 2007 because of the increased amount of US dollar-denominated borrowings. Equity would have been C542 (2007: C157) lower/higher, arising mainly from foreign exchange losses/gains on translation of US dollar-denominated equity securities classified as available for sale. Equity is more sensitive to movement in currency/US dollar exchange rate in 2008 than 2007 because of the increased amount of US dollar-denominated equity securities classified as available for sale.

At 31 December 2008, if the Currency had weakened/strengthened by 4% against the UK pound with all other variables held constant, post-tax profit for the year would have been C135 (2007: C172) lower/higher, mainly as a result of foreign exchange gains/losses on translation of UK pound-denominated trade receivables, financial assets at fair value through profit or loss, debt securities classified as available for sale and foreign exchange losses/gains on translation of UK pound-denominated borrowings.

(ii) Price risk

IFRS7p33(a)(b) The group is exposed to equity securities price risk because of investments held by the group and classified on the consolidated balance sheet either as available for sale or at fair value through profit or loss. The group is not exposed to commodity price risk. To manage its price risk arising from investments in equity securities, the group diversifies its portfolio. Diversification of the portfolio is done in accordance with the limits set by the group.

The group's investments in equity of other entities that are publicly traded are included in one of the following three equity indexes: DAX equity index, Dow Jones equity index and FTSE 100 UK equity index.

IFRS7p40 The table below summarises the impact of increases/decreases of the FTSE 100 on the group's
IFRS7IG36 post-tax profit for the year and on equity. The analysis is based on the assumption that the equity indexes had increased/decreased by 5% with all other variables held constant and all the group's equity instruments moved according to the historical correlation with the index:

IFRS GAAP plc

(Amounts in C thousands unless otherwise stated)

Index	Impact on post-tax profit in C		Impact on other components of equity in C	
	2008	2007	**2008**	2007
DAX	**200**	120	**290**	290
Dow Jones	**150**	120	**200**	70
FTSE 100 UK	**60**	30	**160**	150

Post-tax profit for the year would increase/decrease as a result of gains/losses on equity securities classified as at fair value through profit or loss. Other components of equity would increase/decrease as a result of gains/losses on equity securities classified as available for sale.

IFRS7p33(a)

(iii) Cash flow and fair value interest rate risk

As the group has no significant interest-bearing assets, the group's income and operating cash flows are substantially independent of changes in market interest rates.

IFRS7p33(a)(b),
IFRS7p22(c)

The group's interest rate risk arises from long-term borrowings. Borrowings issued at variable rates expose the group to cash flow interest rate risk. Borrowings issued at fixed rates expose the group to fair value interest rate risk. Group policy is to maintain approximately 60% of its borrowings in fixed rate instruments. During 2008 and 2007, the group's borrowings at variable rate were denominated in the Currency and the UK pound.

IFRS7p22(b)(c)

The group analyses its interest rate exposure on a dynamic basis. Various scenarios are simulated taking into consideration refinancing, renewal of existing positions, alternative financing and hedging. Based on these scenarios, the group calculates the impact on profit and loss of a defined interest rate shift. For each simulation, the same interest rate shift is used for all currencies. The scenarios are run only for liabilities that represent the major interest-bearing positions.

Based on the simulations performed, the impact on post tax profit of a 0.1% shift would be a maximum increase of C41 (2007: C37) or decrease of C34 (2007: C29), respectively. The simulation is done on a quarterly basis to verify that the maximum loss potential is within the limit given by the management.

IFRS7p22(b)(c)

Based on the various scenarios, the group manages its cash flow interest rate risk by using floating-to-fixed interest rate swaps. Such interest rate swaps have the economic effect of converting borrowings from floating rates to fixed rates. Generally, the group raises long-term borrowings at floating rates and swaps them into fixed rates that are lower than those available if the group borrowed at fixed rates directly. Under the interest rate swaps, the group agrees with other parties to exchange, at specified intervals (primarily quarterly), the difference between fixed contract rates and floating-rate interest amounts calculated by reference to the agreed notional amounts.

IFRS7p22(b)(c)

Occasionally the group also enters into fixed-to-floating interest rate swaps to hedge the fair value interest rate risk arising where it has borrowed at fixed rates in excess of the 60% target.

IFRS7p40
IFRS7IG36

At 31 December 2008, if interest rates on Currency-denominated borrowings had been 0.1% higher/lower with all other variables held constant, post-tax profit for the year would have been C22 (2007: C21) lower/higher, mainly as a result of higher/lower interest expense on floating rate borrowings; other components of equity would have been C5 (2007: C3) lower/higher mainly as a result of a decrease/increase in the fair value of fixed rate financial assets classified as available for sale. At 31 December 2008, if interest rates on UK pound-denominated borrowings at that date had been 0.5% higher/lower with all other variables held constant, post-tax profit for the year would have been C57 (2007: C38) lower/higher, mainly as a result of higher/lower interest expense on floating rate borrowings; other components of equity would have been C6 (2007: C4) lower/higher mainly as a result of a decrease/increase in the fair value of fixed rate financial assets classified as available for sale.

(b) Credit risk

IFRS7p33(a)(b)
IFRS7p34(a)

Credit risk is managed on group basis. Credit risk arises from cash and cash equivalents, derivative financial instruments and deposits with banks and financial institutions, as well as credit exposures to wholesale and retail customers, including outstanding receivables and committed transactions. For banks and financial institutions, only independently rated parties with a minimum rating of 'A' are accepted. If wholesale customers are independently rated, these ratings are used. If there is no independent rating, risk control assesses the credit quality of the customer, taking into account its financial position, past experience and other factors. Individual risk limits are set based on internal or external ratings in accordance with limits set by

IFRS GAAP plc

(Amounts in C thousands unless otherwise stated)

the board. The utilisation of credit limits is regularly monitored. Sales to retail customers are settled in cash or using major credit cards. See note 9 for further disclosure on credit risk.

No credit limits were exceeded during the reporting period, and management does not expect any losses from non-performance by these counterparties.

(c) Liquidity risk

IFRS7p33, 39(b) Prudent liquidity risk management implies maintaining sufficient cash and marketable securities, the availability of funding through an adequate amount of committed credit facilities and the ability to close out market positions. Due to the dynamic nature of the underlying businesses, group treasury maintains flexibility in funding by maintaining availability under committed credit lines.

IFRS7p34(a) Management monitors rolling forecasts of the group's liquidity reserve (comprises undrawn borrowing facility (note 21) and cash and cash equivalents (note 15)) on the basis of expected cash flow. This is generally carried out at local level in the operating companies of the group in accordance with practice and limits set by the group. These limits vary by location to take into account the liquidity of the market in which the entity operates. In addition, the group's liquidity management policy involves projecting cashflows in major currencies and considering the level of liquid assets necessary to meet these; monitoring balance sheet liquidity ratios against internal and external regulatory requirements; and maintaining debt financing plans.

IFRS7p39(a) The table below analyses the group's financial liabilities and net-settled derivative financial liabilities into relevant maturity groupings based on the remaining period at the balance sheet to the contractual maturity date. The amounts disclosed in the table are the contractual undiscounted cash flows[1]. Balances due within 12 months equal their carrying balances as the impact of discounting is not significant.

At 31 December 2008	Less than 1 year[2]	Between 1 and 2 years[2]	Between 2 and 5 years[2]	Over 5 Years[2]
Borrowings (excluding finance lease liabilities)	20,496	22,002	67,457	38,050
Finance lease liabilities	2,749	1,573	4,719	2,063
Derivative financial instruments	12	10	116	41
Trade and other payables	15,6683	–	–	–

At 31 December 2007	Less than 1 year[2]	Between 1 and 2 years[2]	Between 2 and 5 years[2]	Over 5 Years[2]
Borrowings (excluding finance lease liabilities)	16,258	11,575	58,679	38,103
Finance lease liabilities	3,203	1,790	5,370	2,891
Derivative financial instruments	19	15	81	50
Trade and other payables	11,518[3]	–	–	–

IFRS7p39(a) [1] As the amounts included in the table are the contractual undiscounted cash flows, these amounts will not reconcile to the amounts disclosed on the balance sheet for borrowings, derivative financial instruments and trade and other payables. Entities can choose to add a reconciling column and a final total which ties into the balance sheet if they so wish.
[2] The maturity analysis applies to financial instruments only and therefore statutory liabilities are not included.

IFRS7p39(a)
IFRS7AppxB15 The table below analyses the group's derivative financial instruments which will be settled on a gross basis into relevant maturity groupings based on the remaining period at the balance sheet to the contractual maturity date. The amounts disclosed in the table are the contractual undiscounted cash flows. Balances due within 12 months equal their carrying balances as the impact of discounting is not significant.

IFRS GAAP plc 63

(Amounts in C thousands unless otherwise stated)

At 31 December 2008	Less than 1 year[2]	Between 1 and 2 years[2]	Between 2 and 5 years[2]	Over 5 Years[2]
Forward foreign exchange contracts – cash flow hedges[1]				
Outflow	78,241	–	–	–
Inflow	78,756	–	–	–
Forward foreign exchange contracts – held-for-trading[1]				
Outflow	14,129	–	–	–
Inflow	14,222	–	–	–

IFRS7p39(a) IFRS7AppxB15 DV *(applies to the above section)*

At 31 December 2007	Less than 1 year[2]	Between 1 and 2 years[2]	Between 2 and 5 years[2]	Over 5 Years[2]
Forward foreign exchange contracts – cash flow hedges[1]				
Outflow	83,077	–	–	–
Inflow	83,366	–	–	–
Forward foreign exchange contracts – held-for-trading[1]				
Outflow	6,612	–	–	–
Inflow	6,635			

IFRS7p39(a)

[1] The specific time buckets presented are not mandated by the standard but are based on a choice by management.

[2] IFRS 7 requires a maturity analysis only for financial liabilities [IFRS 7 para 39(a)]. In addition, IFRS 7 appendix B paragraph 14(d) specifies that contractual gross cash flows to be exchanged in a derivative contract should be presented in that analysis. In our view, as a minimum, for financial instruments that are liabilities at the balance sheet date, the cash outflows should be included in the maturity analysis. This will include the pay legs of gross-settled derivatives and commodity contracts that are liabilities at the balance sheet date. While the standard only requires the gross cash outflows (that is, the pay leg) to be included in the maturity analysis, separate disclosure of the corresponding inflows (that is, the receive leg) might make the information more meaningful.

1p124A,124B, IG5

3.2 Capital risk management

The group's objectives when managing capital are to safeguard the group's ability to continue as a going concern in order to provide returns for shareholders and benefits for other stakeholders and to maintain an optimal capital structure to reduce the cost of capital.

In order to maintain or adjust the capital structure, the group may adjust the amount of dividends paid to shareholders, return capital to shareholders, issue new shares or sell assets to reduce debt.

Consistent with others in the industry, the group monitors capital on the basis of the gearing ratio. This ratio is calculated as net debt divided by total capital. Net debt is calculated as total borrowings (including 'current and non-current borrowings' as shown in the consolidated balance sheet) less cash and cash equivalents. Total capital is calculated as 'equity' as shown in the consolidated balance sheet plus net debt.

During 2008, the group's strategy, which was unchanged from 2007, was to maintain the gearing ratio within 45% to 50% and a BB credit rating. The gearing ratios at 31 December 2008 and 2007 were as follows:

IFRS GAAP plc 64

(Amounts in C thousands unless otherwise stated)

	2008	2007
Total borrowings (note 21)	126,837	114,604
Less: cash and cash equivalents (note 15)	(17,928)	(34,062)
Net debt	108,909	80,542
Total equity	131,773	88,946
Total capital	240,682	169,488
Gearing ratio	**45%**	48%

The decrease in the gearing ratio during 2008 resulted primarily from the issue of share capital as part of the consideration for the acquisition of a subsidiary (notes 17 and 38).

3.3 Fair value estimation

IFRS7p27 The fair value of financial instruments traded in active markets (such as trading and available-for-sale securities) is based on quoted market prices at the balance sheet date. The quoted market price used for financial assets held by the group is the current bid price.

The fair value of financial instruments that are not traded in an active market (for example, over-the-counter derivatives) is determined by using valuation techniques. The group uses a variety of methods and makes assumptions that are based on market conditions existing at each balance sheet date. Quoted market prices or dealer quotes for similar instruments are used for long-term debt. Other techniques, such as estimated discounted cash flows, are used to determine fair value for the remaining financial instruments. The fair value of interest rate swaps is calculated as the present value of the estimated future cash flows. The fair value of forward foreign exchange contracts is determined using quoted forward exchange rates at the balance sheet date.

IFRS7p29(a) The carrying value less impairment provision of trade receivables and payables are assumed to
IFRS7p27(a) approximate their fair values. The fair value of financial liabilities for disclosure purposes is estimated by discounting the future contractual cash flows at the current market interest rate that is available to the group for similar financial instruments.

4 Critical accounting estimates and judgements

Group
Estimates and judgements are continually evaluated and are based on historical experience and other factors, including expectations of future events that are believed to be reasonable under the circumstances.

1p116 **4.1 Critical accounting estimates and assumptions**

The group makes estimates and assumptions concerning the future. The resulting accounting estimates will, by definition, seldom equal the related actual results. The estimates and assumptions that have a significant risk of causing a material adjustment to the carrying amounts of assets and liabilities within the next financial year are addressed below.

(a) Estimated impairment of goodwill
The group tests annually whether goodwill has suffered any impairment, in accordance with the accounting policy stated in note 2.6. The recoverable amounts of cash-generating units have been determined based on value-in-use calculations. These calculations require the use of estimates (note 7).

1p120, An impairment charge of C4,650 arose in the wholesale CGU in Step-land (included in the
36p134(f)(i)-(iii) Russian operating segment) during the course of the 2008 year, resulting in the carrying amount of the CGU being written down to its recoverable amount. If the budgeted gross margin used in the value-in-use calculation for the wholesale CGU in Step-land had been 10% lower than management's estimates at 31 December 2008 (for example, 46% instead of 56%), the group would have recognised a further impairment of goodwill by C100 and would need to reduce the carrying value of property, plant and equipment by C300.

If the estimated pre-tax discount rate applied to the discounted cash flows for the wholesale CGU in Step-land had been 1% higher than management's estimates (for example, 13.8% instead of 12.8%), the group would have recognised a further impairment against goodwill by C300.

IFRS GAAP plc   65

(Amounts in C thousands unless otherwise stated)

(b) Income taxes

The group is subject to income taxes in numerous jurisdictions. Significant judgement is required in determining the worldwide provision for income taxes. There are many transactions and calculations for which the ultimate tax determination is uncertain. The group recognises liabilities for anticipated tax audit issues based on estimates of whether additional taxes will be due. Where the final tax outcome of these matters is different from the amounts that were initially recorded, such differences will impact the current and deferred income tax assets and liabilities in the period in which such determination is made.

Were the actual final outcome (on the judgement areas) to differ by 10% from management's estimates, the group would need to:

– increase the income tax liability by C120 and the deferred tax liability by C230, if unfavourable; or
– decrease the income tax liability by C110 and the deferred tax liability by C215, if favourable.

(c) Fair value of derivatives and other financial instruments

IFRS7p27(a) The fair value of financial instruments that are not traded in an active market (for example, over-the-counter derivatives) is determined by using valuation techniques. The group uses its judgement to select a variety of methods and make assumptions that are mainly based on market conditions existing at each balance sheet date. The group has used discounted cash flow analysis for various available-for-sale financial assets that are not traded in active markets.

The carrying amount of available-for-sale financial assets would be an estimated C12 lower or C15 higher were the discount rate used in the discount cash flow analysis to differ by 10% from management's estimates.

(d) Revenue recognition

The group uses the percentage-of-completion method in accounting for its fixed-price contracts to deliver design services. Use of the percentage-of-completion method requires the group to estimate the services performed to date as a proportion of the total services to be performed. Were the proportion of services performed to total services to be performed to differ by 10% from management's estimates, the amount of revenue recognised in the year would be increased by C175 if the proportion performed were increased, or would be decreased by C160 if the proportion performed were decreased.

(e) Pension benefits

The present value of the pension obligations depends on a number of factors that are determined on an actuarial basis using a number of assumptions. The assumptions used in determining the net cost (income) for pensions include the discount rate. Any changes in these assumptions will impact the carrying amount of pension obligations.

The group determines the appropriate discount rate at the end of each year. This is the interest rate that should be used to determine the present value of estimated future cash outflows expected to be required to settle the pension obligations. In determining the appropriate discount rate, the group considers the interest rates of high-quality corporate bonds that are denominated in the currency in which the benefits will be paid, and that have terms to maturity approximating the terms of the related pension liability.

Other key assumptions for pension obligations are based in part on current market conditions. Additional information is disclosed in note 23.

Were the discount rate used to differ by 10% from management's estimates, the carrying amount of pension obligations would be an estimated C425 lower or C450 higher.

1p113 **4.2 Critical judgements in applying the entity's accounting policies**

(a) Revenue recognition

The group has recognised revenue amounting to C950 for sales of goods to L&Co in the UK during 2008. The buyer has the right to return the goods if their customers are dissatisfied. The group believes that, based on past experience with similar sales, the dissatisfaction rate will not exceed 3%. The group has, therefore, recognised revenue on this transaction with a corresponding provision against revenue for estimated returns. If the estimate changes by 1%, revenue will be reduced/increased by C10.

IFRS GAAP plc 66
(Amounts in C thousands unless otherwise stated)

(b) Impairment of available-for-sale financial assets
The group follows the guidance of IAS 39 to determine when an available-for-sale financial asset is impaired. This determination requires significant judgement. In making this judgement, the group evaluates, among other factors, the duration and extent to which the fair value of an investment is less than its cost; and the financial health of and short-term business outlook for the investee, including factors such as industry and sector performance, changes in technology and operational and financing cash flow.

If all of the declines in fair value below cost were considered significant or prolonged, the group would suffer an additional loss of C1,300 in its 2008 financial statements, being the transfer of the accumulated fair value adjustments recognised in equity on the impaired available-for-sale financial assets to the income statement.

5 Segment information

Group

IFRS8p22(a)   Management has determined the operating segments based on the reports reviewed by the strategic steering committee that are used to make strategic decisions.

IFRS8p22(a)   The committee considers the business from both a geographic and product perspective. Geographically, management considers the performance of wholesale in the UK, US, China, Russia and Europe. The UK and US are further segregated into retail and wholesale, as all of the retail business is located in these two geographic areas.

IFRS8p22(a)   Although the China segment does not meet the quantitative thresholds required by IFRS 8, management has concluded that this segment should be reported, as it is closely monitored by the strategic steering committee as a potential growth region and is expected to materially contribute to group revenue in the future.

IFRS8p22(b)   The reportable operating segments derive their revenue primarily from the manufacture and sale of shoes on a wholesale basis, with the exception of the UK and US, which are further segregated into retail shoe and leather goods sales.

IFRS8p16   Other services included within the European and UK segments include the sale of design services and goods transportation services to other shoe manufacturers. These are not included within the reportable operating segments, as they are not included in the reports provided to the strategic steering committee. The wholesale shoe revenue from the Central American region, mainly Mexico, is also not included, as this information is not reviewed by the strategic steering committee. The results of these operations are included in the 'all other segments' column.

IFRS GAAP plc

(Amounts in C thousands unless otherwise stated)

The segment information provided to the strategic steering committee for the reportable segments for the year ended 31 December 2008 is as follows:

		UK		US		Russia	China	Europe	All other segments	Total
		Wholesale	Retail	Wholesale	Retail					
IFRS8p23(b)	Total segment revenue	46,638	43,257	28,820	42,672	26,273	5,818	40,273	13,155	246,906
	Inter-segment revenue	(11,403)	–	(7,364)	–	(5,255)	(1,164)	(8,055)	(2,631)	(35,872)
IFRS8p23, p33(a)	Revenue from external customers	35,235	43,257	21,456	42,672	21,018	4,654	32,218	10,524	211,034
IFRS8p23	Adjusted EBITDA	17,298	9,550	9,146	9,686	12,322	2,323	16,003	3,504	79,832
IFRS8p23(e)	Depreciation and amortisation	(3,226)	(3,830)	(1,894)	(3,789)	(2,454)	(386)	(2,706)	(269)	(18,554)
IFRS8p23(i) IAS36p129(a)	Goodwill impairment	–	–	–	–	(4,650)	–	–	–	(4,650)
IFRS8p23(i)	Restructuring costs	–	–	–	–	(1,986)	–	–	–	(1,986)
IFRS8p23(h)	Income tax expense	(2,550)	(2,840)	(1,395)	(3,100)	(1,591)	(365)	(2,551)	(400)	(14,792)
IFRS8p23(g)	Share of profit/ (loss) from associates	200	–	–	–	–	–	(389)	15	(174)
IFRS8p23	**Total assets**	**45,201**	**24,495**	**41,195**	**13,988**	**15,067**	**24,899**	**33,571**	**61,285**	**259,701**
	Total assets includes:									
IFRS8p24(a)	Investments in associates	7,207	–	–	–	–	–	–	6,166	13,373
IFRS8p24(b)	Additions to non-current assets (other than financial instruments and deferred tax assets)	–	35,543	–	39,817	–	11,380	–	1,500	88,204
IFRS8p23	**Total liabilities[1]**	**3,207**	**6,700**	**5,900**	**3,500**	**700**	**1,200**	**1,500**	**2,140**	**24,847**

[1] The measure of liabilities has been disclosed for each reportable segment as is regularly provided to the chief operating desion-maker.

IFRS GAAP plc

(Amounts in C thousands unless otherwise stated)

68

The segment information for the year ended 31 December 2007 is as follows:

		UK		US		Russia	China	Europe	All other segments	Total
		Wholesale	Retail	Wholesale	Retail					
	Total segment revenue	57,284	1,682	33,990	2,390	8,778	3,209	26,223	5,724	139,280
IFRS8p23(b)	Inter-segment revenue	(11,457)	–	(6,798)	–	(1,756)	(642)	(5,245)	(1,022)	(26,920)
IFRS8p23(a), 33(a)	Revenue from external customers	45,827	1,682	27,192	2,390	7,022	2,567	20,978	4,702	112,360
IFRS8p23	Adjusted EBITDA	17,183	800	10,369	1,298	3,471	1,506	10,755	1,682	47,064
IFRS8p23(e)	Depreciation and amortisation	(3,801)	(201)	(2,448)	(199)	(453)	(286)	(2,701)	(138)	(10,227)
IFRS 8p23(h)	Income tax expense	(2,772)	(650)	(1,407)	(489)	(509)	(150)	(2,201)	(687)	(8,865)
IFRS8p23(g)	Share of profit/ (loss) from associates	155							(10)	145
IFRS8p23	**Total assets**	**43,320**	**9,580**	**32,967**	**8,550**	**5,067**	**20,899**	**36,450**	**49,270**	**206,103**
	Total assets includes:									
IFRS8p24(a)	Investments in associates	7,050	–	–	–	–	–	–	6,194	13,244
IFRS8p24(b)	Additions to non-current assets (other than financial instruments and deferred tax assets)	–	47	–	46	–	2,971	–	3,678	6,742
IFRS 8p23	**Total liabilities**[1]	**4,221**	**55**	**6,054**	**–**	**250**	**800**	**2,537**	**3,464**	**17,381**

[1] The measure of liabilities has been disclosed for each reportable segment as is regularly provided to the chief operating desion-maker.

During 2007, retail did not qualify as a reportable operating segment. However, with the acquisition in 2008, of Your Shoes Group (note 38), retail qualifies as a reportable operating segment and, therefore, the comparatives are consistent in this regard.

IFRS 8p23(i) See note 7 for details of the impairment of goodwill of C4,650 in the Russian operating segment in 2008 relating to the decision to reduce manufacturing output. There has been no further impact on the measurement of the company's assets and liabilities. There was no impairment charge or restructuring costs recognised in 2007.

IFRS 8p27(a) Sales between segments are carried out at arm's length. The revenue from external parties reported to the strategic steering committee is measured in a manner consistent with that in the income statement.

IFRS8p27(b), 28 The strategic steering committee assesses the performance of the operating segments based on a measure of adjusted EBITDA. This measurement basis excludes the effects of non-recurring expenditure from the operating segments such as restructuring costs, legal expenses and goodwill impairments when the impairment is the result of an isolated, non-recurring event. The measure also excludes the effects of equity-settled share-based payments and unrealised gains/losses on financial instruments. Interest income and expenditure are not allocated to segments, as this type of activity is driven by the central treasury function, which manages the cash position of the group. Since the strategic steering committee reviews adjusted EBITDA, the results of discontinued operations are not included in the measure of adjusted EBITDA.

IFRS GAAP plc 69

(Amounts in C thousands unless otherwise stated)

IFRS 8p28(b) A reconciliation of adjusted EBITDA to profit before tax and discontinued operations is provided as follows:

	2008	2007
Adjusted EBITDA for reportable segments	76,328	45,382
Other segments EBITDA	3,504	1,682
Depreciation	(17,754)	(9,662)
Amortisation	(800)	(565)
Restructuring costs	(1,986)	–
Legal expenses	(737)	(855)
Goodwill impairment	(4,650)	–
Unrealised financial instrument gains	102	101
Share options granted to directors and employees	(690)	(820)
Finance costs – net	(6,443)	(10,588)
Other	(48)	243
Profit before tax and discontinued operations	46,826	24,918

The amounts provided to the strategic steering committee with respect to total assets are measured in a manner consistent with that of the financial statements. These assets are allocated based on the operations of the segment and the physical location of the asset.

Investment in shares (classified as available-for-sale financial assets or financial assets at fair value through profit or loss) held by the group are not considered to be segment assets but rather are managed by the treasury function.

IFRS8p27(c) Reportable segments' assets are reconciled to total assets as follows:

	2008	2007
Segment assets for reportable segments	198,416	156,833
Other segments assets	61,285	49,270
Unallocated:		
Deferred tax	3,520	3,321
Available-for-sale financial assets	19,370	14,910
Financial assets at fair value through the profit and loss	11,820	7,972
Derivatives	1,464	1,196
Assets of disposal group classified as held for resale	3,333	–
Total assets per the balance sheet	299,208	233,502

The amounts provided to the strategic steering committee with respect to total liabilities are measured in a manner consistent with that of the financial statements. These liabilities are allocated based on the operations of the segment.

The group's interest-bearing liabilities are not considered to be segment liabilities but rather are managed by the treasury function.

IFRS8p27(d) Reportable segments' liabilities are reconciled to total liabilities as follows:

	2008	2007
Segment liabilities for reportable segments	22,707	13,917
Other segments liabilities	2,140	3,464
Unallocated:		
Deferred tax	12,370	9,053
Current tax	2,566	2,771
Current borrowings	11,716	18,258
Non-current borrowings	115,121	96,346
Derivatives	595	747
Liabilities of disposal group classified as held for resale	220	–
Total liabilities per the balance sheet	167,435	144,556

IFRS GAAP plc   70

(Amounts in C thousands unless otherwise stated)

IFRS8p27(f)	Due to the European operations utilising excess capacity in certain Russian assets that are geographically close to the European region, a portion of the depreciation charge of C197 (2007: C50) relating to the Russian assets has been allocated to the European segment to take account of this.
IFRS8p32	Revenues from external customers are derived from the sales of shoes on a wholesale and retail basis. The breakdown of retail and wholesale results are provided above. The wholesale of shoes relates only to the group's own brand, Footsy Tootsy. The retail sales comprise not only the group's own brand, but other major retail shoe brands.

Breakdown of the revenue from all services is as follows:

Analysis of revenue by category	2008	2007
Sales of goods	202,884	104,495
Revenue from services	8,000	7,800
Royalty income	150	65

IFRS8p33(a)	The entity is domiciled in the UK. The result of its revenue from external customers in the UK is C50,697 (2007: C48,951), and the total of revenue from external customers from other countries is C160,337 (2007: C63,409). The breakdown of the major component of the total of revenue from external customers from other countries is disclosed above.
IFRS8p33(b)	The total of non-current assets other than financial instruments and deferred tax assets (there are no employment benefit assets and rights arising under insurance contracts) located in the UK is C49,696 (2007: C39,567), and the total of these non-current assets located in other countries is C146,762 (2007: C93,299).
IFRS8p34	Revenues of approximately C32,023 (2007: C28,034) are derived from a single external customer. These revenues are attributable to the US retail and wholesale segments.

IFRS GAAP plc

(Amounts in C thousands unless otherwise stated)

71

6 Property, plant and equipment

1p75(a)

		Group	Land and buildings	Vehicles and machinery	Furniture, fittings and equipment	Total
16p73(d)		**At 1 January 2007**				
		Cost or valuation	39,664	71,072	20,025	130,761
		Accumulated depreciation	(2,333)	(17,524)	(3,690)	(23,547)
		Net book amount	37,331	53,548	16,335	107,214
16p73(e)		**Year ended 31 December 2007**				
		Opening net book amount	37,331	53,548	16,335	107,214
16p73(e)(viii)		Exchange differences	(381)	(703)	(423)	(1,507)
16p73(e)(iv)		Revaluation surplus (note 19)	1,133	–	–	1,133
16p73(e)(i)		Additions	1,588	2,970	1,484	6,042
16p73(e)(ix)		Disposals (note 35)	–	(2,607)	(380)	(2,987)
16p73(e)(vii)		Depreciation charge (note 28)	(636)	(4,186)	(4,840)	(9,662)
		Closing net book amount	39,035	49,022	12,176	100,233
16p73(d)		**At 31 December 2007**				
		Cost or valuation	40,232	68,125	20,026	128,383
		Accumulated depreciation	(1,197)	(19,103)	(7,850)	(28,150)
		Net book amount	39,035	49,022	12,176	100,233
		Year ended 31 December 2008				
16p73(e)		Opening net book amount	39,035	49,022	12,176	100,233
16p73(e)(viii)		Exchange differences	1,601	1,280	342	3,223
16p73(e)(iv)		Acquisition of subsidiary (note 38)	49,072	5,513	13,199	67,784
16p73(e)(i)		Additions	7,126	427	2,202	9,755
16p73(e)(ix)		Disposals (note 35)	(2,000)	(3,729)	(608)	(6,337)
16p73(e)(vii)		Depreciation charge (note 28)	(3,545)	(4,768)	(9,441)	(17,754)
IFRS5p38		Transferred to disposal group classified as held for sale	(341)	(1,222)	–	(1,563)
16p73(d)		**Closing net book amount**	90,948	46,523	17,870	155,341
16p73(d)		**At 31 December 2008**				
		Cost or valuation	95,129	58,268	26,927	180,324
		Accumulated depreciation	(4,181)	(11,745)	(9,057)	(24,983)
		Net book amount	90,948	46,523	17,870	155,341

DV   Property, plant and equipment transferred to the disposal group classified as held for sale amounts to C1,563 and relates to assets which are used by Shoes Limited (part of the wholesale segment). See note 16 for further details regarding the disposal group held for sale.

16p77(a-d), 1p76(b)   The group's land and buildings were last revalued on 1 January 2007 by independent valuers. Valuations were made on the basis of recent market transactions on arm's length terms. The revaluation surplus net of applicable deferred income taxes was credited to 'other reserves in shareholders' equity (note 19).

DV1p93   Depreciation expense of C8,054 (2007: C5,252) has been charged in 'cost of goods sold', C5,568 (2007: C2,410) in 'selling and marketing costs' and C4,132 (2007: C2,000) in 'administrative expenses'.

17p35(c)   Lease rentals amounting to C1,172 (2007: C895) and C9,432 (2007: C7,605) relating to the lease of machinery and property, respectively, are included in the income statement (note 28).

IFRS GAAP plc

72

(Amounts in C thousands unless otherwise stated)

16p77(e)   If land and buildings were stated on the historical cost basis, the amounts would be as follows:

	2008	2007
Cost	93,079	37,684
Accumulated depreciation	(6,131)	(2,197)
Net book amount	**86,948**	35,487

16p74(a)   Bank borrowings are secured on land and buildings for the value of C37,680 (2007: C51,306) (note 21).

Vehicles and machinery includes the following amounts where the group is a lessee under a finance lease:

	2008	2007
Cost – capitalised finance leases	13,996	14,074
Accumulated depreciation	(5,150)	(3,926)
Net book amount	**8,846**	10,148

17p35(d)   The group leases various vehicles and machinery under non-cancellable finance lease agreements. The lease terms are between three and 15 years, and ownership of the assets lie within the group.

   1077

IFRS GAAP plc 73

(Amounts in C thousands unless otherwise stated)

7 Intangible assets

	Group	Goodwill	Trademarks and licences	Contractual customer Relationships	Internally generated software development costs	Total
38p118(c)	**At 1 January 2007**					
IFRS3p75(a)	Cost	12,546	8,301	–	1,455	22,302
IFRS3p75(a)	Accumulated amortisation and impairment	–	(330)	–	(510)	(840)
	Net book amount	12,546	7,971	–	945	21,462
38p118(e)	**Year ended 31 December 2007**					
IFRS3p74	Opening net book amount	12,546	7,971	–	945	21,462
IFRS3p75(f)	Exchange differences	(546)	(306)	–	(45)	(897)
38p118(e)(i)	Additions	–	700	–	–	700
IFRS3p75(a)	Amortisation charge (note 28)	–	(365)	–	(200)	(565)
	Closing net book amount	12,000	8,000	–	700	20,700
38p118(c)	**At 31 December 2007**					
IFRS3p75(a)	Cost	12,000	8,710	–	1,400	22,110
IFRS3p75(a)	Accumulated amortisation and impairment	–	(710)	–	(700)	(1,410)
IFRS3p75(a)	**Net book amount**	12,000	8,000	–	700	20,700
38p118(e)	**Year ended 31 December 2008**					
IFRS3p74	Opening net book amount	12,000	8,000	–	700	20,700
IFRS3p75(f)	Exchange differences	341	96	–	134	571
38p118(e)(i)	Additions	–	684	–	2,366	3,050
IFRS3p75(b)	Acquisition of subsidiary (note 38)	4,501	3,000	1,000	–	8,501
IFRS3p75(e)	Impairment charge (note 28)	(4,650)	–	–	–	(4,650)
IFRS3p75(a)	Amortisation charge (note 28)	–	(402)	(278)	(120)	(800)
IFRS5p38	Transferred to disposal group classified as held for sale		(1,000)	–	(100)	(1,100)
	Closing net book amount	12,192	10,378	722	2,980	26,272
38p118(c)	**At 31 December 2008**					
IFRS3p75(a)	Cost	16,842	11,480	1,000	3,800	33,122
IFRS3p75(a)	Accumulated amortisation and impairment	(4,650)	(1,102)	(278)	(820)	(6,850)
	Net book amount	12,192	10,378	722	2,980	26,272

36p126(a) The carrying amount of the segment has been reduced to its recoverable amount through recognition of an impairment loss against goodwill. This loss has been included in 'cost of goods sold' in the income statement.

38p118(d) Amortisation of C40 (2007: C100) is included in the 'cost of goods sold' the income statement; C680 (2007: C365) in 'selling, and marketing costs; and C80 (2007: C100) in 'administrative expenses'.

DV The trademark transferred to the disposal group classified as held for sale relates to the Shoes Limited trademark (part of the wholesale segment), which was previously recognised by the group on the acquisition of the entity in 2005. A further net book amount of C100 transferred to the disposal group relates to software that was specifically developed for Shoes Limited. See note 16 for further details regarding the disposal group held-for-sale.

Impairment tests for goodwill

36p134(d) Goodwill is allocated to the group's cash-generating units (CGUs) identified according to operating segment.

IFRS GAAP plc 74

(Amounts in C thousands unless otherwise stated)

An operating segment-level summary of the goodwill allocation is presented below.

36p134(a)

	2008			2007		
	Wholesale	**Retail**	**Total**	**Wholesale**	**Retail**	**Total**
UK	**6,250**	**1,051**	**7,301**	5,970	120	6,090
US	**325**	**2,501**	**2,826**	125	30	155
Europe	**1,609**	**–**	**1,609**	705	–	705
Russia	**100**	**–**	**100**	4,750	–	4,750
China	**146**	**–**	**146**	100	–	100
All other segments	**210**	**–**	**210**	200	–	200
	8,640	**3,552**	**12,192**	11,850	150	12,000

During 2007, retail did not qualify as a reportable operating segment. However, with the acquisition in 2008 of Your Shoes Group (note 38), retail qualifies as a separate reportable operating segment, and therefore the comparatives are consistent.

36p130(e)
36p134(c)
36p134(d)(iii)

The recoverable amount of a CGU is determined based on value-in-use calculations. These calculations use pre-tax cash flow projections based on financial budgets approved by management covering a five-year period. Cash flows beyond the five-year period are extrapolated using the estimated growth rates stated below. The growth rate does not exceed the long-term average growth rate for the shoe business in which the CGU operates.

36p134(d)(i)

The key assumptions used for value-in-use calculations are as follows:

		Wholesale					Retail		
		UK	US	Europe	Russia	China	All Other Segments	UK	US
36p134(d)	Gross margin[1]	60.0%	59.0%	60.0%	55.5%	57.0%	56.0%	58.0%	56.0%
36p134 (d)(iv)	Growth rate[2]	1.8%	1.8%	1.8%	2.0%	2.0%	1.9%	1.1%	1.3%
36p134 (d)(v) 36p130(g)	Discount rate[3]	10.5%	10.0%	10.7%	12.8%	12.0%	12.8%	11.5%	11.0%

36p134(d)(ii) These assumptions have been used for the analysis of each CGU within the operating segment.

36p134(d)(ii) Management determined budgeted gross margin based on past performance and its expectations of market development. The weighted average growth rates used are consistent with the forecasts included in industry reports. The discount rates used are pre-tax and reflect specific risks relating to the relevant operating segments.

36p130(a) The impairment charge arose in a wholesale CGU in Step-land (included in the Russian operating segment) following a decision in early 2008 to reduce the manufacturing output allocated to these operations (note 24). This was a result of a redefinition of the group's allocation of manufacturing volumes across all CGUs in order to benefit from advantageous market conditions. Following this decision, the group reassessed the depreciation policies of its property, plant and equipment in this country and estimated that their useful lives would not be affected. No other class of asset than goodwill was impaired. The pre-tax discount rate used in the previous years for the wholesale CGU in Step-land was 12.0%.

[1] Budgeted gross margin.
[2] Weighted average growth rate used to extrapolate cash flows beyond the budget period.
[3] Pre-tax discount rate applied to the cash flow projections.

IFRS GAAP plc

75

(Amounts in C thousands unless otherwise stated)

8a Investments in subsidiaries

		2008	2007
27p42	**Company** Shares in group undertakings		
	Beginning of year	**22,786**	21,964
	Additions in year (Note 38)	**14,250**	–
	Capital contribution relating to share based payment	**173**	206
	End of year	**36,592**	22,170

27p42(c) Investments in group undertakings are recorded at cost, which is the fair value of the consideration paid.

DV The capital contribution relating to share based payment relates to 1,210 share options granted by the company to employees of subsidiary undertakings in the group. Refer to note 17 for further details on the group's share option schemes.

8b Investments in associates

		2008	2007
	Group		
	At 1 January	**13,244**	13,008
	Acquisition of subsidiary (note 38)	**389**	–
28p38	Share of (loss)/profit[1]	**(174)**	145
	Exchange differences (note 19)	**(74)**	105
	Other equity movements: available-for-sale reserve (note 19)	**(12)**	(14)
28p38	**At 31 December**	**13,373**	13,244

IFRS3p29, 28p23 Investments in associates at 31 December 2008 include goodwill of C1,020 (2007: C1,020).

28p37(b) The group's share of the results of its principal associates, all of which are unlisted, and its aggregated assets (including goodwill) and liabilities, are as follows[2]:

Name	Country of incorporation	Assets	Liabilities	Revenues	Profit/ (Loss)	% interest held
2007						
Alfa Limited	Cyprus	27,345	20,295	35,012	155	25
Beta SA	Greece	9,573	3,379	10,001	(10)	30
		36,918	23,674	45,013	145	
2008						
Alfa Limited	Cyprus	32,381	25,174	31,123	200	25
Beta SA	Greece	12,115	5,949	9,001	15	30
Delta Limited	UK	15,278	15,278	25,741	(389)	42
		59,774	46,401	65,865	(174)	

28p37(g) The group has not recognised losses amounting to C20 (2007: nil) for Delta Limited. The accumulated losses not recognised were C20 (2007: nil).

[1] Share of profit/(loss) is after tax and minority interest in associates (IG14).
[2] An alternative method of presentation is to give the gross amounts of assets and liabilities (excluding goodwill) of associates and not of the group's share.

IFRS GAAP plc   76

(Amounts in C thousands unless otherwise stated)

9a Financial instruments by category

IFRS7p6

Group	Loans and receivables	Assets at fair value through the profit and loss	Derivatives used for hedging	Available-for-sale	Total
31 December 2008					
Assets as per balance sheet					
Available-for-sale financial assets	–	–	–	19,370	19,370
Derivative financial instruments	–	361	1,103	–	1,464
Trade and other receivables excluding pre-payments[1]	20,787	–	–	–	20,787
Financial assets at fair value through profit or loss	–	11,820	–	–	11,820
Cash and cash equivalents	22,228	–	–	–	22,228
Total	**43,015**	**12,181**	**1,103**	**19,370**	**75,669**

	Liabilities at fair value through the profit and loss	Derivatives used for hedging	Other financial liabilities at amortised cost	Total
Liabilities as per balance sheet				
Borrowings (excluding finance lease liabilities) [2]	–	–	117,839	117,839
Finance lease liabilities[2]			8,998	8,998
Derivative financial instruments	268	327	–	595
Trade and other payables excluding statutory liabilities[3]	–	–	15,668	15,668
Total	**268**	**327**	**142,505**	**143,100**

	Loans and receivables	Assets at fair value through the profit and loss	Derivatives used for hedging	Available-for-sale	Total
31 December 2007					
Assets as per balance sheet					
Available-for-sale financial assets	–	–	–	14,910	14,910
Derivative financial instruments	–	321	875	–	1,196
Trade and other receivables excluding pre-payments[4]	18,536	–	–	–	18,536
Financial assets at fair value through profit or loss	–	7,972	–	–	7,972
Cash and cash equivalents	36,212	–	–	–	36,212
Total	**54,748**	**8,293**	**875**	**14,910**	**78,826**

[1] Pre-payments are excluded from the trade and other receivables balance as this analysis is required only for financial instruments.

[2] The categories in this disclosure are determined by IAS 39. Finance leases are mostly outside the scope of IAS 39, but they remain within the scope of IFRS 7. Therefore finance leases have been shown separately.

[3] Statutory liabilities are excluded from the trade payables balance, as this analysis is required only for financial instruments.

[4] Prepayments are excluded from the trade and other receivables balance as this analysis is required only for financial instruments.

IFRS GAAP plc

77

(Amounts in C thousands unless otherwise stated)

	Liabilities at fair value through the profit and loss	Derivatives used for hedging	Other financial liabilities	Total
Liabilities as per balance sheet				
Borrowings (excluding finance lease liabilities)[1]	–	–	104,006	104,006
Finance lease liabilities[1]			10,598	10,598
Derivative financial instruments	298	449	–	747
Trade and other payables excluding statutory liabilities[2]	–	–	11,518	11,518
Total	**298**	**449**	**126,122**	**126,869**

Company	Loans and receivables	Assets at fair value through the profit and loss	Derivatives used for hedging	Available-for-sale	Total
31 December 2008					
Assets as per balance sheet					
Trade and other receivables	41,147	–	–	–	41,147
Cash and cash equivalents	3,261	–	–	–	3,261
Total	**44,408**	**–**	**–**	**–**	**44,408**

	Loans and receivables	Assets at fair value through the profit and loss	Derivatives used for hedging	Available for sale	Total
31 December 2007					
Assets as per balance sheet					
Trade and other receivables	31,296	–	–	–	31,296
Cash and cash equivalents	6,234	–	–	–	6,234
Total	**37,530**	**–**	**–**	**–**	**37,530**

[1] The categories in this disclosure are determined by IAS 39. Finance leases are mostly outside the scope of IAS 39, but they remain within the scope of IFRS 7. Therefore finance leases have been shown separately.
[2] Statutory liabilities are excluded from the trade payables balance, as this analysis is required only for financial instruments.

IFRS GAAP plc   78

(Amounts in C thousands unless otherwise stated)

9b Credit quality of financial assets

IFRS7p36(c)

The credit quality of financial assets that are neither past due nor impaired can be assessed by reference to external credit ratings (if available) or to historical information about counterparty default rates:

Group	2008	2007
Trade receivables		
Counterparties with external credit rating (Moody's)		
A	**5,895**	5,757
BB	**3,200**	3,980
BBB	**1,500**	1,830
	10,595	11,567
Counterparties without external credit rating		
Group 1	**750**	555
Group 2	**4,950**	3,668
Group 3	**1,770**	1,312
	7,470	5,535
Total trade receivables	**18,065**	17,102
Cash at bank and short-term bank deposits[1]		
AAA	**8,790**	15,890
AA	**5,300**	7,840
A	**6,789**	11,257
	20,879	34,987
Available-for-sale debt securities		
AA	**347**	264
	347	264
Derivative financial assets		
AAA	**1,046**	826
AA	**418**	370
	1,464	1,196
Loans to related parties		
Group 2	**2,501**	1,301
Group 3	**167**	87
	2,668	1,388

- Group 1 – new customers/related parties (less than 6 months).
- Group 2 – existing customers/related parties (more than 6 months) with no defaults in the past.
- Group 3 – existing customers/related parties (more than 6 months) with some defaults in the past. All defaults were fully recovered.

IFRS7p36(d)

None of the financial assets that are fully performing has been renegotiated in the last year. None of the loans to related parties is past due but not impaired.

---

[1] The rest of the balance sheet item 'cash and cash equivalents' is cash on hand.

IFRS GAAP plc

(Amounts in C thousands unless otherwise stated)

10 Available-for-sale financial assets

Group	2008	2007
At 1 January	**14,910**	14,096
Exchange differences	**646**	(435)
Acquisition of subsidiary (note 38)	**473**	–
Additions	**2,781**	1,126
Net gains/(losses) transfer from equity (note 19)	**(130)**	(152)
Net gains/(losses) transfer to equity (note 19)	**690**	275
At 31 December	**19,370**	14,910
Less: non-current portion	**(17,420)**	(14,910)
Current portion	**1,950**	–

1p76(b)

1p57

1p57

IFRS7p20(a)(ii) The group removed profits of C217 (2007: C187) and losses C87 (2007: C35) from equity into the income statement. Losses in the amount of C55 (2007: C20) were due to impairments.

IFRS7p27(b),31, Available-for-sale financial assets include the following:
34

	2008	2007
Listed securities:		
– Equity securities – UK	**8,335**	8,300
– Equity securities – Europe	**5,850**	2,086
– Equity securities – US	**4,550**	4,260
– Debentures with fixed interest of 6.5% and maturity date of 27 August 2012	**210**	–
– Non-cumulative 9.0% non-redeemable preference shares	**78**	–
Unlisted securities:		
– Debt securities with fixed interest ranging from 6.3% to 6.5% and maturity dates between July 2011 and May 2013	**347**	264
	19,370	14,910

IFRS7p34(c) Available-for-sale financial assets are denominated in the following currencies:

	2008	2007
UK pound	**7,897**	8,121
Euros	**5,850**	2,086
US dollar	**4,550**	4,260
Other currencies	**1,073**	443
	19,370	14,910

IFRS7p27(a), (b), The fair values of unlisted securities are based on cash flows discounted using a rate based on the
1p76(b) market interest rate and the risk premium specific to the unlisted securities (2008: 6%; 2007: 5.8%).

IFRS7p36(a) The maximum exposure to credit risk at the reporting date is the carrying value of the debt securities classified as available for sale.

IFRS7p36(c) None of these financial assets is either past due or impaired.

5 Sch 23-25 A 20% (2007: 20%) interest in the nominal value of ordinary shares is held by the group in
CA06 Invest AG which is incorporated in Germany. The aggregate capital and reserves of Invest AG
SI 2008/410 4 as at 31 December 2008 is C205,000 (2007: C180,000), and profit after tax for the year ended 31
Shc 4-6 December 2008 is C25,067 (2007: C32,456).

IFRS GAAP plc   80

(Amounts in C thousands unless otherwise stated)

11 Derivative financial instruments

Group		2008		2007	
		Assets	**Liabilities**	Assets	Liabilities
IFRS7p22(a)(b)	Interest rate swaps – cash flow hedges	**351**	**110**	220	121
IFRS7p22(a)(b)	Interest rate swaps – fair value hedges	**57**	**37**	49	11
IFRS7p22(a)(b)	Forward foreign exchange contracts – cash flow hedges	**695**	**180**	606	317
	Forward foreign exchange contracts – held-for-trading	**361**	**268**	321	298
	Total	**1,464**	**595**	1,196	747
1p57	Less non-current portion:				
	Interest rate swaps – cash flow hedges	**345**	**100**	200	120
	Interest rate swaps – fair value hedges	**50**	**35**	45	9
		395	**135**	245	129
1p57	**Current portion**	**1,069**	**460**	951	618

Trading derivatives are classified as a current asset or liability. The full fair value of a hedging derivative is classified as a non-current asset or liability if the remaining maturity of the hedged item is more than 12 months and, as a current asset or liability, if the maturity of the hedged item is less than 12 months.

IFRS7p24   The ineffective portion recognised in the profit or loss that arises from fair value hedges amounts to a loss of C1 (2007: loss of C1) (note 25). The ineffective portion recognised in the profit or loss that arises from cash flow hedges amounts to a gain of C17 (2007: a gain of C14) (note 25). There was no ineffectiveness to be recorded from net investment in foreign entity hedges.

(a) Forward foreign exchange contracts

IFRS7p31   The notional principal amounts of the outstanding forward foreign exchange contracts at 31 December 2008 were C92,370 (2007: C89,689).

IFRS7p23(a) 39p100, 1p76(b)   The hedged highly probable forecast transactions denominated in foreign currency are expected to occur at various dates during the next 12 months. Gains and losses recognised in the hedging reserve in equity (note 19) on forward foreign exchange contracts as of 31 December 2008 are recognised in the income statement in the period or periods during which the hedged forecast transaction affects the income statement. This is generally within 12 months from the balance sheet date unless the gain or loss is included in the initial amount recognised for the purchase of fixed assets, in which case recognition is over the lifetime of the asset (five to 10 years).

(b) Interest rate swaps

IFRS7p31   The notional principal amounts of the outstanding interest rate swap contracts at 31 December 2008 were C4,314 (2007: C3,839).

IFRS7p23(a)   At 31 December 2008, the fixed interest rates vary from 6.9% to 7.4% (2007: 6.7% to 7.2%), and the main floating rates are EURIBOR and LIBOR. Gains and losses recognised in the hedging reserve in equity (note 19) on interest rate swap contracts as of 31 December 2008 will be continuously released to the income statement until the repayment of the bank borrowings (note 21).

(c) Hedge of net investment in foreign entity

IFRS7p22, 1p76(b)   A proportion of the group's US dollar-denominated borrowing amounting to C321 (2007: C321) is designated as a hedge of the net investment in the group's US subsidiary. The fair value of the borrowing at 31 December 2008 was C370 (2007: C279). The foreign exchange loss of C45 (2007: gain of C40) on translation of the borrowing to currency at the balance sheet date is recognised in other reserves, in shareholders' equity (note 19).

IFRS7p36(a)   The maximum exposure to credit risk at the reporting date is the fair value of the derivative assets in the balance sheet.

IFRS GAAP plc
(Amounts in C thousands unless otherwise stated)

81

12 Trade and other receivables

		Group		Company	
		2008	2007	**2008**	2007
IFRS7p36, 1p74	Trade receivables	**18,174**	17,172	–	–
	Less: provision for impairment of trade receivables	**(109)**	(70)	–	–
1p75(b)	Trade receivables – net	**18,065**	17,102	–	–
1p75(b)	Prepayments	**1,300**	1,146	–	–
1p75(b), 24p17(b)	Receivables from related parties (note 39)	**54**	46	**41,147**	31,296
1p75(b), 24p17(b)	Loans to related parties (note 39)	**2,668**	1,388	–	–
		22,087	19,682	**41,147**	31,296
1p75(b), 1p57	Less non-current portion: loans to related parties	**(2,322)**	(1,352)	–	–
1p57	**Current portion**	**19,765**	18,330	**41,147**	31,296

Group
All non-current receivables are due within five years from the balance sheet date.

IFRS7p25   The fair values of trade and other receivables are as follows:

	2008	2007	**2008**	2007
Trade receivables	**18,065**	17,172	–	–
Receivables from related parties	**54**	46	**41,147**	31,296
Loans to related parties	**2,722**	1,398	–	–
	20,841	18,616	**41,147**	31,296

IFRS7p27(a)   The fair values of loans to related parties are based on cash flows discounted using a rate based on the borrowings rate of 7.5% (2007: 7.2%). The discount rate equals to LIBOR plus appropriate credit rating.

24p17(b)(i)   The effective interest rates on non-current receivables were as follows:

	2008	2007
Loans to related parties (note 39)	6.5-7.0%	6.5-7.0%

IFRS7p14   Certain European subsidiaries of the group transferred receivable balances amounting to C1,014 to a bank in exchange for cash during the year ended 31 December 2008. The transaction has been accounted for as a collateralised borrowing (note 21). In case the entities default under the loan agreement, the bank has the right to receive the cash flows from the receivables transferred. Without default, the entities will collect the receivables and allocate new receivables as collateral.

DV   As of 31 December 2008, trade receivables of C17,670 (2007:C16,595) were fully performing.

IFRS7p37(a)   As of 31 December 2008, trade receivables of C277 (2007: C207) were past due but not impaired. These relate to a number of independent customers for whom there is no recent history of default. The ageing analysis of these trade receivables is as follows:

	2008	2007
Up to 3 months	**177**	108
3 to 6 months	**100**	99
	277	207

IFRS7p37(b)   As of 31 December 2008, trade receivables of C227 (2007: C142) were impaired and provided for. The amount of the provision was C109 as of 31 December 2008 (2007: C70). The individually impaired receivables mainly relate to wholesalers, which are in unexpectedly difficult economic situations. It was assessed that a portion of the receivables is expected to be recovered. The ageing of these receivables is as follows:

IFRS GAAP plc

82

(Amounts in C thousands unless otherwise stated)

	2008	2007
3 to 6 months	177	108
Over 6 months	50	34
	227	142

The carrying amounts of the group's trade and other receivables are denominated in the following currencies:

	2008	2007
UK pound	9,846	8,669
Euros	5,987	6,365
US dollar	6,098	4,500
Other currencies	156	148
	22,087	19,682

IFRS7p16	Movements on the group provision for impairment of trade receivables are as follows:

	2008	2007
At 1 January	70	38
Provision for receivables impairment	74	61
Receivables written off during the year as uncollectible	(28)	(23)
Unused amounts reversed	(10)	(8)
Unwind of discount (note 30)	3	2
At 31 December	109	70

IFRS7p20(e) (appears against "Provision for receivables impairment")

The creation and release of provision for impaired receivables have been included in 'other expenses' in the income statement (note 28). Unwind of discount is included in 'finance costs' in the income statement (note 30). Amounts charged to the allowance account are generally written off, when there is no expectation of recovering additional cash.

IFRS7p16	The other classes within trade and other receivables do not contain impaired assets.
IFRS7p36(a)	The maximum exposure to credit risk at the reporting date is the carrying value of each class of receivable mentioned above. The group does not hold any collateral as security.

Company

IFRS7p25   The fair values of trade and other receivables are as follows:

	Company 2008	Company 2007
Receivables from related parties	41,147	31,296
	41,147	31,296

DV	As of 31 December 2008, company receivables from related parties of C14,120 (2007: 16,279) were fully performing.
IFRS7p37(a) IFRS7p36(c)	As of 31 December 2008, receivables of C27,027 (2007: C15, 017) were past due but not impaired. These relate to subsidiary undertakings for which there is no history of default. The ageing analysis of these trade receivables is as follows:

	2008	2007
3 to 6 months	27,027	15,017
	27,027	15,017

IFRS7p31, 34(c)   The carrying amounts of the company's receivables are denominated in the following currencies:

	2008	2007
UK pound	41,147	31,296

IFRS GAAP plc

83

(Amounts in C thousands unless otherwise stated)

13 Inventories

2p36(b), 1p75(c)

Group	2008	2007
Raw materials	**7,622**	7,612
Work in progress	**1,810**	1,796
Finished goods[1]	**15,268**	8,774
	24,700	18,182

2p36(d), 38

The cost of inventories recognised as expense and included in 'cost of sales' amounted to C60,252 (2007: C29,545).

2p36 (f)(g)
36p126(b)
36p130(a)

The group reversed C603 of a previous inventory write-down in July 2007. The group has sold all the goods that were written down to an independent retailer in Australia at original cost. The amount reversed has been included in 'cost of sales' in the income statement.

14 Financial assets at fair value through profit or loss

Group	2008	2007
Listed securities – held-for-trading		
– Equity securities – UK	**5,850**	3,560
– Equity securities – Europe	**4,250**	3,540
– Equity securities – US	**1,720**	872
	11,820	7,972

IFRS7p8(a), 27(b), 31, 34(c)

7p15

Financial assets at fair value through profit or loss are presented within 'operating activities' as part of changes in working capital in the cash flow statement (note 35).

Changes in fair values of financial assets at fair value through profit or loss are recorded in 'other (losses)/gains – net' in the income statement (note 25).

IFRS7p27(b)

The fair value of all equity securities is based on their current bid prices in an active market.

15 Cash and cash equivalents

	Group		Company	
	2008	2007	2008	2007
Cash at bank and on hand	**8,398**	28,648	**3,261**	6,234
Short-term bank deposits	**9,530**	5,414	**–**	–
	17,928	34,062	**3,261**	6,234

7p45

Cash, cash equivalents and bank overdrafts include the following for the purposes of the cash flow statement:

	Group		Company	
	2008	2007	2008	2007
Cash and cash equivalents	**17,928**	34,062	**3,261**	6,234
Bank overdrafts (note 21)	**(2,650)**	(6,464)	**–**	–
	15,278	27,598	**3,261**	6,234

7p8

[1] Separate disclosure of finished goods at fair value less cost to sell is required, where applicable.

IFRS GAAP plc

84

(Amounts in C thousands unless otherwise stated)

16 Assets of disposal group classified as held-for-sale and discontinued operations

Group

IFRS5p41
(a)(b)(d)

The assets and liabilities related to company Shoes Limited (part of the wholesale segment) have been presented as held for sale following the approval of the group's management and shareholders on 23 September 2008 to sell company Shoes Limited in the UK. The completion date for the transaction is expected by May 2009.

Group and company	2008	2007
Operating cash flows[1]	300	190
Investing cash flows[1]	(103)	(20)
Financing cash flows[1]	(295)	(66)
Total cash flows	**(98)**	**104**

IFRS5p33(c)
IFRS5p33(c)
IFRS5p33(c)

IFRS5p38

(a) Assets of disposal group classified as held for sale

	2008	2007
Property, plant and equipment	1,563	–
Intangible assets	1,100	–
Inventory	442	–
Other current assets	228	–
Total	**3,333**	**–**

IFRS5p38

(b) Liabilities of disposal group classified as held for sale

	2008	2007
Trade and other payables	104	–
Other current liabilities	20	–
Provisions	96	–
Total	**220**	**–**

IFRS5p38

(c) Cumulative income or expense recognised directly in equity relating to disposal group classified as held for sale

	2008	2007
Foreign exchange translation adjustments[2]	–	–
	–	–

---

[1] Under this approach, the entity presents the cash flow statement as if no discontinued operation has occurred and makes the required IFRS 5 para 33 disclosures in the notes. It would also be acceptable to present the three categories separately on the face of the cash flow statement and present the line-by-line breakdown of the categories, either in the notes or on the face of the cash flow statement. It would not be acceptable to present all cash flows from discontinued operations in one line either as investing or operating activity.

[2] IFRS 5 requires the separate presentation of any cumulative income or expense recognised directly in equity relating to a non-current asset (or disposal group) classified as held for sale. There are no items recognised directly in equity relating to the disposal group classified as held-for-sale, but the line items are shown for illustrative purposes.

IFRS GAAP plc

85

(Amounts in C thousands unless otherwise stated)

IFRS5p33 (b) Analysis of the result of discontinued operations, and the result recognised on the remeasurement of assets or disposal group, is as follows[1]:

	2008	2007
Revenue	**1,200**	1,150
Expenses	**(960)**	(950)
Profit before tax of discontinued operations	**240**	200
Tax	**(96)**	(80)
Profit after tax of discontinued operations	**144**	120
Pre-tax gain/(loss) recognised on the remeasurement of assets of disposal group	**(73)**	–
Tax	**29**	–
After tax gain/(loss) recognised on the remeasurement of assets of disposal group	**(44)**	–
Profit for the year from discontinued operations	**100**	120

12p81(h)(ii) (Tax rows as above)

12p81(h)(ii)

17 Share capital and premium

1p76

Group and company	Number of shares (thousands)	Ordinary shares	Share premium	Total
At 1 January 2007	20,000	20,000	10,424	30,424
Employee share option scheme:				
– Proceeds from shares issued	1,000	1,000	70	1,070
At 31 December 2007	21,000	21,000	10,494	31,494
Employee share option scheme:				
– Proceeds from shares issued	750	750	200	950
Acquisition of subsidiary (note 38)	3,550	3,550	6,450	10,000
At 31 December 2008	**25,300**	**25,300**	**17,144**	**42,444**

1p97(a), (c) (Proceeds from shares issued row)

1p97(a), (c)
IFRS3p67(d)(ii)

1p76(a)

1p76(a) The total authorised number of ordinary shares is 50 million shares (2007: 50 million shares) with a par value of C1 per share (2007: C1 per share). All issued shares are fully paid.

1p76(a) The company acquired 875,000 of its own shares through purchases on the EuroMoney stock exchange on 18 April 2008. The total amount paid to acquire the shares, net of income tax, was C2,564 and has been deducted from retained earnings[2] within shareholders' equity (note 18). The shares are held as 'treasury shares'. The company has the right to re-issue[3] these shares at a later date. All shares issued by the company were fully paid.

10p21 The company reissued 500,000 treasury shares for a total consideration of C1,500 on 15 January 2008.

Share options

IFRS2p45(a) Share options are granted to directors and to selected employees. The exercise price of the granted options is equal to the market price of the shares less 15% on the date of the grant. Options are conditional on the employee completing three year's service (the vesting period). The options are exercisable starting three years from the grant date, subject to the group achieving its target growth in earnings per share over the period of inflation plus 4%; the options have a contractual option term of five years. The group has no legal or constructive obligation to repurchase or settle the options in cash.

---

[1] These disclosures can also be given on the face of the primary financial statements.

[2] The accounting treatment of treasury shares should be recorded in accordance with local company law and practice. Treasury shares may be disclosed separately on the balance sheet or deducted from retained earnings or a specific reserve.

[3] Depending on the company law, the company could have the right to resell the treasury shares.

IFRS GAAP plc 86

(Amounts in C thousands unless otherwise stated)

Movements in the number of share options outstanding and their related weighted average exercise prices are as follows:

		2008		2007	
		Average exercise price in C per share	Options (thousands)	Average exercise price in C per share	Options (thousands)
IFRS2p45 (b)(i)	At 1 January	1.73	4,744	1.29	4,150
IFRS2p45 (b)(ii)	Granted	2.95	964	2.38	1,827
IFRS2p45 (b)(iii)	Forfeited	–	–	2.00	(200)
IFRS2p45 (b)(iv)	Exercised	1.28	(750)	1.08	(1,000)
IFRS2p2 (b)(v)	Expired	2.30	(125)	0.80	(33)
IFRS2p2 (b)(vi)	**At 31 December**	2.03	4,833	1.73	4,744

IFRS2p45 (b)(vii), Out of the 4,833 thousand outstanding options (2007: 4,744 thousand options), 400 thousand
IFRS2p45(c) options (2007: 600 thousand) were exercisable. Options exercised in 2008 resulted in 750 thousand shares (2007: 1,000 thousand shares) being issued at a weighted average price of C1.28 each (2007: C1.08 each). The related weighted average share price at the time of exercise was C2.85 (2007: C2.65) per share. The related transaction costs amounting to C10 (2007: C10) have been netted off with the proceeds received.

IFRS2p45(d) Share options outstanding at the end of the year have the following expiry date and exercise prices:

Expiry date – 1 July	Exercise price in C per share	Shares	
		2008	2007
2008	1.10	–	500
2009	1.20	800	900
2010	1.35	1,200	1,250
2011	2.00	217	267
2012	2.38	1,777	1,827
2013	2.95	964	–
		4,958	4,744

IFRS2p47(a) The weighted average fair value of options granted during the period determined using the Black-Scholes valuation model was C0.86 per option (2007: C0.66). The significant inputs into the model were weighted average share price of C3.47 (2007: C2.80) at the grant date, exercise price shown above, volatility of 30% (2007: 27%), dividend yield of 4.3% (2007: 3.5%), an expected option life of three years, and an annual risk-free interest rate of 5% (2007: 4%). The volatility measured at the standard deviation of continuously compounded share returns is based on statistical analysis of daily share prices over the last three years. See note 29 for the total expense recognised in the income statement for share options granted to directors and employees.

33p71(c) On 1 January 2009, 1,200 thousand share options were granted to directors and employees with
10p21, 22(f) an exercise price set at the market share prices less 15% on that date of C3.20 per share (share price: C3.68) (expiry date: 31 December 2014).

The group issued 3,550 thousand shares on 1 March 2008 (14.5% of the total ordinary share capital issued) to the shareholders of Your Shoes Group as part of the purchase consideration for 70% of its ordinary share capital. The ordinary shares issued have the same rights as the other shares in issue. The fair value of the shares issued amounted to C10.05 million (C2.82 per share). The related transaction costs amounting to C50 each have been netted off with the deemed proceeds.

IFRS GAAP plc

(Amounts in C thousands unless otherwise stated)

18 Retained earnings

		Group	Company
1p97(b)	At 1 January 2007	**48,470**	16,036
	Profit for the year	**15,512**	10,491
1p97(a)	Dividends paid relating to 2006	**(15,736)**	(15,736)
IFRS2p50	Value of employee services[1]	**822**	822
16p41	Depreciation transfer on land and buildings net of tax	**87**	–
12p68C	Tax credit relating to share option scheme	**20**	–
19p93A	Actuarial loss on post employment benefit obligations net of tax	**(494)**	–
	At 31 December 2007	**48,681**	11,613
1p97(b)	At 1 January 2008	**48,681**	11,613
	Profit for the year	**29,767**	9,098
1p97(a)	Dividends relating to 2007	**(10,102)**	(10,102)
IFRS2p50	Value of employee services[1]	**690**	690
16p41	Depreciation transfer on land and buildings net of tax	**100**	–
12p68C	Tax credit relating to share option scheme	**30**	–
1p97(a)	Purchase of treasury shares[2]	**(2,564)**	(2,564)
19p93A	Actuarial loss on post employment benefit obligations net of tax	**–**	–
12p80(d)	Impact of change in UK tax rate on deferred tax[3]	**(10)**	–
	At 31 December 2008	**66,592**	8,735

[1] The credit entry to equity in respect of the IFRS 2 charge should be recorded in accordance with local company law and practice. This may be a specific reserve, retained earnings or share capital.

[2] The accounting treatment of treasury shares should be recorded in accordance with local company law and practice. Treasury shares may be disclosed separately on the balance sheet or deducted from retained earnings or a specific reserve.

[3] Solely for illustrative purposes, a change in tax rates has been assumed to have taken place in 2008. UK companies with 31 December 2008 year ends will have reflected an actual change in tax rates in 2007.

IFRS GAAP plc
88

(Amounts in C thousands unless otherwise stated)

19 Other reserves

	Group	Convertible bond	Land and buildings revaluation[1]	Hedging reserve	Available-for-sale Investments	Translation	Asset revaluation surplus	Total
	At 1 January 2007	–	1,152	65	1,320	3,827	–	6,364
16p39, IFRS7p20(a)(ii)	Revaluation – gross (notes 6 and 10)	–	1,133	–	275	–	–	1,408
	Revaluation transfer – gross	–	–	–	(152)	–	–	(152)
12p61, 81(a)	Revaluation – tax (note 31)	–	(374)	–	(61)	–	–	(435)
28p39	Revaluation – associates (note 8)	–	–	–	(14)	–	–	(14)
16p41	Depreciation transfer – gross	–	(130)	–	–	–	–	(130)
16p41	Depreciation transfer – tax	–	43	–	–	–	–	43
1p96(b)	Cash flow hedges:							
IFRS7p23(c)	– Fair value gains in year	–	–	300	–	–	–	300
12p61, 81(a)	– Tax on fair value gains (note 31)	–	–	(101)	–	–	–	(101)
IFRS7p23(d)	– Transfers to sales	–	–	(236)	–	–	–	(236)
12p61, 81(a)	– Tax on transfers to sales (note 31)	–	–	79	–	–	–	79
IFRS7p23(e)	– Transfers to inventory	–	–	(67)	–	–	–	(67)
12p61, 81(a)	– Tax on transfers to inventory (note 31)	–	–	22	–	–	–	22
39p102(a)	Net investment hedge (note 11)	–	–	–	–	40	–	40
1p96(b)	Currency translation differences:							
21p52(b)	– Group	–	(50)	–	–	(171)	–	(221)
28p39	– Associates	–	–	–	–	105	–	105
	At 31 December 2007	–	1,774	62	1,368	3,801	–	7,005
16p39, IFRS7p20(a)(ii)	Revaluation – gross (note 10)	–	–	–	690	–	–	690
	Revaluation transfer – gross	–	–	–	(130)	–	–	(130)
12p61, 81(a)	Revaluation – tax (note 31)	–	–	–	(198)	–	–	(198)
28p39	Revaluation – associates (note 8)	–	–	–	(12)	–	–	(12)
16p41	Depreciation transfer – gross	–	(149)	–	–	–	–	(149)
16p41	Depreciation transfer – tax	–	49	–	–	–	–	49
1p96(b) IFRS7p23(c)	Cash flow hedges: – Fair value gains in year	–	–	368	–	–	–	368
12p61, 81(a)	– Tax on fair value gains (note 31)	–	–	(123)	–	–	–	(123)
IFRS7p23(d)	– Transfers sales	–	–	(120)	–	–	–	(120)
12p61, 81(a)	– Tax on transfers to sales (note 31)	–	–	40	–	–	–	40
IFRS7p23(e)	– Transfers to inventory	–	–	(151)	–	–	–	(151)
12p61, 81(a)	– Tax on transfers to inventory (note 31)	–	–	50	–	–	–	50
39p102(a)	Net investment hedge (note 11)	–	–	–	–	(45)	–	(45)
1p96(b),	Currency translation differences:							
21p52(b)	– Group	–	15	–	–	2,051	–	2,066
28p39	– Associates	–	–	–	–	(74)	–	(74)
	Convertible bond – equity component (note 21)	7,761	–	–	–	–	–	7,761
12p61, 81(a)	Tax on equity component on convertible bond (note 31)	(2,328)	–	–	–	–	–	(2,328)
	Increase in fair values of proportionate holding of Your Shoes Group (note 38)	–	–	–	–	–	850	850
	At 31 December 2008	5,433	1,689	126	1,718	5,733	850	15,549

[1] An entity should disclose in its financial statements whether there are any restrictions on the distribution of the 'land and buildings' fair value reserve to the equity holders of the company (IAS16p77(f)).

[2] It is assumed that the tax base on the convertible bond is not split between the debt and equity elements. If the tax base were split, this would impact the deferred tax position.

IFRS GAAP plc 89

(Amounts in C thousands unless otherwise stated)

20 Trade and other payables

	Group		Company	
	2008	2007	**2008**	2007
Trade payables	**10,983**	9,495	**–**	–
Amounts due to related parties (note 39)	**2,202**	1,195	**29,662**	16,452
Social security and other taxes	**2,002**	960	**21**	16
Accrued expenses	**1,483**	828	**138**	125
	16,670	12,478	**29,821**	16,593

(1p74, 24p17 in margin)

21 Borrowings

Group	2008	2007
Non-current		
Bank borrowings	**32,193**	40,244
Convertible bond	**42,822**	–
Debentures and other loans	**3,300**	18,092
Redeemable preference shares	**30,000**	30,000
Finance lease liabilities	**6,806**	8,010
	115,121	96,346
Current		
Bank overdrafts (note 15)	**2,650**	6,464
Collateralised borrowings (note 12)	**1,014**	–
Bank borrowings	**3,368**	4,598
Debentures and other loans	**2,492**	4,608
Finance lease liabilities	**2,192**	2,588
	11,716	18,258
Total borrowings	**126,837**	114,604

(a) Bank borrowings

IFRS7p31 Bank borrowings mature until 2014 and bear average coupons of 7.5% annually (2007: 7.4% annually).

IFRS7p14 Total borrowings include secured liabilities (bank and collateralised borrowings) of C37,680 (2007: C51,306). Bank borrowings are secured by the land and buildings of the group (note 6). Collateralised borrowings are secured by trade receivables (note 12).

IFRS7p31 The exposure of the group's borrowings to interest rate changes and the contractual repricing dates at the balance sheet dates are as follows:

	2008	2007
6 months or less	**10,496**	16,748
6-12 months	**36,713**	29,100
1-5 years	**47,722**	38,555
Over 5 years	**31,906**	30,201
	126,837	114,604

IFRS7p25 The carrying amounts and fair value of the non-current borrowings are as follows:

	Carrying amount		Fair value	
	2008	2007	**2008**	2007
Bank borrowings	**32,193**	40,244	**32,590**	39,960
Redeemable preference shares	**30,000**	30,000	**28,450**	28,850
Debentures and other loans	**3,300**	18,092	**3,240**	17,730
Convertible bond	**42,822**	–	**42,752**	–
Finance lease liabilities	**6,806**	8,010	**6,205**	7,990
	115,121	96,346	**113,237**	94,530

IFRS GAAP plc

(Amounts in C thousands unless otherwise stated)

IFRS7p29(a) The fair value of current borrowings equals their carrying amount, as the impact of discounting is not significant. The fair values are based on cash flows discounted using a rate based on the borrowing rate of 7.5% (2007: 7.2%).

IFRS7p25 The carrying amounts of short-term borrowings approximate their fair value.

IFRS7p31, 34(c) The carrying amounts of the group's borrowings are denominated in the following currencies:

	2008	2007
UK pound	**80,100**	80,200
Euros	**28,353**	16,142
US dollar	**17,998**	17,898
Other currencies	**386**	364
	126,837	114,604

DV7p50(a) The group has the following undrawn borrowing facilities:

	2008	2007
Floating rate:		
– Expiring within one year	**6,150**	4,100
– Expiring beyond one year	**14,000**	8,400
Fixed rate:		
– Expiring within one year	**18,750**	12,500
	38,900	25,000

The facilities expiring within one year are annual facilities subject to review at various dates during 2008. The other facilities have been arranged to help finance the proposed expansion of the group's activities in Europe.

(b) Convertible bond

IFRS7p17, 1p76(b) The company issued 500,000 5.0% convertible bonds at a par value of C50 million[1] on 2 January 2008. The bonds mature five years from the issue date at their nominal value of C50 million[1] or can be converted into shares at the holder's option at the maturity date at the rate of 33 shares per C500[1]. The values of the liability component and the equity conversion component were determined at issuance of the bond.

The bonds mature five years from the issue date at their nominal value of C50 million[1] or can be converted into shares at the holder's option at the rate of 33 shares per C500.

32p28, 32p31, 1p76(b) The fair value of the liability component, included in non-current borrowings, was calculated using a market interest rate for an equivalent non-convertible bond. The residual amount, representing the value of the equity conversion option, is included in shareholders' equity in other reserves (note 19), net of income taxes.

The convertible bond recognised in the balance sheet is calculated as follows:

		2008	2007
	Face value of convertible bond issued on 2 January 2008	**50,000**	–
12AppxBEx4	Equity component (note 19)	**(7,761)**	–
	Liability component on initial recognition at 2 January 2008	**42,239**	–
	Interest expense (note 30)	**3,083**	–
	Interest paid	**(2,500)**	–
	Liability component at 31 December 2008	**42,822**	–

IFRS7p27(a) The fair value of the liability component of the convertible bond at 31 December 2008 amounted to C42,617. The fair value is calculated using cash flows discounted at a rate based on the borrowings rate of 7.5%.

[1] These amounts are not in C thousands.

IFRS GAAP plc   91

(Amounts in C thousands unless otherwise stated)

(c) Redeemable preference shares

<table>
<tr><td>32p15, 32p18(a)</td><td>The group issued 30 million cumulative redeemable preference shares with a par value of C1 per share on 4 January 2007. The shares are mandatorily redeemable at their par value on 4 January 2013, and pay dividends at 6.5% annually.</td></tr>
<tr><td>10p21</td><td>On 1 February 2008, the group issued C6,777 6.5% US dollar bonds to finance its expansion programme and working capital requirements in the US. The bonds are repayable on 31 December 2013.</td></tr>
</table>

(d) Finance lease liabilities

Lease liabilities are effectively secured as the rights to the leased asset revert to the lessor in the event of default

	2008	2007
17p31(b) Gross finance lease liabilities – minimum lease payments		
No later than 1 year	**2,749**	3,203
Later than 1 year and no later than 5 years	**6,292**	7,160
Later than 5 years	**2,063**	2,891
	11,104	13,254
Future finance charges on finance leases	**(2,106)**	(2,656)
Present value of finance lease liabilities	**8,998**	10,598

	2008	2007
17p31(b) The present value of finance lease liabilities is as follows:		
No later than 1 year	**2,192**	2,588
Later than 1 year and no later than 5 years	**4,900**	5,287
Later than 5 years	**1,906**	2,723
	8,998	10,598

22 Deferred income tax

12p74   Deferred income tax assets and liabilities are offset when there is a legally enforceable right to offset current tax assets against current tax liabilities and when the deferred income taxes assets and liabilities relate to income taxes levied by the same taxation authority on either the taxable entity or different taxable entities where there is an intention to settle the balances on a net basis. The offset amounts are as follows:

Group	2008	2007
Deferred tax assets:		
1p52 – Deferred tax asset to be recovered after more than 12 months	**(2,873)**	(3,257)
– Deferred tax asset to be recovered within 12 months	**(647)**	(64)
	(3,520)	(3,321)
Deferred tax liabilities:		
– Deferred tax liability to be recovered after more than 12 months	**10,743**	8,016
– Deferred tax liability to be recovered within 12 months	**1,627**	1,037
	12,370	9,053
Deferred tax liabilities (net)	**8,850**	5,732

The gross movement on the deferred income tax account is as follows:

	2008	2007
At 1 January	**5,732**	3,047
Exchange differences	**(1,753)**	(154)
Acquisition of subsidiary (note 38)	**1,953**	–
Income statement charge (note 31)	**379**	2,635
Tax charged directly to equity (note 19)	**2,539**	204
At 31 December .	**8,850**	5,732

IFRS GAAP plc

(Amounts in C thousands unless otherwise stated)

12p81(g)(i)
12p81(g)(ii)
The movement in deferred income tax assets and liabilities during the year, without taking into consideration the offsetting of balances within the same tax jurisdiction, is as follows:

Deferred tax liabilities	Accelerated tax depreciation	Fair value gains	Convertible bond	Other	Total
At 1 January 2007	6,058	272	–	284	6,614
Charged/(credited) to the income statement	1,786	–	–	799	2,585
Charged directly to equity	–	435	–	–	435
Exchange differences	241	100	–	–	341
At 31 December 2007	8,085	807	–	1,083	9,975
Charged/(credited) to the income statement	425	–	(193)	138	370
Charged directly to equity	–	231	2,328	–	2,559
Acquisition of subsidiary	553	1,375	–	275	2,203
Exchange differences	(571)	(263)	–	(123)	(957)
At 31 December 2008	**8,492**	**2,150**	**2,135**	**1,373**	**14,150**

Row tags: 12p81(g)(i) · 12p81(g)(ii) · 12p81(a) (Charged directly to equity/Exchange differences) · 12p81(g)(i), 12p81(g)(ii) (At 31 December 2007/Charged) · 12p81(a) · 12p81(g)(i) (At 31 December 2008)

Deferred tax assets	Retirement benefit obligation	Provisions	Impairment losses	Tax losses	Other	Total
At 1 January 2007	(428)	(962)	(732)	(1,072)	(373)	(3,567)
Charged/(credited) to the income statement	–	181	–	–	(131)	50
Charged/(credited) directly to equity	(211)	–	–	–	(20)	(231)
Exchange differences	–	(35)	–	(460)	–	(495)
At 31 December 2007	(639)	(816)	(732)	(1,532)	(524)	(4,243)
(Credited)/charged to the income statement	–	(538)	(322)	1,000	(131)	9
Charged/(credited) directly to equity	10	–	–	–	(30)	(20)
Acquisition of subsidiary (note 38)	(250)	–	–	–	–	(250)
Exchange differences	–	(125)	(85)	(350)	(236)	(796)
At 31 December 2008	**(879)**	**(1,479)**	**(1,139)**	**(882)**	**(921)**	**(5,300)**

Row tags: 12p81(g)(i) · 12p81(g)(ii) · 12p81(a) · 12p81(g)(i) (At 31 December 2007) · 12p81(a) · 12p81(g)(i) (At 31 December 2008)

12p81(e)
Deferred income tax assets are recognised for tax loss carry-forwards to the extent that the realisation of the related tax benefit through future taxable profits is probable. The group did not recognise deferred income tax assets of C333 (2007: C1,588) in respect of losses amounting to C1,000 (2007: C5,294) that can be carried forward against future taxable income. Losses amounting to C900 (2007: C5,294) and C100 (2007: nil) expire in 2011 and 2012 respectively.

12p81(f)
Deferred income tax liabilities of C3,141 (2007: C2,016) have not been recognised for the withholding tax and other taxes that would be payable on the unremitted earnings of certain subsidiaries. Such amounts are permanently reinvested. Unremitted earnings totalled C30,671 at 31 December 2008 (2007: C23,294).

IFRS GAAP plc 93

(Amounts in C thousands unless otherwise stated)

23 Retirement benefit obligations

Group	2008	2007
Balance sheet obligations for:		
Pension benefits	**3,225**	1,532
Post-employment medical benefits	**1,410**	701
	4,635	2,233
Income statement charge for (note 29):		
Pension benefits	**755**	488
Post-employment medical benefits	**149**	107
	904	595

		2008	2007
19p120A(h)	Actuarial losses recognised in the SORIE in the period (before tax)	–	705
19p120A(i)	Cumulative actuarial losses recognised in the SORIE (before tax)	**203**	203

(a) Pension benefits

DV The group operates defined benefit pension plans in the UK and the US based on employee pensionable remuneration and length of service. The majority of plans are externally funded. Plan assets are held in trusts, foundations or similar entities, governed by local regulations and practice in each country, as is the nature of the relationship between the group and the trustees (or equivalent) and their composition.

19p120A(d)(f)   The amounts recognised in the balance sheet are determined as follows:

	2008	2007
Present value of funded obligations	**6,155**	2,943
Fair value of plan assets	**(5,991)**	(2,797)
	164	146
Present value of unfunded obligations	**3,206**	1,549
Unrecognised past service cost	**(145)**	(163)
Liability in the balance sheet	**3,225**	1,532

19p120A(c)   The movement in the defined benefit obligation over the year is as follows:

	2008	2007
At 1 January	**4,492**	3,479
Current service cost	**751**	498
Interest cost	**431**	214
Contributions by plan participants	**55**	30
Actuarial losses/(gains)	**(15)**	495
Exchange differences	**(43)**	(103)
Benefits paid	**(66)**	(121)
Liabilities acquired in a business combination (note 38)	**3,691**	–
Curtailments	**65**	–
Settlements[1]	–	–
At 31 December	**9,361**	4,492

---

[1] IAS 19 requires the disclosure of settlements as part of the reconciliation of the opening and closing balances of the present value of the defined benefit obligation. There is no such movement on the defined benefit obligation relating to pension plans in these financial statements, but the line item has been shown for illustrative purposes.

IFRS GAAP plc 94

(Amounts in C thousands unless otherwise stated)

	2008	2007
19p120A(e) The movement in the fair value of plan assets of the year is as follows:

	2008	2007
At 1 January	2,797	2,264
Expected return on plan assets	510	240
Actuarial (losses)/gains	(15)	(5)
Exchange differences	25	(22)
Employer contributions	908	411
Employee contributions	55	30
Benefits paid	(66)	(121)
Business combinations (note 38)	1,777	–
At 31 December	**5,991**	**2,797**

19p120A(g) The amounts recognised in the income statement are as follows:

	2008	2007
Current service cost	751	498
Interest cost	431	214
Expected return on plan assets	(510)	(240)
Past service cost	18	16
Losses on curtailment	65	–
Total, included in staff costs (note 29)	**755**	**488**

19p120A(g) Of the total charge, C516 (2007: C319) and C239 (2007: C169) were included in 'cost of goods sold' and 'administrative expenses' respectively.

19p120A(m) The actual return on plan assets was C495 (2007: C235).

The principal actuarial assumptions used were as follows:

19p120A(n)

	2008		2007	
	UK	US	UK	US
Discount rate	6.0%	6.1%	5.5%	5.6%
Inflation rate	3.6%	3.0%	3.3%	2.7%
Expected return on plan assets	8.5%	8.3%	8.7%	8.7%
Future salary increases	5.0%	4.5%	4.5%	4.0%
Future pension increases	3.6%	2.8%	3.1%	2.7%

Assumptions regarding future mortality experience are set based on actuarial advice in accordance with published statistics and experience in each territory. Mortality assumptions for the most important countries are based on the following post-retirement mortality tables: (i) UK: PNMA 00 and PNFA 00 with medium cohort adjustment subject to a minimum annual improvement of 1% and scaling factors of 110% for current male pensioners, 125% for current female pensioners and 105% for future male and female pensioners; and (ii) US: RP2000 with a projection period of 10-15 years.

These tables translate into an average life expectancy in years of a pensioner retiring at age 65:

	2008		2007	
	UK	US	UK	US
Retiring at the balance sheet date:				
– Male	22	20	22	20
– Female	25	24	25	24
Retiring 20 years after the balance sheet date:				
– Male	24	23	24	23
– Female	27	26	27	26

IFRS GAAP plc

(Amounts in C thousands unless otherwise stated)

DV

The sensitivity of the overall pension liability to changes in the weighted principal assumptions is:

	Change in assumption	Impact on overall liability
Discount rate	Increase/decrease by 0.5%	Increase/decrease by 7.2%
Inflation rate	Increase/decrease by 0.5%	Increase/decrease by 5.1%
Salary growth rate	Increase/decrease by 0.5%	Increase/decrease by 3.3%
Rate of mortality	Increase by 1 year	Increase by 5.2%

19p122(b)

(b) Post-employment medical benefits

The group operates a number of post-employment medical benefit schemes, principally in the US. The method of accounting, assumptions and the frequency of valuations are similar to those used for defined benefit pension schemes. The majority of these plans are unfunded.

19p120A(n)

In addition to the assumptions set out above, the main actuarial assumption is a long-term increase in health costs of 8.0% a year (2007: 7.6%).

19p120A(d)(f)

The amounts recognised in the balance sheet were determined as follows:

	2008	2007
Present value of funded obligations	705	340
Fair value of plan assets	(620)	(302)
	85	38
Present value of unfunded obligations	1,325	663
Liability in the balance sheet	**1,410**	701

19p120A(c)

Movement in the defined benefit obligation is as follows:

	2008	2007
At 1 January	1,003	708
Current service cost	153	107
Interest cost	49	25
Contributions by plan participants[1]	–	–
Actuarial losses/(gains)	(2)	204
Exchange differences	25	(41)
Benefits paid[1]	–	–
Liabilities acquired in a business combination (note 38)	802	–
Curtailments[1]	–	–
Settlements[1]	–	–
At 31 December	**2,030**	1,003

19p120A(e)

The movement in the fair value of plan assets of the year is as follows:

	2008	2007
At 1 January	302	207
Expected return on plan assets	53	25
Actuarial gains/(losses)	(2)	(1)
Exchange differences	5	(2)
Employer contributions	185	73
Employee contributions[1]	–	–
Benefits paid[1]	–	–
Business combinations (note 38)	77	–
At 31 December	**620**	302

[1] IAS 19 requires the disclosure of contributions by plan participants, benefits paid, curtailments and settlements as part of the reconciliation of the opening and closing balances of the present value of the defined benefit obligation. There is no such movement on the defined benefit obligation relating to post-employment medical benefits in these financial statements, but the line items have been shown for illustrative purposes.

IFRS GAAP plc 96

(Amounts in C thousands unless otherwise stated)

19p120A(g) The amounts recognised in the income statement were as follows[1]:

	2008	2007
Current service cost	153	107
Interest cost	49	25
Expected return on plan assets	(53)	(25)
Total, included in staff costs (note 29)	**149**	107

19p120A(g) Of the total charge, C102 (2007: C71) and C47 (2007: C36) respectively were included in cost of goods sold and administrative expenses.

19p120A(m) The actual return on plan assets was C51 (2007: C24).

19p120A(o) The effect of a 1% movement in the assumed medical cost trend rate is as follows:

	Increase	Decrease
Effect on the aggregate of the current service cost and interest cost	24	(20)
Effect on the defined benefit obligation	366	(313)

(c) Post-employment benefits (pension and medical)

19p120A(j) Plan assets are comprised as follows:

	2008		2007	
Equity instruments	3,256	49%	1,224	40%
Debt instruments	1,524	23%	571	18%
Property	1,047	16%	943	30%
Other	784	12%	361	12%
	6,611	100%	3,099	100%

DV Investments are well diversified, such that the failure of any single investment would not have a material impact on the overall level of assets. The largest proportion of assets is invested in equities, although the group also invests in property, bonds, hedge funds and cash. The group believes that equities offer the best returns over the long term with an acceptable level of risk. The majority of equities are in a globally diversified portfolio of international blue chip entities, with a target of 60% of equities held in the UK and Europe, 30% in the US and the remainder in emerging markets.

19p120A(k) Pension plan assets include the company's ordinary shares with a fair value of C136 (2007: C126) and a building occupied by the group with a fair value of C612 (2007: C609).

19p120A(l) The expected return on plan assets is determined by considering the expected returns available on the assets underlying the current investment policy. Expected yields on fixed interest investments are based on gross redemption yields as at the balance sheet date. Expected returns on equity and property investments reflect long-term real rates of return experienced in the respective markets.

19p120(q) Expected contributions to post-employment benefit plans for the year ending 31 December 2008 are C1,150.

DV The group has agreed that it will aim to eliminate the deficit over the next nine years. Funding levels are monitored on an annual basis and the current agreed regular contribution rate is 14% of pensionable salaries in the UK and 12% in the US. The next triennial valuation is due to be completed as at 31 December 2009. The group considers that the contribution rates set at the last valuation date are sufficient to eliminate the deficit over the agreed period and that regular contributions, which are based on service costs, will not increase significantly.

DV An alternative method of valuation to the projected unit credit method is a buy-out valuation. This assumes that the entire post-employment benefit liability will be settled by transferring all obligations to a suitable insurer. The group estimates the amount required to settle the post-employment benefit liabilities at the balance sheet date would be C15,500.

[1] IAS 19 requires the disclosure of employee contributions and employee contributions as part of the reconciliation of the opening and closing balances of plan assets. There is no such movement on the plan assets relating to post-employment medical benefits in these financial statements, but the line items have been shown for illustrative purposes.

IFRS GAAP plc 97

(Amounts in C thousands unless otherwise stated)

19p120A(p)

At 31 December	2008	2007	2006	2005[1]
Present value of defined benefit obligation	**11,391**	5,495	4,187	3,937
Fair value of plan assets	**6,611**	3,099	2,471	2,222
Deficit/(surplus) in the plan	**4,780**	2,396	1,716	1,715
Experience adjustments on plan liabilities	**(326)**	125	55	–
Experience adjustments on plan assets	**(17)**	(6)	(197)	–

24 Provisions for other liabilities and charges

1p75(d)

Group	Environmental restoration	Restructuring	Legal claims	Profit-sharing and bonuses	Contingent liability arising on a business combination	Total
37p84(a) At 1 January 2008	842	–	828	1,000	–	2,670
Charged/(credited) to the income statement:						
37p84(b) – Additional provisions/fair value adjustment on acquisition of Your Shoes Group	316	1,986	2,405	500	1,000	6,207
37p84(d) – Unused amounts reversed	(15)	–	(15)	(10)	–	(40)
37p84(e) – Unwinding of discount	40	–	–	–	4	44
37p84(c) Used during year	(233)	(886)	(3,059)	(990)	–	(5,168)
Exchange differences	(7)	–	(68)	–	–	(75)
IFRS5p38 Transferred to disposal group/ classified as held for sale	(96)	–	–	–	–	(96)
37p84(a) **At 31 December 2008**	**847**	**1,100**	**91**	**500**	**1,004**	**3,542**

Analysis of total provisions:

	2008	2007
1p60 Non-current (environmental restoration)	**1,320**	274
1p60 Current	**2,222**	2,396
	3,542	2,670

(a) Environmental restoration

37p85 (a)-(c) The group uses various chemicals in working with leather. A provision is recognised for the present value of costs to be incurred for the restoration of the manufacturing sites. It is expected that C531 will be used during 2009 and C320 during 2010. Total expected costs to be incurred are C880 (2007: C760).

DV The provision transferred to the disposal group classified as held for sale amounts to C96 and relates to an environmental restoration provision for Shoes Limited (part of the wholesale segment). See note 16 for further details regarding the disposal group held for sale.

[1] IAS 19 requires a five-year record, but this does not have to be applied retrospectively (IAS 19p160).

IFRS GAAP plc

(Amounts in C thousands unless otherwise stated)

(b) Restructuring

37p85(a)-(c) The reduction of the volumes assigned to manufacturing operations in Step-land (a subsidiary) will result in the reduction of a total of 155 jobs at two factories. An agreement was reached with the local union representatives that specifies the number of staff involved and the voluntary redundancy compensation package offered by the group, as well as amounts payable to those made redundant, before the financial year-end. The estimated staff restructuring costs to be incurred are C799 at 31 December 2008 (note 29). Other direct costs attributable to the restructuring, including lease termination, are C1,187. These costs were fully provided for in 2008. The provision of C1,100 at 31 December 2008 is expected to be fully utilised during the first half of 2009.

36p130 A goodwill impairment charge of C4,650 was recognised in the cash-generating unit relating to Step-land as a result of this restructuring (note 7).

(c) Legal claims

37p85(a)-(c) The amounts represent a provision for certain legal claims brought against the group by customers of the wholesale segment. The provision charge is recognised in profit or loss within 'administrative expenses'. The balance at 31 December 2008 is expected to be utilised in the first half of 2009. In the directors' opinion, after taking appropriate legal advice, the outcome of these legal claims will not give rise to any significant loss beyond the amounts provided at 31 December 2008.

(d) Profit-sharing and bonuses

19p8(c),10 DV, The provision for profit-sharing and bonuses is payable within three month of finalisation of the
37p859(a) audited financial statements.

(e) Contingent liability

A contingent liability of C1,000 has been recognised on the acquisition of Your Shoes Group for a pending lawsuit in which the entity is a defendant. The claim has arisen from a customer alleging defects on products supplied to them. It is expected that the courts will have reached a decision on this case by the end of 2010. The potential undiscounted amount of all future payments that the group could be required to make if there was an adverse decision related to the lawsuit is estimated to be between C500 and C1,500. As of 31 December 2008, there has been no change in the amount recognised (except for the unwinding of the discount of C4) for the liability at 31 March 2008, as there has been no change in the probability of the outcome of the lawsuit.

The selling shareholders of Your Shoes Group have contractually agreed to indemnify IFRS GAAP plc for the claim that may become payable in respect of the above-mentioned lawsuit. This possible compensation will not be recognised until virtually certain and will be adjusted against goodwill once received from the vendor.

25 Other (losses)/gains — net

Group	2008	2007
IFRS7p20(a)(i) Financial assets at fair value through profit or loss (note 14):		
– Fair value losses	**(508)**	(238)
– Fair value gains	**593**	–
IFRS7p20(a)(i) Foreign exchange forward contracts:		
– Held for trading	**86**	88
21p52(a) – Net foreign exchange gains/(losses) (note 32)	**(277)**	200
IFRS7p24(a) Ineffectiveness on fair value hedges (note 11)	**(1)**	(1)
IFRS7p24(b) Ineffectiveness on cash flow hedges (note 11)	**17**	14
	(90)	63

IFRS GAAP plc 99

(Amounts in C thousands unless otherwise stated)

26 Other income

	Group	
	2008	2007
18p35(b)(v) Dividend income on available-for-sale financial assets	**1,100**	883
18p35(b)(v) Dividend income on financial assets at fair value through profit or loss	**800**	310
Investment income	**1,900**	1,193
Insurance reimbursement	**–**	66
	1,900	1,259

The insurance reimbursement relates to the excess of insurance proceeds over the carrying values of goods damaged.

27 Loss on expropriated land

Group

During 2008, undeveloped land owned by the group in the UK was expropriated following works for the enlargement of a motorway adjacent to the group's manufacturing facilities. Losses relating to the expropriation are C1,117 as of 31 December 2008 (2007: nil).

28a Expenses by nature

	Group		Company	
	2008	2007	**2008**	2007
1p93 Changes in inventories of finished goods and work in progress	**6,950**	(2,300)	**–**	–
1p93 Raw materials and consumables used	**53,302**	31,845	**–**	–
1p93 Employee benefit expense (note 29)	**40,082**	15,492	**4,573**	4,190
1p93 Depreciation, amortisation and impairment charges (notes 6 and 7)	**23,204**	10,227	**–**	–
1p93 Transportation expenses	**8,584**	6,236	**–**	–
1p93 Advertising costs	**12,759**	6,662	**–**	–
1p93 Operating lease payments (note 6)	**10,604**	8,500	**–**	–
1p93 Other expenses	**2,799**	1,659	**–**	–
Total cost of sales, distribution costs and administrative expenses	**158,284**	78,321	**4,573**	4,190

IFRS GAAP plc 100

(Amounts in C thousands unless otherwise stated)

28b Auditor remuneration

Tech 06/06 **Services provided by the company's auditor and its associates[1]**

SI 2005/2417 During the year the group (including its overseas subsidiaries) obtained the following services from the company's auditor and its associates:

Group	2008	2007
Fees payable to company's auditor for the audit of parent company and consolidated financial statements	738	625
Fees payable to the company's auditor and its associates for other services:		
– The audit of company's subsidiaries pursuant to legislation	901	543
– Other services pursuant to legislations[2]	312	154
– Tax services	107	143
	2,058	1,465

	2008	2007
Fees in respect of the IFRS GAAP plc pension scheme:		
Audit	1,204	931
Other services pursuant to legislation	123	–
	1327	931

29a Employee benefit expense

		Group		Company	
		2008	2007	2008	2007
19p142	Wages and salaries, including restructuring costs C799 (2007: nil) (note 24) and other termination benefits C1,600 (2007: nil)	28,363	10,041	2,824	2,486
	Social security costs	9,369	3,802	1,160	1,087
IFRS2p51(a)	Share options granted to directors and employees	690	822	518	617
19p46	Pension costs – defined contribution plans	756	232	72	–
19p120A(g)	Pension costs – defined benefit plans (note 23)	755	488	–	–
19p120A(g)	Other post-employment benefits (note 23)	149	107	–	–
		40,082	15,492	4,573	4,190

29b Average number of people employed

Group	2008 Number	2007 Number
S231A(1)(a)-(b) Average number of people (including executive directors) employed:		
Wholesale	257	95
Retail	178	75
Administration	100	40
Total average headcount	535	210

Company
The average number of administration staff employed by the company during the year, including executive directors was 50 (2007: C48).

C.C.D3 [1] The annual report should outline how the directors ensure that the independence of the group's auditors has not been compromised by the provision of non-audit services. For listed companies, guidance on independence is included in the Combined Code. This disclosure may be given as part of the corporate governance statement or disclosure in the annual report.
[2] Includes fees for interim review.

1105

IFRS GAAP plc

(Amounts in C thousands unless otherwise stated)

30 Finance income and costs

	Group	2008	2007
IFRS7p20(b)	Interest expense:		
	– Bank borrowings	**(5,242)**	(10,646)
	– Dividend on redeemable preference shares (note 21)	**(1,950)**	(1,950)
	– Convertible bond (note 21)	**(3,083)**	–
	– Finance lease liabilities	**(550)**	(648)
37p84(e)	– Provisions: unwinding of discount (note 24)	**(44)**	(37)
21p52(a)	Net foreign exchange gains on financing activities (note 32)	**2,594**	996
	Fair value gains on financial instruments:		
IFRS7p23(d)	– Interest rate swaps: cash flow hedges, transfer from equity	**102**	88
IFRS7p24(a)(i)	– Interest rate swaps: fair value hedges	**16**	31
IFRS7p24(a)(ii)	Fair value adjustment of bank borrowings attributable to interest rate risk	**(16)**	(31)
	Finance costs	**(8,173)**	(12,197)
	Finance income:		
21p52(a)	– Interest income on short-term bank deposits	**550**	489
IFRS7p20(b)	– Interest income on available-for-sale financial assets	**963**	984
IFRS7p20(b)	– Interest income on loans to related parties (note 39)	**217**	136
	Finance income	**1,730**	1,609
	Net finance costs	**(6,443)**	(10,588)

31 Income tax expense

	Group	2008	2007
	Current tax:		
12p80(a)	Current tax on profits for the year	**14,082**	6,035
12p80(b)	Adjustments in respect of prior years	**150**	–
	Total current tax	**14,232**	6,035
	Deferred tax (note 22)		
12p80(c)	Origination and reversal of temporary differences	**476**	2,635
12p80(d)	Impact of change in the UK tax rate[1]	**(97)**	–
	Total deferred tax	**379**	2,635
	Income tax expense	**14,611**	8,670

12p81(c) The tax on the group's profit before tax differs from the theoretical amount that would arise using the weighted average tax rate applicable to profits of the consolidated entities as follows:

	2008	2007
Profit before tax	**46,826**	24,918
Tax calculated at domestic tax rates applicable to profits in the respective countries	**15,453**	7,475
Tax effects of:		
– Associates' results reported net of tax	**57**	(44)
– Income not subject to tax	**(1,072)**	(212)
– Expenses not deductible for tax purposes	**1,540**	1,104
– Utilisation of previously unrecognised tax losses	**(1,450)**	–
– Tax losses for which no deferred income tax asset was recognised	**30**	347
Remeasurement of deferred tax – change in the UK tax rate[1]	**(97)**	–
Adjustment in respect of prior years	**150**	–
Tax charge	**14,611**	8,670

[1] Solely for illustrative purposes, a change in tax rates has been assumed to have taken place in 2008. UK companies with 31 December 2008 year ends will have reflected an actual change in tax rates in 2007.

IFRS GAAP plc
(Amounts in C thousands unless otherwise stated)

102

12p81(d)	During the year, as a result of the change in the UK corporation tax rate from 30% to 28% that was substantively enacted on 26 June 2008 and that will be effective from 1 April 2009, deferred tax balances have been remeasured. Deferred tax expected to reverse in the year to 31 December 2009 has been measured using the effective rate that will apply in the UK for the period $(28.5\%)^2$.

12p81(d)	The weighted average applicable tax rate was 33% (2007: 30%). The increase is caused by a change in the profitability of the group's subsidiaries in the respective countries net against the impact of the reduction in the UK tax rate.

12p81(a) The income tax charged/(credited) to equity during the year is as follows:

	2008	2007
Current tax[1]:		
Share option scheme	–	–
Retirement benefit scheme	–	–
Deferred tax:		
Fair value reserves in shareholders' equity:		
– Land and buildings (note 19)	-	374
– Hedging reserve (note 19)	33	–
– Available-for-sale financial assets (note 19)	198	61
Share option scheme	(30)	(20)
Convertible bond – equity component[2] (note 19)	2,328	–
Tax on actuarial loss on retirement benefits scheme	–	(211)
12p80(d) Impact of change in the UK tax rate on deferred tax[3]	10	–
	2,539	204

In addition, deferred income tax of C49 (2007: C43) was transferred from other reserves (note 19) to retained earnings (note 18). This represents deferred tax on the difference between the actual depreciation on buildings and the equivalent depreciation based on the historical cost of buildings.

32 Net foreign exchange gains/(losses)

21p52(a) The exchange differences (charged)/credited to the income statement are included as follows:

Group	2008	2007
Other (losses)/gains – net (note 25)	(277)	200
Net finance costs (note 30)	2,594	996
	2,317	1,196

33 Earnings per share

(a) Basic
Basic earnings per share is calculated by dividing the profit attributable to equity holders of the company by the weighted average number of ordinary shares in issue during the year excluding ordinary shares purchased by the company and held as treasury shares (note 17).

Group	2008	2007
33p70(a) Profit attributable to equity holders of the company	29,767	15,512
Profit from discontinued operation attributable to equity holders of the company	100	120
	29,867	15,632
33p70(b) Weighted average number of ordinary shares in issue (thousands)	23,454	20,500

[1] IAS 12 requires disclosure of current tax charged/credited to equity, in addition to deferred tax. There are no current tax items shown in equity in these financial statements, but the line items are shown for illustrative purposes.
[2] It is assumed that the tax base on the convertible bond is not split between the debt and equity elements. If the tax base were split, this would impact the deferred tax position.
[3] Solely for illustrative purposes, a change in tax rates has been assumed to have taken place in 2008. UK companies with 31 December 2008 year ends will have reflected an actual change in tax rates in 2007.

IFRS GAAP plc

(Amounts in C thousands unless otherwise stated)

(b) Diluted

Diluted earnings per share is calculated by adjusting the weighted average number of ordinary shares outstanding to assume conversion of all dilutive potential ordinary shares. The company has two categories of dilutive potential ordinary shares: convertible debt and share options. The convertible debt is assumed to have been converted into ordinary shares, and the net profit is adjusted to eliminate the interest expense less the tax effect. For the share options, a calculation is done to determine the number of shares that could have been acquired at fair value (determined as the average annual market share price of the company's shares) based on the monetary value of the subscription rights attached to outstanding share options. The number of shares calculated as above is compared with the number of shares that would have been issued assuming the exercise of the share options.

	2008	2007
Earnings		
Profit attributable to equity holders of the company	29,767	15,512
Interest expense on convertible debt (net of tax)	2,158	–
Profit used to determine diluted earnings per share	31,925	15,512
Profit from discontinued operations attributable to equity holders of the company	100	120
	32,025	15,632
Weighted average number of ordinary shares in issue (thousands)	23,454	20,500
Adjustments for:		
– Assumed conversion of convertible debt (thousands)	3,030	–
– Share options (thousands)	1,213	1,329
Weighted average number of ordinary shares for diluted earnings per share (thousands)	27,697	21,829

33p70(a) — (Profit used to determine diluted earnings per share row)

33p70(b) — (Weighted average number of ordinary shares for diluted earnings per share row)

34 Dividends per share

Group

1p95, 1p125(a)
10p12

The dividends paid in 2008 and 2007 were C10,102 (C0.48 per share) and C15,736 (C0.78 per share) respectively. A dividend in respect of the year ended 31 December 2008 of C0.51 per share, amounting to a total dividend of C12,945, is to be proposed at the annual general meeting on 30 April 2008. These financial statements do not reflect this dividend payable.

IFRS GAAP plc   104

(Amounts in C thousands unless otherwise stated)

35 Cash generated from operations

	Group 2008	2007	Company 2008	2007
7p18(b), 20 Profit before income tax including discontinued operations	**47,066**	25,118	**9,098**	10,491
Adjustments for:			–	–
– Depreciation (note 6)	**17,754**	9,662	–	–
– Amortisation (note 7)	**800**	565	–	–
– Goodwill impairment charge (note 7)	**4,650**	–	–	–
– (Profit)/loss on disposal of property, plant and equipment (see below)	**(17)**	8	–	–
– Share-based payment and increase in retirement benefit obligations	**509**	1,470	–	–
– Fair value gains on derivative financial instruments (note 25)	**(86)**	(88)	–	–
– Fair value (gains)/losses on financial assets at fair value through profit or loss (note 25)	**(85)**	238	–	–
– Dividend income on available-for-sale financial assets (note 26)	**(1,100)**	(883)	**(13,809)**	(14,806)
– Dividend income on financial assets at fair value through profit or loss (note 26)	**(800)**	(310)	–	–
– Finance costs – net (note 30)	**6,443**	10,588	–	–
– Share of loss/(profit) from associates (note 8)	**174**	(145)	–	–
– Foreign exchange losses/(gains) on operating activities (note 32)	**(277)**	(200)	–	–
Changes in working capital (excluding the effects of acquisition and exchange differences on consolidation):			–	–
– Inventories	**(6,077)**	(966)	–	–
– Trade and other receivables	**(1,339)**	(2,966)	–	–
– Financial assets at fair value through profit or loss	**(3,747)**	(858)	–	–
– Trade and other payables	**(7,634)**	543	**18**	–
Cash generated from operations	**56,234**	41,776	**(4,693)**	(4,316)

In the cash flow statement, proceeds from sale of property, plant and equipment comprise:

Group	2008	2007
Net book amount (note 6)	**6,337**	2,987
Profit/(loss) on disposal of property, plant and equipment	**17**	(8)
Proceeds from disposal of property, plant and equipment	**6,354**	2,979

Non-cash transactions

7p43 The principal non-cash transaction is the issue of shares as consideration for the acquisition discussed in note 16.

IFRS GAAP plc

(Amounts in C thousands unless otherwise stated)

36 Contingencies

Group

37p86   The group has contingent liabilities in respect of legal claims arising in the ordinary course of business.

It is not anticipated that any material liabilities will arise from the contingent liabilities other than those provided for (note 24).

In respect of the acquisition of Your Shoes Group on 1 March 2008 (note 38), additional consideration of 5% of the profit of Your Shoes Group may be payable in cash if the acquired operations achieve sales in excess of C7,500 for 2009, up to a maximum undiscounted amount of C2,500. At the date of acquisition, it was not considered probable that these monies would be payable. They were, therefore, not included as consideration for the business combination. There is no change in this assessment at the year end.

37p89   The group entered into an 'earn-out' agreement in connection with the disposal on 30 December 2006 of Leather Goods Limited. Additional cash consideration will be payable to the group if the future performance of Leather Goods Limited reaches a certain level. No gain has been recognised in the financial statements, as the amount of the earn-out is dependent on the aggregate result of Leather Goods Limited for the 39-month period ending 31 March 2010.

37 Commitments

(a) Capital commitments
Capital expenditure contracted for at the balance sheet date but not yet incurred is as follows:

Group	2008	2007
Property, plant and equipment	**3,593**	3,667
Intangible assets	**460**	474
	4,053	4,141

16p74(c), 38p122(e)

(b) Operating lease commitments – group company as lessee

17p35(d)   The group leases various retail outlets, offices and warehouses under non-cancellable operating lease agreements. The lease terms are between five and 10 years, and the majority of lease agreements are renewable at the end of the lease period at market rate.

17p35(d)   The group also leases various plant and machinery under cancellable operating lease agreements. The group is required to give a six-month notice for the termination of these agreements. The lease expenditure charged to the income statement during the year is disclosed in note 28.

17p35(a)   The future aggregate minimum lease payments under non-cancellable operating leases are as follows:

Group	2008	2007
No later than 1 year	**11,664**	10,604
Later than 1 year and no later than 5 years	**45,651**	45,651
Later than 5 years	**15,710**	27,374
	73,025	83,629

38 Business combinations

Group

IFRS3p66(a), IFRS3p67(a-c), IFRS3p70(a), IFRS3p67(i), IFRS3p70(b)   On 30 June 2007, the group acquired 15% of the share capital of Your Shoes Group. On 1 March 2008, the group acquired a further 55% of the share capital and obtained the control of Your Shoes Group, a shoe and leather goods retailer operating in the US and most western European countries. The acquired business contributed revenues of C44,709 and net profit of C2,762 to the group for the period from1 March 2008 to 31 December 2008. If the acquisition had occurred on 1 January 2008, group revenue would have been C220,345, and profit before allocations would have been C33,126. These amounts have been calculated using the group's accounting policies and by adjusting the results of the subsidiary to reflect the additional

IFRS GAAP plc 106

(Amounts in C thousands unless otherwise stated)

depreciation and amortisation that would have been charged assuming the fair value adjustments to property, plant and equipment and intangible assets had applied from 1 January 2008, together with the consequential tax effects.

Details of net assets acquired and goodwill are as follows:

IFRS3p67(d) 7p40(b)	Purchase consideration:	
	– Cash paid	4,050
	– Direct costs relating to the acquisition	200
IFRS3p67(d)(i)	– Fair value of shares issued (note 17)	10,000
7p40(a)	**Total purchase consideration**	**14,250**

IFRS3p67(h) The goodwill is attributable to the acquired customer base and economies of scale expected from combining the operations of the group and Your Shoes Group.

IFRS3p67(d)(ii) The fair value of the shares issued was based on the published share price (1 March 2008).

IFRS3p67(f) The assets and liabilities as of 1 March 2008 arising from the acquisition are as follows:

	Fair value	Acquiree's carrying amount
Cash and cash equivalents	300	300
Property, plant and equipment (note 6)	67,784	63,562
Trademarks (included in intangibles) (note 7)	2,000	–
Licences (included in intangibles) (note 7)	1,000	–
Contractual customer relationship (included in intangibles) (note 7)	1,000	–
Investment in associates (note 8)	389	329
Available-for-sale financial assets (note 10)	473	473
Inventories	1,122	672
Trade and other receivables	585	585
Trade and other payables	(12,461)	(12,461)
Retirement benefit obligations:		
– Pensions (note 23)	(1,914)	(1,901)
– Other post-retirement obligations (note 23)	(725)	(725)
Borrowings	(41,459)	(41,459)
Contingent liability	(1,000)	–
Deferred tax liabilities (note 22)	(1,953)	(410)
Fair value of net assets	**15,141**	**8,965**
Minority interests (30%)	(4,542)	
Asset revaluation surplus (note 19)	(850)	
Goodwill (note 7)	4,501	
Total purchase consideration	**14,250**	

	Purchase consideration settled in cash	4,250
7p40(c)	Cash and cash equivalents in subsidiary acquired	(300)
	Cash outflow on acquisition	**3,950**

There were no acquisitions in the year ended 31 December 2007.

See note 40 for disclosures regarding the business combination that took place after the balance sheet date but before the approval of these financial statements.

IFRS GAAP plc

(Amounts in C thousands unless otherwise stated)

39 Related-party transactions

Group

1p126(c)
24p12
The group is controlled by M Limited (incorporated in the UK), which owns 57% of the company's shares. The remaining 43% of the shares are widely held. The ultimate parent of the group is G Limited (incorporated in the UK). The ultimate controlling party of the group is Mr Power.

24p17, 18, 22   The following transactions were carried out with related parties:

24p17(a)   *(a) Sales of goods and services*

	2008	2007
Sales of goods:		
– Associates	1,123	291
Sales of services:		
– The ultimate parent (legal and administration services)	67	127
– Close family members of the ultimate controlling party (design services)	100	104
	1,290	522

Goods are sold based on the price lists in force and terms that would be available to third parties[1]. Sales of services are negotiated with related parties on a cost-plus basis, allowing a margin ranging from 15% to 30% (2007: 10% to 18%).

24p17(a)   *(b) Purchases of goods and services*

	2008	2007
Purchases of goods:		
– Associates	3,054	3,058
Purchases of services:		
– An entity controlled by key management personnel	83	70
– The immediate parent (management services)	295	268
	3,432	3,396

24p21
Goods and services are bought from associates and an entity controlled by key management personnel on normal commercial terms and conditions. The entity controlled by key management personnel is a firm belonging to Mr Chamois, a non-executive director of the company. Management services are bought from the immediate parent on a cost-plus basis, allowing a margin ranging from 15% to 30% (2007: 10%).

24p16   *(c) Key management compensation*

Key management includes directors (executive and non-executive), members of the Executive Committee, the Company Secretary and the Head of Internal Audit. The compensation paid or payable to key management for employee services is shown below:

	2008	2007
24p16(a) Salaries and other short-term employee benefits	2,200	1,890
24p16(d) Termination benefits	1,600	–
24p16(b) Post-employment benefits	123	85
24p16(c) Other long-term benefits	26	22
24p16(e) Share-based payments	150	107
	4,099	2,104

[1] Management should disclose that related-party transactions were made on an arm's length basis only when such terms can be substantiated (IAS24p21).

IFRS GAAP plc
108

(Amounts in C thousands unless otherwise stated)

CA06 s412 — *(d) Directors*

	2008	2007
Aggregate emoluments	**860**	661
Aggregate gains made on the exercise of share options	**311**	157
Aggregate amounts receivable under long-term incentive schemes	**211**	239
Company contributions to money purchase pension scheme	**72**	–
	1,273	1,061

6 Sch 1(1)(a)
SI 2008/410
5 Sch 1(1)(a)
6 Sch 1(1)(b)
SI 2008/410
S Sch 1 (1)(b)
6 Sch 1(1)(c)
SI 2008/410
S Sch 1 (1)(c)
6 Sch 1(1)(d)
SI 2008/410
S Sch 1 (1)(d)

Refer to the director's remuneration report for further details of remuneration of directors employed by the Company.

24p17(b), 1p74 — *(e) Year-end balances arising from sales/purchases of goods/services*

	2008	2007
Receivables from related parties (note 12):		
– Ultimate parent	**50**	40
– Close family members of key management personnel	**4**	6
Payables to related parties (note 20):		
– Immediate parent	**200**	190
– Associates	**1,902**	1, 005
– Entity controlled by key management personnel	**100**	–

The receivables from related parties arise mainly from sale transactions and are due two months after the date of sales. The receivables are unsecured in nature and bear no interest. There are no provisions held against receivables from related parties (2007: nil).

The payables to related parties arise mainly from purchase transactions and are due two months after the date of purchase. The payables bear no interest.

24p17, 1p74 — *(e) Loans to related parties*

	2008	2007
Loans to key management of the company (and their families)[1]:		
At 1 January	**196**	168
Loans advanced during year	**343**	62
Loan repayments received	**(49)**	(34)
Interest charged	**30**	16
Interest received	**(30)**	(16)
At 31 December	**490**	196
Loans to associates:		
At 1 January	**1,192**	1,206
Loans advanced during year	**1,000**	50
Loan repayments received	**(14)**	(64)
Interest charged	**187**	120
Interest received	**(187)**	(120)
At 31 December	**2,178**	1,192
Total loans to related parties:		
At 1 January	**1,388**	1,374
Loans advanced during year	**1,343**	112
Loan repayments received	**(63)**	(98)
Interest charged	**217**	136
Interest received (note 30)	**(217)**	(136)
At 31 December (note 12)	**2,668**	1,388

[1] None of the loans made to members of key management has been made to directors.

IFRS GAAP plc

(Amounts in C thousands unless otherwise stated)

24p17(b)(i) The loans advanced to key management have the following terms and conditions:

Name of key management	Amount of loan	Term	Interest rate
2008			
Mr Brown	C173	Repayable monthly over 2 years	6.3%
Mr White	C170	Repayable monthly over 2 years	6.3%
2007			
Mr Black	C20	Repayable monthly over 2 years	6.5%
Mr White	C42	Repayable monthly over 1 year	6.5%

IFRS7p15 Certain loans advanced to associates during the year amounting to C1,500 (2007: C500) are collateralised by shares in listed companies. The fair value of these shares was C65 at the balance sheet date (2007: C590).

The loans to associates are due on 1 January 2009 and carry interest at 7.0% (2007:8%). The fair values and the effective interest rates of loans to associates are disclosed in note 12.

24p17(c) No provision has been required in 2008 and 2007 for the loans made to key management personnel and associates.

24p18(a) **Company**
The following transactions with subsidiaries occurred in the year

	2008	2007
24p17(a) Dividends received	13,809	14,806

24p17(a)
24p17(b) Treasury Limited, an indirect subsidiary of the company provided the company with additional cash funding of C13,210 on 1 March 2008. The funding was used to partially finance the acquisition of 'Your Shoes Group', which resulted in a C4,250 cash outflow and the acquistion of 875,000 of the company's own shares on 18 April 2008 which resulted in cash outflow of C2,564. No interest is repayable on the outstanding loan of C29,662 as at 31 December 2008 (2007:C16,452) from Treasury Limited, which is repayable on demand. See note 20 for further details.

24p17(a), (b) Short term cash financing is provided to subsidiary undertakings in the group. The monies advanced are generally repayable within 3 months. The outstanding receivable balance is C41,147 as at 31 December 2008 (2007:C31,296). See note 12 for further details.

No purchase or sales transactions were entered into between the company and subsidiary undertakings.

40 Events after the balance sheet date

Group

(a) Business combinations

10p21,
IFRS3p66(b),
IFRS3p67 (a-c) The group acquired 100% of the share capital of K&Co, a group of companies specialising in the manufacture of shoes for extreme sports, for a cash consideration of C5,950 on 1 February 2009.

Details of net assets acquired and goodwill are as follows:

IFRS3p67(d) Purchase consideration:	
– Cash paid	5,950
– Direct cost relating to the acquisition	150
7p40(a) Total purchase consideration	6,100
Fair value of assets acquired (see below)	(5,145)
Goodwill	955

IFRS3p67(h)
IFRS3p67(f) The above goodwill is attributable to K&Co's strong position and profitability in trading in the niche market for extreme-sports equipment.

IFRS GAAP plc
110

(Amounts in C thousands unless otherwise stated)

The assets and liabilities arising from the acquisition, provisionally determined, are as follows:

	Fair value	Acquiree's carrying amount
Cash and cash equivalents	195	195
Property, plant and equipment	29,056	28,234
Trademarks	1,000	–
Licences	700	–
Customer relationships	1,850	–
Favourable lease agreements	800	–
Inventories	995	495
Trade and other receivables	855	855
Trade and other payables	(9,646)	(9,646)
Retirement benefit obligations	(1,425)	(1,300)
Borrowings	(19,259)	(19,259)
Deferred tax assets	24	519
Net assets acquired	**5,145**	**93**

(b) Associates

10p21 · The group acquired 40% of the share capital of L&Co, a group of companies specialising in the manufacture of leisure shoes, for a cash consideration of C2,050 on 25 January 2009.

Details of net assets acquired and goodwill are as follows:

Purchase consideration:	
– Cash paid	2,050
– Direct cost relating to the acquisition	70
Total purchase consideration	2,120
Share of fair value of net assets acquired (see below)	(2,000)
Goodwill	**120**

DV · The goodwill is attributable to L&Co's strong position and profitability in trading in the market of leisure shoes and to its workforce, which cannot be separately recognised as an intangible asset.

DV · The assets and liabilities arising from the acquisition, provisionally determined, are as follows:

	Fair value	Acquiree's carrying amount
Contractual customer relationships	380	–
Property, plant and equipment	3,200	2,400
Inventory	500	500
Cash	220	220
Trade creditors	(420)	(350)
Borrowings	(1,880)	(1,420)
Net assets acquired	**2,000**	**1,350**

(c) Equity transactions

10p21 · 33p71(c) · 10p21, 22(f) · On 1 January 2009, 1,200 thousand share options were granted to directors and employees with an exercise price set at the market share prices less 15% on that date of C3.13 per share (share price: C3.68) (expiry date: 31 December 2013).

The company re-issued 500,000 treasury shares for a total consideration of C1,500 on 15 January 2009.

(d) Borrowings

10p21 · On 1 February 2009, the group issued C6,777 6.5% US dollar bonds to finance its expansion programme and working capital requirements in the US. The bonds are repayable on 31 December 2013 (note 21).

IFRS GAAP plc

(Amounts in C thousands unless otherwise stated)

41 Principal subsidiaries and associates

Group and Company

27p42(b)
5 Sch 15 (1)-(5)
SI 2008/410
4 Sch 1(1)-(3),
16(1)-(3)
5 Sch 16
SI 2008/410
4 Sch17

Name	Country of incorporation	Nature of business	Proportion of ordinary shares held by parent	Proportion of ordinary shares held by the group	Proportion of preference shares held by the group
Treasury Limited	UK	Head office financing company	100%	0%	0%
A Limited	UK	Intermediate holding company	0%	100%	100%
O Limited	UK	Shoe manufacturer and wholesaler	0%	100%	0%
Shoe Retailer Limited	UK	Shoe and leather goods retailer	0%	100%	0%
Transport Limited	UK	Logistics company	100%	0%	0%
Design Limited	UK	Design services	100%	0%	0%
Your Shoes Group	US	Shoe and leather goods retailer	70%	0%	0%
European Shoes GbmH	Europe	Shoe manufacturer and wholesaler	0%	100%	0%
Transport SARL	Europe	Logistics company	0%	100%	0%
Design GbmH	Europe	Design services	0%	100%	0%
China Shoes Group	China	Shoe manufacturer and wholesaler	0%	100%	0%
Russia Shoes Group	Russia	Shoe manufacturer and wholesaler	0%	100%	0%

All subsidiary undertakings are included in the consolidation. The proportion of the voting rights in the subsidiary undertakings held directly by the parent company do not differ from the proportion of ordinary shares held. The parent company further does not have any shareholdings in the preference shares of subsidiary undertakings included in the group.

Refer to note 8b for details of group holdings in associates.

IFRS GAAP plc   112
(Amounts in C thousands unless otherwise stated)

Appendices

Appendix I — Alternative presentation of primary statements

Consolidated income statement – by nature of expense

As an alternative to the presentation of costs by function shown in the above illustrative corporate consolidated financial statements, the group is permitted to present the analysis of costs using the nature of expenditure format. The following disclosures would be made on the face of the income statement:

		Note	Year ended 31 December	
			2008	2007
1p91	Revenue		**211,034**	112,360
1p83	Other income	26	**1,900**	1,259
	Changes in inventories of finished goods and work in progress	13	**(6,950)**	2,300
	Raw materials and consumables used	13	**(53,302)**	(31,845)
	Employee benefits expense	29	**(40,082)**	(15,492)
	Impairment	7	**(4,650)**	–
	Depreciation and amortisation	6, 7	**(18,554)**	(10,227)
	Transportation expense		**(8,584)**	(6,236)
	Advertising costs		**(12,759)**	(6,662)
	Operating lease payments		**(10,604)**	(8,500)
1p83	Other (losses)/gains – net	25	**(90)**	63
1p83	Loss on expropriated land	27	**(1,117)**	–
	Other expenses		**(2,799)**	(1,659)
	Operating profit		**53,443**	35,361
1p81(b)	Finance income	30	**1,730**	1,609
1p83	Finance costs	30	**(8,173)**	(12,197)
1p83	Finance costs – net	30	**(6,443)**	(10,588)
1p81(c)	Share of (loss)/profit of associate	8	**(174)**	145
1p81(f)	**Profit before income tax**		**46,826**	24,918
1p81(e), 12p77	Income tax expense		**(14,611)**	(8,670)
1p81(f)	**Profit for the year from continuing operations**		**32,215**	16,248
IFRS5p34	**Discontinued operations:**			
12p81(b)				
	Profit for the year from discontinued operations		**100**	120
1p81(f)	**Profit for the year**		**32,315**	16,368
1p82	**Attributable to:**			
1p82(b)	Equity holders of the company		**29,767**	15,512
1p82(a)	Minority interest		**2,548**	856
			32,315	16,368

Earnings per share for profit attributable and profit from discontinued operations to the equity holders of the company during the year (expressed in C per share)

	Basic earnings per share	Note	**2008**	2007
33p66	From continuing operations	33	**1.26**	0.75
33p68	From discontinuing operations		**0.01**	0.01
			1.27	0.76
	Diluted earnings per share[1]			
33p66	From continuing operations	33	**1.15**	0.71
33p68	From discontinuing operations		**0.01**	0.01
			1.16	0.72

[1] EPS for discontinued operations may be given in the notes to the accounts instead of the face of the income statement.

The notes on pages 43 to 111 are an integral part of these consolidated financial statements.

IFRS GAAP plc

113

(Amounts in C thousands unless otherwise stated)

Consolidated statement of changes in equity

As an alternative to the presentation of changes in equity in the illustrative corporate consolidated financial statements (statement of recognised income and expense (SORIE) and reconciliation of opening and closing balances of share capital, reserves and retained earnings in the notes), the group would normally be permitted to present the statement of changes in equity (SOCIE)[1] as a primary statement. As the group chose to record all actuarial gains and losses directly in equity, they were required to present the SORIE as a primary statement. If the group had chosen to record actuarial gains and losses in accordance with the 'corridor approach' (see related policy and note disclosure below), it would be permitted to present the statement of changes in equity (SOCIE) below as a primary statement.

1,96, 1p97, 1p36

1p104		Note	Share capital	Share premium	Other reserves	Retained earnings	Total	Minority interest	Total equity
1p97(c)	Balance at 1 January 2007		20,000	10,424	6,364	47,976	84,764	1,500	86,264
1p96(b)	Fair value gains, net of tax[2]:								
16p77(f)	– Land and buildings[3]	19	–	–	759	–	759	–	759
IFRS7p20(a)(ii)	– Available-for-sale financial assets	19	–	–	48	–	48	–	48
1p96(b), 16p41	Depreciation transfer on land and buildings, net of tax	18, 19	–	–	(87)	87	–	–	–
1p96(b)	Cash flow hedges, net of tax	19	–	–	(3)	–	(3)	–	(3)
1p96(b), 39p102(a)	Net investment hedge	19	–	–	40	–	40	–	40
1p96(b),	Currency translation differences	19	–	–	(116)	–	(116)	(40)	(156)
1p96(b)	Net income/(expense) recognised directly in equity		–	–	641	87	728	(40)	688
1p96(a)	Profit for the year		–	–	–	15,512	15,512	856	16,368
1p96(c)	**Total recognised income and expense for 2007**		–	–	641	15,599	16,240	816	17,056
1p97(a)	Employees share option scheme:								
IFRS2p50	– Value of employee services	18	–	–	–	822[4]	822	–	822
IFRS2p50	– Proceeds from shares issued	17	1,000	70	–	–	1,070	–	1,070
1p97(b)	– Tax credit relating to share option scheme	18	–	–	–	20	20	–	20
1p97(a)	Dividend relating to 2006	34	–	–	–	(15,736)	(15,736)	(550)	(16,286)
			1,000	70	–	(14,894)	(13,824)	(550)	(14,374)
1p97(c)	**Balance at 31 December 2007**		21,000	10,494	7,005	48,681	87,180	1,766	88,946

Attributable to equity holders of the Company (spanning Share capital, Share premium, Other reserves, Retained earnings, Total)

[1] If, according to IAS 19 para 93A, actuarial gains and losses are recognised outside the income statement in the period in which they occur, a statement of recognised income and expense should be presented.

[2] Line items can be presented either net of tax as above or gross with a separate line item for the total tax impact (see IAS 1 para IG 4).

[3] IAS16 para 77(f) requires disclosure of any restrictions on the distribution of the land and buildings fair value reserve to shareholders.

[4] The credit entry to equity in respect of the IFRS 2 charge should be recorded in accordance with local company law and practice. This may be a specific reserve, retained earnings or share capital.

IFRS GAAP plc

114

(Amounts in C thousands unless otherwise stated)

		Note	Share capital	Share premium	Other reserves	Retained earnings	Total	Minority interest	Total equity
			Attributable to equity holders of the Company						
1p97(c)	Balance at 1 January 2008		21,000	10,494	7,005	48,681	87,180	1,766	188,946
1p96(b)	Fair value gains, net of tax:								
IFRS7p20(a)(ii)	– Available-for-sale financial assets	19	–	–	350	–	350	–	350
1p96(b), 16p41	Depreciation transfer on land and buildings, net of tax	18, 19	–	–	(100)	100	–	–	–
1p96(b)	Cash flow hedges, net of tax	19	–	–	64	–	64	–	64
1p96(b), 39p102(a)	Net investment hedge	19	–	–	(45)	–	(45)	–	(45)
1p96(b),21p52(b)	Currency translation differences	19	–	–	1,992	–	1,992	252	2,244
IFRS3p59	Increase in fair values of proportionate holding of Your Shoes Group (note 38)	19	–	–	850	–	850	–	850
12p80(d)	Impact of the change in the UK tax rate on deferred tax[5]	22	–	–	–	(10)	(10)	–	(10)
1p96(b)	Net income recognised directly in equity	19	–	–	3,111	90	3,201	252	3,453
1p96(a)	Profit for the year	19	–	–	–	29,767	29,767	2,548	32,315
1p96(c)	**Total recognised income and expense for 2008**		**–**	**–**	**3,111**	**29,857**	**32,968**	**2,800**	**35,768**
1p97(a)	Employee share option scheme:								
IFRS2p50	– Value of employee services	18	–	–	–	690[6]	690	–	690
IFRS2p50	– Proceeds from shares issued	17	750	200	–	–	950	–	950
197(b)	– Tax credit relating to share option scheme	18	–	–	–	30	30	–	30
1p97(a)	Issue of share capital – business combination	17	3,550	6,450	–	–	10,000	–	10,000
1p97(a)	Purchase of treasury shares	18	–	–	–	(2,564)	(2,564)	–	(2,564)
1p97(a), 32p28	Convertible bond – equity component	19	–	–	5,433	–	5,433	–	5,433
1p97(a)	Dividend relating to 2007	34	–	–	–	(10,102)	(10,102)	(1,920)	(12,022)
1p97(a)	Minority interest arising on business combinations	38	–	–	–	–	–	4,542	4,542
			4,300	6,650	5,433	(11,946)	4,437	2,622	7,059
1p97(c)	**Balance at 31 December 2008**		**25,300**	**17,144**	**15,549**	**66,592**	**124,585**	**7,188**	**131,773**

---

[5] Solely for illustrative purposes, a change in tax rates has been assumed to have taken place in 2008. UK companies with 31 December 2008 year ends will have reflected an actual change in tax rates in 2007.

[6] The credit entry to equity in respect of the IFRS 2 charge should be recorded in accordance with local company law and practice. This may be a specific reserve, retained earnings or share capital.

IFRS GAAP plc   115

(Amounts in C thousands unless otherwise stated)

IAS 19 – Employee benefits

Included below is the illustrative disclosure for post-employment benefits using the option in IAS 19 to recognise actuarial gains and losses using the corridor approach.

Note – Accounting policies

Employee benefits

1p110	*(a) Pension obligations*
19p27	Group companies operate various pension schemes. The schemes are generally funded through
19p25	payments to insurance companies or trustee-administered funds, determined by periodic
19p7	actuarial calculations. The group has both defined benefit and defined contribution plans. A
19p120A(b)	defined contribution plan is a pension plan under which the group pays fixed contributions into

a separate entity. The group has no legal or constructive obligations to pay further contributions if the fund does not hold sufficient assets to pay all employees the benefits relating to employee service in the current and prior periods. A defined benefit plan is a pension plan that is not a defined contribution plan. Typically, defined benefit plans define an amount of pension benefit that an employee will receive on retirement, usually dependent on one or more factors such as age, years of service and compensation.

19p79	The liability recognised in the balance sheet in respect of defined benefit pension plans is the present value of the defined benefit obligation at the balance sheet date less the fair value of plan
19p80	assets, together with adjustments for unrecognised actuarial gains or losses and past service
19p64	costs. The defined benefit obligation is calculated annually by independent actuaries using the

projected unit credit method. The present value of the defined benefit obligation is determined by discounting the estimated future cash outflows using interest rates of high-quality corporate bonds that are denominated in the currency in which the benefits will be paid and that have terms to maturity approximating to the terms of the related pension liability.

19p92	Actuarial gains and losses arising from experience adjustments and changes in actuarial
19p93	assumptions in excess of the greater of 10% of the fair value of plan assets or 10% of the present
19p120A(a)	value of the defined benefit obligation are charged or credited to income over the employees'

expected average remaining working lives.

19p96	Past-service costs are recognised immediately in income, unless the changes to the pension plan are conditional on the employees remaining in service for a specified period of time (the vesting period). In this case, the past-service costs are amortised on a straight-line basis over the vesting period.

19p44	For defined contribution plans, the group pays contributions to publicly or privately administered pension insurance plans on a mandatory, contractual or voluntary basis. The group has no further payment obligations once the contributions have been paid. The contributions are recognised as employee benefit expense when they are due. Prepaid contributions are recognised as an asset to the extent that a cash refund or a reduction in the future payments is available.

1p110	*(b) Other post-employment obligations*
19p120A(a)	Some group companies provide post-retirement healthcare benefits to their retirees. The
19p120A(b)	entitlement to these benefits is usually conditional on the employee remaining in service up to

retirement age and the completion of a minimum service period. The expected costs of these benefits are accrued over the period of employment using the same accounting methodology as used for defined benefit pension plans. Actuarial gains and losses arising from experience adjustments, and changes in actuarial assumptions in excess of the greater of 10% of the fair value of plan assets or 10% of the present value of the defined benefit obligation, are charged or credited to income over the expected average remaining working lives of the related employees. These obligations are valued annually by independent qualified actuaries.

1p110	*(c) Share-based compensation*
IFRS2p15(b)	The group operates a number of equity-settled, share-based compensation plans, under which
IFRS2p19	the entity receives services from employees as consideration for equity instruments (options) of

the group. The fair value of the employee services received in exchange for the grant of the options is recognised as an expense. The total amount to be expensed is determined by reference to the fair value of the options granted, excluding the impact of any non-market service and performance vesting conditions (for example, profitability, sales growth targets and remaining an employee of the entity over specified time period). Non-market vesting conditions are included in assumptions about the number of options that are expected to vest. The total

IFRS GAAP plc

(Amounts in C thousands unless otherwise stated)

amount to be expensed is recognised over the vesting period, which is the period over which all the specified vesting conditions are to be satisfied. At each balance sheet date, the entity revises its estimates of the number of options that are expected to vest based on the non-market vesting conditions. It recognises the impact of the revision of original estimates, if any, in the income statement, with a corresponding adjustment to equity.

The proceeds received net of any directly attributable transaction costs are credited to share capital (nominal value) and share premium when the options are exercised.

<table>
<tr><td>1p110
19p133</td><td>*(d) Termination benefits*
Termination benefits are payable when employment is terminated by the group before the normal retirement date, or whenever an employee accepts voluntary redundancy in exchange for</td></tr>
<tr><td>19p134
19p139</td><td>these benefits. The group recognises termination benefits when it is demonstrably committed to either: terminating the employment of current employees according to a detailed formal plan without possibility of withdrawal; or providing termination benefits as a result of an offer made to encourage voluntary redundancy. Benefits falling due more than 12 months after the balance sheet date are discounted to present value.</td></tr>
<tr><td>1p110
19p17</td><td>*(e) Profit-sharing and bonus plans*
The group recognises a liability and an expense for bonuses and profit-sharing, based on a formula that takes into consideration the profit attributable to the company's shareholders after certain adjustments. The group recognises a provision where contractually obliged or where there is a past practice that has created a constructive obligation.</td></tr>
</table>

Note – Retirement benefit obligation

	2008	2007
Balance sheet obligations for:		
Pension benefits	3,138	1,438
Post-employment medical benefits	1,402	692
	4,540	2,130
Income statement charge for (note 29):		
Pension benefits	762	496
Post-employment medical benefits	150	107
	912	603

(a) Pension benefits
The group operates defined benefit pension plans in the UK and the US based on employee pensionable remuneration and length of service. The majority of plans are externally funded. Plan assets are held in trusts, foundations or similar entities, governed by local regulations and practice in each country, as is the nature of the relationship between the group and the trustees (or equivalent) and their composition.

19p120A(d)(f) The amounts recognised in the balance sheet are determined as follows:

	2008	2007
Present value of funded obligations	6,155	2,943
Fair value of plan assets	(5,991)	(2,797)
	164	146
Present value of unfunded obligations	3,206	1,549
Unrecognised actuarial losses	(87)	(94)
Unrecognised past service cost	(145)	(163)
Liability in the balance sheet	3,138	1,438

IFRS GAAP plc
117

(Amounts in C thousands unless otherwise stated)

19p120A(c)   The movement in the defined benefit obligation over the year is as follows:

	2008	2007
At 1 January	4,492	3,479
Current service cost	751	498
Interest cost	431	214
Contributions by plan participants	55	30
Actuarial losses/(gains)	(15)	495
Exchange differences	(43)	(103)
Benefits paid	(66)	(121)
Liabilities acquired in a business combination (note 38)	3,691	–
Curtailments	65	–
Settlements[1]	–	–
At 31 December	9,361	4,492

19p120A(e)   The movement in the fair value of plan assets of the year is as follows:

	2008	2007
At 1 January	2,797	2,264
Expected return on plan assets	510	240
Actuarial gains/(losses)	(15)	(5)
Exchange differences	25	(22)
Employer contributions	908	411
Employee contributions	55	30
Benefits paid	(66)	(121)
Business combinations (note 38)	1,777	–
At 31 December	5,991	2,797

19p120A(g)   The amounts recognised in the income statement are as follows:

	2008	2007
Current service cost	751	498
Interest cost	431	214
Expected return on plan assets	(510)	(240)
Net actuarial losses recognised during the year	7	8
Past service cost	18	16
Losses on curtailment	65	–
Total, included in staff costs (note 29)	762	496

19p120A(g)   Of the total charge, C521 (2007: C324) and C241 (2007: C172) were included in cost of goods sold and administrative expenses respectively.

19p120A(m)   The actual return on plan assets was C495 (2007: C235).

19p120A(n)   The principal actuarial assumptions used were as follows:

	2008		2007	
19p120A(n)	UK	US	UK	US
Discount rate	6.0%	6.1%	5.5%	5.6%
Inflation rate	3.6%	3.0%	3.3%	2.7%
Expected return on plan assets	8.5%	8.3%	8.7%	8.7%
Future salary increases	5.0%	4.5%	4.5%	4.0%
Future pension increases	3.6%	2.8%	3.1%	2.7%

[1] IAS 19 requires the disclosure of settlements as part of the reconciliation of the opening and closing balances of the present value of the defined benefit obligation. There is no such movement on the defined benefit obligation relating to pension plans in these financial statements, but the line item has been shown for illustrative purposes.

IFRS GAAP plc 118

(Amounts in C thousands unless otherwise stated)

19p120A(n)(vi)   Assumptions regarding future mortality experience are set based on actuarial advice, published statistics and experience in each territory. Mortality assumptions for the most important countries are based on the following post-retirement mortality tables: (i) UK: PNMA 00 and PNFA 00 with medium cohort adjustment subject to a minimum annual improvement of 1% and scaling factors of 110% for current male pensioners, 125% for current female pensioners and 105% for future male and female pensioners; and (ii) US: RP2000 with a projection period of 10-15 years.

These tables translate into an average life expectancy in years of a pensioner retiring at age 65 of:

	2008		2007	
19p120A(n)	**UK**	**US**	UK	US
Retiring at the balance sheet date:				
– Male	**22**	**20**	22	20
– Female	**25**	**24**	25	24
– Retiring 20 years after the balance sheet date:				
– Male	**24**	**23**	24	23
– Female	**27**	**26**	27	26

DV   The sensitivity of the overall pension liability to changes in the weighted principal assumptions is:

	Change in assumption	**Impact on overall liability**
Discount rate	Increase/decrease by 0.5%	Increase/decrease by 7.2%
Inflation rate	Increase/decrease by 0.5%	Increase/decrease by 5.1%
Salary growth rate	Increase/decrease by 0.5%	Increase/decrease by 3.3%
Rate of mortality	Increase by 1 year	Increase by 5.2%

19p122(b)   *(b) Post-employment medical benefits*
The group operates a number of post-employment medical benefit schemes, principally in the US. The method of accounting, assumptions and the frequency of valuations are similar to those used for defined benefit pension schemes. The majority of these plans are unfunded.

19p120A(n)   In addition to the assumptions set out above, the main actuarial assumption is a long-term increase in health costs of 8.0% a year (2007: 7.6%).

19p120A(d)   The amounts recognised in the balance sheet were determined as follows:

19p120A(f)	**2008**	2007
Present value of funded obligations	**705**	340
Fair value of plan assets	**(620)**	(302)
	85	38
Present value of unfunded obligations	**1,325**	663
Unrecognised actuarial losses	**(8)**	(9)
Liability in the balance sheet	**1,402**	692

19p120A(c)   The movement in the defined benefit obligation is as follows:

	2008	2007
Beginning of the year	**1,003**	708
Current service cost	**153**	107
Interest cost	**49**	25
Contributions by plan participants[1]	**–**	–
Actuarial losses/(gains)[1]	**(2)**	204
Exchange differences	**25**	(41)
Benefits paid[1]	**–**	–
Liabilities acquired in a business combination (note 38)	**802**	–
Curtailments[1]	**–**	–
Settlements[1]	**–**	–
At 31 December	**2,030**	1,003

[1] IAS 19 requires the disclosure of contributions by plan participants, benefits paid, curtailments and settlements as part of the reconciliation of the opening and closing balances of the present value of the defined benefit obligation. There is no such movement on the defined benefit obligation relating to post-employment medical benefits in these financial statements, but the line items have been shown for illustrative purposes.

IFRS GAAP plc

(Amounts in C thousands unless otherwise stated)

19p120A(e) The movement in the fair value of plan assets of the year is as follows:

	2008	2007
At 1 January	302	207
Expected return on plan assets	53	25
Actuarial gains/(losses)	(2)	(1)
Exchange differences	5	(2)
Employer contributions	185	73
Employee contributions[1]	–	–
Benefits paid[1]	–	–
Business combinations (note 38)	77	–
At 31 December	**620**	**302**

19p120A(g) The amounts recognised in the income statement were as follows:

	2008	2007
Current service cost	153	107
Interest cost	49	25
Expected return on plan assets	(53)	(25)
Net actuarial losses recognised in year	1	–
Total, included in employee benefits expense (note 29)	**150**	**107**

19p120A(o) The effect of a 1% movement in the assumed medical cost trend rate is as follows:

	Increase	Decrease
Effect on the aggregate of the current service cost and interest cost	24	(20)
Effect on the defined benefit obligation	366	(313)

19p120A(g) Of the total charge, C102 (2007: C71) and C48 (2007: C36) respectively were included in cost of goods sold and administrative expenses.

19p120A(m) The actual return on plan assets was C51 (2007: C24).

(c) Post-employment benefits (pension and medical)

19p120A(j) Plan assets are comprised as follows:

	2008		2007	
Equity instruments	3,256	49%	1,224	40%
Debt instruments	1,524	23%	571	18%
Property	1,047	16%	943	30%
Other	784	12%	361	12%
	6,611	100%	3,099	100%

DV Investments are well diversified, such that the failure of any single investment would not have a material impact on the overall level of assets. The largest proportion of assets is invested in equities, although the group also invests in property, bonds, hedge funds and cash. The group believes that equities offer the best returns over the long-term with an acceptable level of risk. The majority of equities are in a globally diversified portfolio of international blue chip entities, with a target of 60% of equities held in the UK and Europe, 30% in the US and the remainder in emerging markets.

19p120A(k) Pension plan assets include the company's ordinary shares with a fair value of C136 (2007: C126) and a building occupied by the group with a fair value of C612 (2007: C609).

19p120A(l) The expected return on plan assets was determined by considering the expected returns available on the assets underlying the current investment policy. Expected yields on fixed interest investments are based on gross redemption yields as at the balance sheet date. Expected returns on equity and property investments reflect long-term real rates of return experienced in the respective markets.

[1] IAS 19 requires the disclosure of employee contributions and employee contributions as part of the reconciliation of the opening and closing balances of plan assets. There is no such movement on the plan assets relating to post-employment medical benefits in these financial statements, but the line items have been shown for illustrative purposes.

IFRS GAAP plc

(Amounts in C thousands unless otherwise stated)

120

19p120(q)   Expected contributions to post-employment benefit plans for the year ending 31 December 2008 are C1,150.

DV   The group has agreed that it will aim to eliminate the deficit over the next nine years. Funding levels are monitored on an annual basis and the current agreed regular contribution rate is 14% of pensionable salaries in the UK and 12% in the US. The next triennial valuation is due to be completed as at 31 December 2009. The group considers that the contribution rates set at the last valuation date are sufficient to eliminate the deficit over the agreed period and that regular contributions, which are based on service costs, will not increase significantly.

DV   An alternative method of valuation to the projected unit credit method is a buy-out valuation. This assumes that the entire post-employment benefit liability will be settled by transferring all obligations to a suitable insurer. The group estimates the amount required to settle the post-employment benefit liabilities at the balance sheet date would be C15,500.

19p120A(p)

	2008	2007	2006	2005[1]
At 31 December				
Present value of defined benefit obligation	**11,391**	5,495	4,187	3,937
Fair value of plan assets	**6,611**	3,099	2,471	2,222
Deficit/(surplus) in the plan	**4,780**	2,396	1,716	1,715
Experience adjustments on plan liabilities	**(326)**	125	55	–
Experience adjustments on plan assets	**(17)**	(6)	(197)	–

Consolidated cash flow statement – direct method

IAS 7 encourages the use of the 'direct method' for the presentation of cash flows from operating activities. The presentation of cash flows from operating activities using the direct method in accordance with IAS 7 (revised 1994), paragraph 18, is as follows:

Consolidated cash flow statement

1p104, 7p10

		Year ended 31 December	
	Note	**2008**	2007
7p18(a) **Cash flows from operating activities**			
Cash receipts from customers		**212,847**	114,451
Cash paid to suppliers and employees		**(156,613)**	(72,675)
Cash generated from operations		**56,234**	41,776
Interest paid		**(7,835)**	(14,773)
Income taxes paid		**(14,317)**	(10,526)
Net cash flows from operating activities		**34,082**	16,477

7p21 **Cash flows from investing activities**			
7p39 Acquisition of subsidiary, net of cash acquired	38	**(3,950)**	–
7p16(a) Purchases of property, plant and equipment (PPE)	6	**(9,755)**	(6,042)
7p16(b) Proceeds from sale of PPE	35	**6,354**	2,979
7p16(a) Purchases of intangible assets	7	**(3,050)**	(700)
7p16(c) Purchases of available-for-sale financial assets	10	**(2,781)**	(1,126)
7p16(e) Loans granted to associates	39	**(1,000)**	(50)
7p16(f) Loan repayments received from associates	39	**14**	64
7p31 Interest received		**1,254**	1,193
7p31 Dividends received		**1,180**	1,120
Net cash used in investing activities		**(11,734)**	(2,562)

---

[1] IAS 19 requires a five-year record, but this does not have to be applied retrospectively [IAS 19 para 160].

IFRS GAAP plc

121

(Amounts in C thousands unless otherwise stated)

7p21	**Cash flows from financing activities**		
7p17(a)	Proceeds from issuance of ordinary shares	17	950	1,070
7p17(b)	Purchase of treasury shares	17	**(2,564)**	–
7p17(c)	Proceeds from issuance of convertible bond	36	**50,000**	–
7p17(c)	Proceeds from issuance of redeemable preference shares	37	**–**	30,000
7p17(c)	Proceeds from borrowings		**8,500**	18,000
7p17(d)	Repayments of borrowings		**(78,117)**	(34,674)
7p31	Dividends paid to group shareholders		**(10,102)**	(15,736)
7p31	Dividends paid to holders of redeemable preference shares		**(1,950)**	(1,950)
7p31	Dividends paid to minority interests		**(1,920)**	(550)
	Net cash used in financing activities		**(35,203)**	(3,840)
	Net (decrease)/increase in cash, cash equivalents and bank overdrafts		**(12,855)**	10,075
	Cash, cash equivalents and bank overdrafts at beginning of the year		**27,598**	17,587
	Exchange gains/(losses) on cash, cash equivalents and bank overdrafts		**535**	(64)
	Cash, cash equivalents and bank overdrafts at end of the year	15	**15,278**	27,598

The notes on pages 43 to 111 are an integral part of these consolidated financial statements.

Consolidated statement of comprehensive income — single statement (including disclosures of tax effects and reclassifications of components of other comprehensive income)

IAS 1 (revised) will be mandatory for annual periods beginning on or after 1 January 2009. Early adoption is permitted by the standard, but local legal or regulatory requirements such as endorsement by the EU may restrict the ability of entities to early adopt. The illustrative financial statements on pages 6 to 82 do not reflect early adoption of IAS 1 (revised). IAS 1 (revised) is still subject to endorsement by the EU and therefore may not be early adopted by companies domiciled in the EU. The examples below show an alternative presentation and additional disclosures that could be made on adoption of IAS 1 (revised).

IAS 1 (revised) requires, inter alia:

- Recognised income and expenses to be presented in a single statement (a statement of comprehensive income) or in two statements (an income statement and a statement of comprehensive income), separately from owner changes in equity. Components of other comprehensive income may not be presented in the statement of changes in equity. The statement of comprehensive income under the 'two-statement' approach is the same as the 'statement of recognised income and expense' illustrated on page 4. The statement of comprehensive income under the single statement approach is illustrated below; this example presents expenses by function but entities may classify expenses by nature, as shown on page 72.
- Both the statement of comprehensive income and the statement of changes in equity to be included as primary statements (ie, are components of a complete set of financial statements). See page 92 for an illustration of the statement of changes in equity.
- The balance sheet to be referred to as the 'statement of financial position' and the cash flow statement to be referred to as the 'statement of cash flows'.
- The components of other comprehensive income to be shown before tax, with the total tax on those components shown as a separate line item, as illustrated below, or net of tax. Whichever approach is adopted, entities are required to disclose the income tax related to each component of other comprehensive income either in the statement of comprehensive income or in the notes. An example of the disclosure that would be made in the notes is set out below.
- Reclassification adjustments (that is, amounts reclassified to profit or loss in the current period that were recognised as other comprehensive income in previous periods) to be disclosed. An example of the disclosure that would be made in the notes is set out below.
- Entities to present a statement of financial position (that is, a balance sheet) as at the beginning of the earliest comparative period when an entity applies an accounting policy retrospectively or makes a retrospective restatement or reclassifies items in the financial statements. Neither prior period adjustments nor restatements are illustrated in these financial statements.

IFRS GAAP plc

122

(Amounts in C thousands unless otherwise stated)

Consolidated statement of comprehensive income – single statement, by function of expense

1(R)p81-83, 1(R)p103,1(R)p38 1p104		Note	Year ended 31 December 2008	2007
	Continuing operations			
1(R)p82(a)	Revenue	5	211,034	112,360
1(R)p103	Cost of sales		(77,366)	(46,682)
1(R)p103	**Gross profit**		133,668	65,678
1(R)p103	Distribution costs		(52,140)	(21,213)
1(R)p103	Administrative expenses		(28,778)	(10,426)
1(R)p103	Other income	26	1,900	1,259
1(R)p85	Other (losses)/gains – net	25	(90)	63
1(R)p85	Loss on expropriated land	27	(1,117)	–
1(R)p85	**Operating profit**		53,443	35,361
1(R)p85	Finance income	30	1,730	1,609
1(R)p82(b)	Finance costs	30	(8,173)	(12,197)
1(R)p85	Finance costs – net	30	(6,443)	(10,558)
1(R)p82(c)	Share of (loss)/profit of associates	8	(174)	145
1(R)p103	**Profit before income tax**		46,826	24,918
1(R)p82(d), 12p77	Income tax expense	31	(14,611)	(8,670)
1(R)p82(f)	Profit for the year from continuing operations		32,215	16,248
IFRS5p34, 12p81(b)	**Discontinued operations:**			
	Profit for the year from discontinued operations		100	120
1(R)p82(f)	**Profit for the year**		32,315	16,368
1(R)p82(g), 91(a)	**Other comprehensive income:**			
1(R)p82(g)	**Gains/losses recognised directly in equity**			
1(R)p82(g), 16p77(f)	Gains on revaluation of land and buildings	19	–	1,133
1(R)p82(g), 91(a) IFRS7p20(a)(ii)	Available-for-sale financial assets	19	560	123
IAS28p39, 1(R)p82(b)	Share of other comprehensive income of associates	19	(12)	(14)
1(R)p82(g), 19p93A	Actuarial loss on retirement benefit obligations		–	(705)
12p80(d)	Impact of change in the UK tax rate on deferred tax[1]	22	(10)	
1(R)p82(g), IFRS7p23(c)	Cash flow hedges	19	97	(3)
1(R)p82(g)	Net investment hedge	19	(45)	40
1(R)p82(g)	Currency translation differences	19	2,244	(156)
IFRS3p59	Increase in fair values of proportionate holding of Your Shoes Group (note 38)	19	850	–
	Income tax relating to components of other comprehensive income		(231)	(224)
	Other comprehensive income for the year, net of tax		3,453	194
1(R)p82(i)	**Total comprehensive income for the year**		35,768	16,562
1(R)p83(a)	**Profit attributable to:**			
1(R)p83(a)(ii)	Equity holders of the company		29,767	15,512
1(R)p83(a)(i)	Minority interest		2,548	856
			32,315	16,368
1(R)p83(b)	**Total comprehensive income attributable to:**			
1(R)p83(b)(i)	Equity holders of the company		32,968	15,746
1(R)p83(b)(i)	Minority interest		2,800	816
			35,768	16,562

[1] Solely for illustrative purposes, a change in tax rates has been assumed to have taken place in 2008. UK companies with 31 December 2008 year ends will have reflected an actual change in tax rates in 2007.

IFRS GAAP plc

(Amounts in C thousands unless otherwise stated)

Earnings per share for profit attributable and profit from discontinued operations to the equity holders of the company during the year (expressed in C per share)

Basic earnings per share

33p66	From continuing operations	33	**1.26**	0.75
33p68	From discontinuing operations		**0.01**	0.01
			1.27	0.76

Diluted earnings per share[1]

33p66	From continuing operations	33	**1.15**	0.71
33p68	From discontinuing operations		**0.01**	0.01
			1.16	0.72

The notes on pages 43 to 111 are an integral part of these consolidated financial statements.

Note – Income tax expense

Tax effects of components of other comprehensive income[2]

(This note could be included in note 31, 'Income tax expense', which sets out tax charged/credited to equity.)

		Year ended 31 December					
1(R)p90		2008			2007		
		Before tax	Tax (charge) credit	After tax	Before tax	Tax (charge) credit	After tax
1(R)p90	Fair value gains:						
1(R)p90	– Land and buildings	–	–	–	1,133	(374)	759
1(R)p90	– Available-for-sale financial assets	560	(198)	362	123	(61)	62
1(R)p90	Share of other comprehensive income of associates	(12)	–	(12)	(14)	–	(14)
1(R)p90	Actuarial loss on retirement benefit obligations	–	–	–	(705)	211	(494)
1(R)p90							
1(R)p90	Impact of change in the UK tax rate on deferred tax[3]	–	(10)	(10)	–	–	–
1(R)p90	Cash flow hedges	97	(33)	64	(3)	–	(3)
1(R)p90	Net investment hedge	(45)	–	(45)	40	–	40
1(R)p90	Currency translation differences	2,244	–	2,244	(156)	–	(156)
IFRS3p59	Increase in fair values of proportionate holding of Your Shoes Group (note 38)	850	–	850	–	–	–
	Other comprehensive income	**3,694**	**(241)**	**3,453**	418	(224)	194

[1] EPS for discontinued operations may be given in the notes to the accounts instead of the face of the income statement.

[2] This disclosure may be included in note 31, which sets out tax charged/credited to equity.

[3] Solely for illustrative purposes, a change in tax rates has been assumed to have taken place in 2008. UK companies with 31 December 2008 year ends will have reflected an actual change in tax rates in 2007.

IFRS GAAP plc

124

(Amounts in C thousands unless otherwise stated)

Note – Other reserves

Components of other comprehensive income[1]

(This note could be included within note 19)

	31 December	
	2008	2007
Gain on revaluation of land and buildings	–	1,133
Available-for-sale financial assets/associates:		
Gains arising during the year	**678**	261
Reclassification for gains included in profit or loss	**(130)**	(152)
	548	109
Actuarial loss on retirement benefit obligations	–	(705)
Cash flow hedges:		
Gains arising during the year	**368**	300
Reclassification to inventory	**(151)**	(67)
Reclassification for gains included in profit or loss	**(120)**	(236)
	97	(3)
Net investment hedge	**(45)**	40
Currency translation differences	**2,244**	(156)
Increase in fair values of proportionate holding of Your Shoes Group (note 38)	**850**	–
Income tax relating to components of other comprehensive income	**(241)**	(224)
Other comprehensive income	**3,453**	194

(Margin references, left column: 1(R)p90, 1(R)p90, 1(R)p90, 1(R)p90, 1(R)p90, 1(R)p90, 1(R)p90, 1(R)p90, IFRS3p59)

---

[1] This disclosure may be included within note 19. When an entity chooses an aggregated presentation in the statement of comprehensive income, the amounts for reclassification adjustments and current year gain or loss are presented in the notes. This disclosure may be included within note 19.

IFRS GAAP plc   125

(Amounts in C thousands unless otherwise stated)

Appendix II — Policies and disclosures for areas not relevant to IFRS GAAP plc

Investment property[1]

40p5 Investment property is defined as property (land or a building – or part of a building – or both) held (by the owner or by the lessee under a finance lease) to earn rentals or for capital appreciation or both, rather than for: (a) use in the production of supply of goods or services or for administrative purposes; or (b) sale in the ordinary course of business.

Note – Accounting policies

(a) Basis of preparation[2]
The consolidated financial statements have been prepared under the historical cost convention as modified by the revaluation of land and buildings, available-for-sale financial assets, financial assets and financial liabilities at fair value through profit or loss and investment properties, which are carried at fair value.

1p110 *(b) Investment property[2]*
40p75(a)(d) Investment property, principally comprising freehold office buildings, is held for long-term rental yields and is not occupied by the group. Investment property is carried at fair value, representing open market value determined annually by external valuers. Fair value is based on active market prices, adjusted, if necessary, for any difference in the nature, location or condition of the specific asset. If the information is not available, the group uses alternative valuation methods such as recent prices on less active markets or discounted cash flow projections. These valuations are reviewed annually by A [Valuers][3]. Changes in fair values are recorded in the income statement as part of other income.

(c) Rental income
Rental from investment property is recognised in the income statement on a straight-line basis over the term of the lease.

40p6, 25 Land held under operating lease is classified and accounted for as investment property when the rest of the definition of investment property is met. The operating lease is accounted for as if it were a finance lease.

Consolidated balance sheet (extracts)	2008	2007
Assets		
1p51 **Non-current assets**		
1p68(a) Property, plant and equipment	155,341	98,670
1p68(b) Investment property	18,108	15,690

Note – Investment property	2008	2007
40p76 Beginning of the year	15,690	16,043
40p76(e) Exchange differences	748	(1,396)
40p76(d) Fair value gains (included in other gains/(losses) – net)	1,670	1,043
40p76 End of the year	18,108	15,690

40p75(d)(e) The investment properties are valued annually on 31 December at fair value, comprising market value by an independent, professionally qualified valuer.

The following amounts have been recognised in the income statement:

	2008	2007
40p75(f)(i) Rental income	770	620
40p75(f)(ii) Direct operating expenses arising from investment properties that generate rental income	(640)	(550)
40p75(f)(ii) Direct operating expenses that did not generate rental income	(40)	(20)

---

[1] The above investment property disclosures are given for corporate entities that hold property to earn rentals or for capital appreciation or both. It does not cover all the disclosures that would be required for an investment property company. For investment property companies, refer to the PwC industry-specific illustrative financial statements.

[2] To be approximately amended if the cost method is applied.

[3] To include the name of the external valuer.

IFRS GAAP plc 126

(Amounts in C thousands unless otherwise stated)

Note – Capital commitments

Capital expenditure contracted for at the balance sheet date but not recognised in the financial statements is as follows:

		2008	2007
16p74(c)	Property, plant and equipment	**3,593**	3,667
40p75(h)	Investment property	**290**	–
	Investment property – repairs and maintenance:		
40p75(h)	– Contractual obligations for future repairs and maintenance of investment property	**140**	130

Construction contracts

11p3 A construction contract is defined by IAS 11 as a contract specifically negotiated for the construction of an asset.

Note – Accounting policies

Construction contracts

11p39(b)(c) Contract costs are recognised as expenses in the period in which they are incurred.

When the outcome of a construction contract cannot be estimated reliably, contract revenue is recognised only to the extent of contract costs incurred that are likely to be recoverable.

11p31 When the outcome of a construction contract can be estimated reliably and it is probable that the contract will be profitable, contract revenue is recognised over the period of the contract. When it is probable that total contract costs will exceed total contract revenue, the expected loss is recognised as an expense immediately.

Variations in contract work, claims and incentive payments are included in contract revenue to the extent that may have been agreed with the customer and are capable of being reliably measured.

The group uses the 'percentage-of-completion method' to determine the appropriate amount to recognise in a given period. The stage of completion is measured by reference to the contract costs incurred up to the balance sheet date as a percentage of total estimated costs for each contract. Costs incurred in the year in connection with future activity on a contract are excluded from contract costs in determining the stage of completion. They are presented as inventories, prepayments or other assets, depending on their nature.

The group presents as an asset the gross amount due from customers for contract work for all contracts in progress for which costs incurred plus recognised profits (less recognised losses) exceed progress billings. Progress billings not yet paid by customers and retention are included within 'trade and other receivables'.

The group presents as a liability the gross amount due to customers for contract work for all contracts in progress for which progress billings exceed costs incurred plus recognised profits (less recognised losses).

Consolidated balance sheet (extracts)

		Note	2008	2007
1p51	**Current assets**			
1p68(h)	Trade and other receivables	12	**23,303**	20,374
	Inventories	13	**24,885**	18,481
1p51	**Current liabilities**			
1p68(j)	Trade and other payables	20	**17,667**	13,733

IFRS GAAP plc

(Amounts in C thousands unless otherwise stated)

Consolidated income statement (extracts)

	Note	2008	2007
1p81-83			
11p39(a) Contract revenue		**58,115**	39,212
11p16 Contract costs		**(54,729)**	(37,084)
1p92 Gross profit		**3,386**	2,128
1p92 Selling and marketing costs		**(386)**	(128)
1p92 Administrative expenses		**(500)**	(400)

Note – Trade and other receivables (extracts)

	2008	2007
IFRS7p36, 1p75(b) Trade receivables	**18,174**	16,944
Less: Provision for impairment of receivables	**(109)**	(70)
Trade receivables – net	**18,065**	16,874
11p42(a) Amounts due from customers for contract work	**984**	788
11p40(c) Retentions	**232**	132
Prepayments	**1,300**	1,146
1p74, 24p17 Receivables from related parties (note 39)	**54**	46
1p74, 24p17 Loans to related parties (note 39)	**2,668**	1,388
Total	**23,303**	20,374

Note – Trade and other payables (extracts)

	2008	2007
Trade payables	**10,983**	9,495
24p17 Amounts due to related parties (note 39)	**2,202**	1,195
11p42(b) Amounts due to customers for contract work	**855**	900
11p40(b) Advances received for contract work	**142**	355
Social security and other taxes	**2,002**	960
Accrued expenses	**1,483**	828
	17,667	13,733

Note – Inventories (extract)

	2008	2007
Raw materials	**7,622**	7,612
Work in progress (not related to construction contracts)	**1,810**	1,796
Finished goods	**15,268**	8,774
Costs capitalised in relation to construction contracts	**185**	299
	24,885	18,481

Note – Construction contracts

	2008	2007
11p40(a) The aggregate costs incurred and recognised profits (less recognised losses) to date	**69,804**	56,028
Less: Progress billings	**(69,585)**	(56,383)
Net balance sheet position for ongoing contracts	**219**	(355)

Leases: Accounting by lessor

17p4 A lease is an agreement whereby the lessor conveys to the lessee in return for a payment, or series of payments, the right to use an asset for an agreed period of time.

Note – Accounting policies

1p110 When assets are leased out under a finance lease, the present value of the lease payments is recognised as a receivable. The difference between the gross receivable and the present value of the receivable is recognised as unearned finance income.

Lease income is recognised over the term of the lease using the net investment method, which reflects a constant periodic rate of return.

IFRS GAAP plc

128

(Amounts in C thousands unless otherwise stated)

17p49   When assets are leased out under an operating lease, the asset is included in the balance sheet based on the nature of the asset.

17p50   Lease income is recognised over the term of the lease on a straight-line basis.

Note – Property, plant and equipment

The category of vehicles and equipment includes vehicles leased by the group to third parties under operating leases with the following carrying amounts:

	2008	2007
Cost	**70,234**	–
Accumulated depreciation at 1 January	**(14,818)**	–
Depreciation charge for the year	**(5,058)**	–
Net book amount	**50,358**	–

Note – Trade and other receivables

		2008	2007
1p75(b)	**Non-current receivables**		
17p47(a)	Finance leases – gross receivables	**1,810**	630
17p47(b)	Unearned finance income	**(222)**	(98)
		1,588	532
1p75(b)	**Current receivables**		
17p47(a)	Finance leases – gross receivables	**1,336**	316
17p47(b)	Unearned finance income	**(300)**	(98)
		1,036	218
1p75(a)	Gross receivables from finance leases:		
17p47(a)	No later than 1 year	**1,336**	316
	Later than 1 year and no later than 5 years	**1,810**	630
	Later than 5 years	**–**	–
		3,146	946
1p75(b), 17p47(b)	Unearned future finance income on finance leases	**(522)**	(196)
	Net investment in finance leases	**2,624**	750
1p75(a)	The net investment in finance leases may be analysed as follows:		
17p47(a)	– No later than 1 year	**1,036**	218
	– Later than 1 year and no later than 5 years	**1,588**	532
	– Later than 5 years	**–**	–
		2,624	750

Note – Operating leases

17p56(a)   **Operating leases commitments – group company as lessor**

The future minimum lease payments receivable under non-cancellable operating leases are as follows:

	2008	2007
No later than 1 year	**12,920**	12,920
Later than 1 year and no later than 5 years	**41,800**	41,800
Later than 5 years	**840**	10,840
	55,560	65,560

17p56(b)   Contingent-based rents recognised in the income statement were C235 (2007: C40).

17p56(c)   The company lease vehicles under various agreements which terminate between 2008 and 2013. The agreements do not include an extension option.

IFRS GAAP plc   129

(Amounts in C thousands unless otherwise stated)

Investments: held-to-maturity financial assets

Note – Accounting policies

Investments

Held-to-maturity financial assets

1p110, 39p9   Held-to-maturity financial assets are non-derivative financial assets with fixed or determinable payments and fixed maturities that the group's management has the positive intention and ability to hold to maturity. If the group were to sell other than an insignificant amount of held-to-maturity financial assets, the whole category would be tainted and reclassified as available for sale. Held-to-maturity financial assets are included in non-current assets, except for those with maturities less than 12 months from the balance sheet date, which are classified as current assets.

Consolidated balance sheet

	2008	2007
Non-current assets		
Held-to-maturity financial assets	**3,999**	1,099

1p51
1p68(d)

Note – Held-to-maturity financial assets

IFRS7p27(b)   *Held-to-maturity financial assets*

	2008	2007
Listed securities:		
– Debentures with fixed interest of 5% and maturity date of 15 June 2012 – UK	**4,018**	984
– Debentures with fixed interest of 5.5% and maturity date of 15 June 2009 – US	**–**	160
Allowance for impairment	**(19)**	(45)
	3,999	1,099

39AG71-73

The movement in held to maturity of financial assets may be summarised as follows:

	2008	2007
At 1 January	**1,009**	390
Exchange differences	**81**	56
Additions	**3,093**	888
Disposals	**(165)**	(280)
Provision for impairment	**(19)**	(45)
At 31 December	**3,999**	1,009
Less: non-current portion	**(3,999)**	(1,009)
Current portion	**–**	–

1p57

1p57

IFRS7p16   Movements on the provision for impairment of held-to-maturity financial assets are as follows:

	2008	2007
At 1 January	**45**	30
Provision for impairment	**–**	16
Unused amounts reversed	**(26)**	(3)
Unwind of discount (note 30)	**–**	2
At 31 December	**19**	45

IFRS7p20(e)

IFRS7p12(b)   The group has not reclassified any financial assets measured amortised cost rather than fair value during the year (2007: nil).

IFRS7p20(a)(iii)   There were no gains or losses realised on the disposal of held to maturity financial assets in 2008 and 2007, as all the financial assets were disposed of at their redemption date.

IFRS GAAP plc 130

(Amounts in C thousands unless otherwise stated)

IFRS7p25   The fair value of held to maturity financial assets is based on quoted market bid prices (2008: C3,901; 2007: C976).

IFRS7p34(c)   Held-to-maturity financial assets are denominated in the following currencies:

	2008	2007
UK pound	**2,190**	990
US dollar	**1,809**	109
Total	**3,999**	1,099

IFRS7p36(a)   The maximum exposure to credit risk at the reporting date is the carrying amount of held to maturity financial assets.

Government grants[1]

Note – Accounting policies

Government grants

20p39(a)
20p12   Grants from the government are recognised at their fair value where there is a reasonable assurance that the grant will be received and the group will comply with all attached conditions.

Government grants relating to costs are deferred and recognised in the income statement over the period necessary to match them with the costs that they are intended to compensate.

Government grants relating to property, plant and equipment are included in non-current liabilities as deferred government grants and are credited to the income statement on a straight-line basis over the expected lives of the related assets.

Note – Other (losses)/gains

20p39(b)
20p39(c)   The group obtained and recognised as income a government grant of C100 (2007: nil) to compensate for losses caused by flooding incurred in the previous year. The group is obliged not to reduce its average number of employees over the next three years under the terms of this government grant.

The group benefits from government assistance for promoting in international markets products made in the UK; such assistance includes marketing research and similar services provided by various UK government agencies free of charge.

Joint ventures

Note – Accounting policies

1p110   **Consolidation**

(c) Joint ventures

31p57   The group's interests in jointly controlled entities are accounted for by proportionate consolidation. The group combines its share of the joint ventures' individual income and expenses, assets and liabilities and cash flows on a line-by-line basis with similar items in the group's financial statements. The group recognises the portion of gains or losses on the sale of assets by the group to the joint venture that is attributable to the other venturers. The group does not recognise its share of profits or losses from the joint venture that result from the group's purchase of assets from the joint venture until it re-sells the assets to an independent party. However, a loss on the transaction is recognised immediately if the loss provides evidence of a reduction in the net realisable value of current assets, or an impairment loss.

---

[1] There are two approaches to accounting for government grants namely the capital approach, under which a grant is credited directly to shareholder's interest and the income approach, under which a grant is taken to income over one or more periods. The accounting policy and disclosure below reflects the income approach.

IFRS GAAP plc 131

(Amounts in C thousands unless otherwise stated)

Note – Interest in joint venture

31p56   The group has a 50% interest in a joint venture, JV&Co, which provides products and services to the automotive industry. The following amounts represent the group's 50% share of the assets and liabilities, and sales and results of the joint venture. They are included in the balance sheet and income statement:

	2008	2007
Assets:		
Long-term assets	**2,730**	2,124
Current assets	**803**	717
	3,533	2,841
Liabilities:		
Long-term liabilities	**1,114**	1,104
Current liabilities	**355**	375
	1,469	1,479
Net assets	**2,064**	1,362
Income	**5,276**	5,618
Expenses	**(3,754)**	(4,009)
Profit after income tax	**1,522**	1,609
31p55(b) **Proportionate interest in joint venture's commitments**	**90**	92

31p54   There are no contingent liabilities relating to the group's interest in the joint venture, and no contingent liabilities of the venture itself.

Transactions with minority shareholders – 'economic entity approach'

Note – Accounting policies

IFRS3   The group applies a policy of treating transactions with minority interests as transactions with equity owners of the group. For purchases from minority interests, the difference between any consideration paid and the relevant share acquired of the carrying value of net assets of the subsidiary is recorded in equity. Gains or losses on disposals to minority interests are also recorded in equity.

Oil and gas exploration assets

Note – Accounting policies

IFRS6p24   Oil and natural gas exploration and evaluation expenditures are accounted for using the 'successful efforts' method of accounting. Costs are accumulated on a field-by-field basis. Geological and geophysical costs are expensed as incurred. Costs directly associated with an exploration well, and exploration and property leasehold acquisition costs, are capitalised until the determination of reserves is evaluated. If it is determined that commercial discovery has not been achieved, these costs are charged to expense.

Capitalisation is made within property, plant and equipment or intangible assets according to the nature of the expenditure.

Once commercial reserves are found, exploration and evaluation assets are tested for impairment and transferred to development tangible and intangible assets. No depreciation and/or amortisation is charged during the exploration and evaluation phase.

(a) Development tangible and intangible assets
Expenditure on the construction, installation or completion of infrastructure facilities such as platforms, pipelines and the drilling of commercially proven development wells, is capitalised within property, plant and equipment and intangible assets according to nature. When development is completed on a specific field, it is transferred to production or intangible assets. No depreciation or amortisation is charged during the exploration and evaluation phase.

IFRS GAAP plc

(Amounts in C thousands unless otherwise stated)

(b) Oil and gas production assets

Oil and gas production properties are aggregated exploration and evaluation tangible assets, and development expenditures associated with the production of proved reserves.

(c) Depreciation/amortisation

Oil and gas properties intangible assets are depreciated or amortised using the unit-of-production method. Unit-of-production rates are based on proved developed reserves, which are oil, gas and other mineral reserves estimated to be recovered from existing facilities using current operating methods. Oil and gas volumes are considered produced once they have been measured through meters at custody transfer or sales transaction points at the outlet valve on the field storage tank.

(d) Impairment – exploration and evaluation assets

Exploration and evaluation assets are tested for impairment when reclassified to development tangible or intangible assets, or whenever facts and circumstances indicate impairment. An impairment loss is recognised for the amount by which the exploration and evaluation assets' carrying amount exceeds their recoverable amount. The recoverable amount is the higher of the exploration and evaluation assets' fair value less costs to sell and their value in use. For the purposes of assessing impairment, the exploration and evaluation assets subject to testing are grouped with existing cash-generating units of production fields that are located in the same geographical region.

(e) Impairment – proved oil and gas production properties and intangible assets

Proven oil and gas properties and intangible assets are reviewed for impairment whenever events or changes in circumstances indicate that the carrying amount may not be recoverable. An impairment loss is recognised for the amount by which the asset's carrying amount exceeds its recoverable amount. The recoverable amount is the higher of an asset's fair value less costs to sell and value in use. For the purposes of assessing impairment, assets are grouped at the lowest levels for which there are separately identifiable cash flows.

IFRS GAAP plc

133

(Amounts in C thousands unless otherwise stated)

Property, plant and equipment[1]

	Capitalised exploration and evaluation expenditure	Capitalised development expenditure	Subtotal – assets under construction	Production assets	Other businesses and corporate assets	Total
At 1 January 2008						
Cost	218	12,450	12,668	58,720	3,951	75,339
Accumulated amortisation and impairment	(33)	–	(33)	(5,100)	(77)	(5,210)
Net book amount	185	12,450	12,635	53,620	3,874	70,129
Year ended 31 December 2008						
Opening net book amount	185	12,450	12,635	53,620	3,874	70,129
Exchange differences	17	346	363	1,182	325	1,870
Acquisitions	–	386	386	125	4	515
Additions	45	1,526	1,571	5,530	95	7,196
Transfers	(9)	(958)	(967)	1,712	–	745
Disposals	(12)	(1,687)	(1,699)	–	–	(1,699)
Depreciation charge	–	–	–	(725)	(42)	(767)
Impairment charge	(7)	(36)	(43)	(250)	(3)	(296)
Closing net book amount	**219**	**12,027**	**12,246**	**61,194**	**4,253**	**77,693**
At 31 December 2008						
Cost	264	12,027	12,291	67,019	4,330	83,640
Accumulated amortisation and impairment	(45)	–	(45)	(5,825)	(77)	(5,947)
Net book amount	**219**	**12,027**	**12,246**	**61,194**	**4,253**	**77,693**

[1] For the purpose of this illustrative appendix, comparatives for the year ended 31 December 2007 are not disclosed, although they are required by IAS 1.

IFRS GAAP plc

134

(Amounts in C thousands unless otherwise stated)

Intangible assets[1]

	Capitalised exploration and evaluation expenditure	Capitalised development expenditure	Subtotal – intangible assets in progress expenditure	Production assets	Goodwill	Other	Total
At 1 January 2008							
Cost	5,192	750	5,942	3,412	9,475	545	19,374
Accumulated amortisation and impairment	(924)	–	(924)	(852)	(75)	(19)	(1,870)
Net book amount	4,268	750	5,018	2,560	9,400	526	17,504
Year ended 31 December 2008							
Opening net book amount	4,268	750	5,018	2,560	9,400	526	17,504
Exchange differences	152	8	160	195	423	28	806
Acquisitions	26	32	58	5	–	5	68
Additions	381	8	389	15	–	86	490
Transfers	(548)	548	–	–	–	–	–
Transfers to production	–	(850)	(850)	105	–	–	(745)
Disposals	–	(28)	(28)	(15)	–	–	(43)
Amortisation charge	–	–	–	(98)	–	(42)	(140)
Impairment charge	(45)	–	(45)	–	(175)	(5)	(225)
Closing net book amount	**4,234**	**468**	**4,702**	**2,767**	**9,648**	**598**	**17,715**
At 31 December 2008							
Cost	5,203	468	5,671	3,717	9,898	659	19,945
Accumulated amortisation and impairment	(969)	–	(969)	(950)	(250)	(61)	(2,230)
Net book amount	**4,234**	**468**	**4,702**	**2,767**	**9,648**	**598**	**17,715**

Assets and liabilities related to the exploration and evaluation of mineral resources other than those presented above are as follows:

	2008	2007
Receivables from joint venture partners	**25**	22
Payable to subcontractors and operators	**32**	34

Exploration and evaluation activities have led to total expenses of C59,000 (2007: C57,000), of which C52,000 (2007: C43,000) are impairment charges.

In 2008, the disposal of a 16.67% interest in an offshore exploration stage 'Field X' resulted in post-tax profits on sale of C3 million (2007: nil).

Cash payments of C415,000 (2007: C395,000) have been incurred related to exploration and evaluation activities. The cash proceeds due to the disposal of the interest in Field X were C8,000 (2007: nil).

---

[1] For the purpose of this illustrative appendix, comparatives for the year ended 31 December 2007 are not disclosed, although they are required by IAS 1.

IFRS GAAP plc 135

(Amounts in C thousands unless otherwise stated)

Revenue recognition: multiple-element arrangements

Note – Accounting policies

The group offers certain arrangements whereby a customer can purchase a personal computer together with a two-year servicing agreement. When such multiple-element arrangements exist, the amount recognised as revenue upon the sale of the personal computer is the fair value of the computer in relation to the fair value of the arrangement taken as a whole. The revenue relating to the service element, which represents the fair value of the servicing arrangement in relation to the fair value of the arrangement, is recognised over the service period. The fair values of each element are determined based on the current market price of each of the elements when sold separately.

Where the group is unable to determine the fair value of each of the elements in an arrangement, it uses the residual value method. Under this method, the group determines the fair value of the delivered element by deducting the fair value of the undelivered element from the total contract consideration.

To the extent that there is a discount on the arrangement, such discount is allocated between the elements of the contract in such a manner as to reflect the fair value of the elements.

Defaults and breaches of loans payable[1]

Borrowings (extract)

IFRS7p18   The company was overdue paying interests on bank borrowings with a carrying amount of C10,000. The company experienced a temporary shortage of currencies because cash outflows in the second and third quarters for business expansions in the UK were higher than anticipated. As a result, interest payables of C700 due by 30 September 2009 remained unpaid.

The company has paid all outstanding amounts (including additional interests and penalties for the late payment) during the fourth quarter.

Management expects that the company will be able to meet all contractual obligations from borrowings on a timely basis going forward.

IFRS7p19   *Covenants*

Some of the company's credit contracts are subject to covenant clauses, whereby the company is required to meet certain key performance indicators. The company did not fulfil the debt/equity ratio as required in the contract for a credit line of C30,000, of which the company has currently drawn an amount of C15,000.

Due to this breach of the covenant clause, the bank is contractually entitled to request early repayment of the outstanding amount of C15,000. The outstanding balance was reclassified as a current liability[2]. Management started renegotiating the terms of the loan agreement when it became likely that the covenant clause may be breached.

The bank has not requested early repayment of the loan as of the date when these financial statements were approved by the board of directors. Management expects that a revised loan agreement will be in place during the first quarter of 2008.

---

[1] These events or conditions may cast significant doubt about company's ability to continue as a going concern. When events or conditions have been identified that may cast significant doubt on a company's ability to continue as a going concern, the auditor should: 1) Review management's plans for future actions based on its going concern assessment; 2) Gather sufficient appropriate audit evidence to confirm or dispel whether or not a material uncertainty exists through carrying out audit procedures considered necessary, including considering the effect of any plans of management and other mitigating factors; 3) Seek written representations from management regarding its plans for future action. If a material uncertainty related to events or conditions that may cast significant doubt on a company's ability to continue as a going concern exists, disclosure is required in the auditor's report. ISA 570, 'Going concern', establishes standards and provides guidance on the auditor's responsibility in the audit of financial statements with respect to the going concern assumption used in the preparation of the financial statements, including considering management's assessment of the entity's ability to continue as a going concern.

[2] The reclassification of non-current debt to current liabilities would still be required if the terms of the loan were successfully renegotiated after the balance sheet date.

IFRS GAAP plc   136

(Amounts in C thousands unless otherwise stated)

Appendix III — Critical accounting estimates and judgements not relevant to IFRS GAAP plc

Critical accounting estimates

1p116   The following critical accounting estimates may be applicable, among many other possible areas not presented in IFRS GAAP plc's consolidated financial statements.

(a) Useful lives of technology division's plant and equipment
The group's management determines the estimated useful lives and related depreciation charges for its plant and equipment. This estimate is based on projected product lifecycles for its high-tech segment. It could change significantly as a result of technical innovations and competitor actions in response to severe industry cycles. Management will increase the depreciation charge where useful lives are less than previously estimated lives, or it will write-off or write-down technically obsolete or non-strategic assets that have been abandoned or sold.

Were the actual useful lives of the technology division plant and equipment to differ by 10% from management's estimates, the carrying amount of the plant and equipment would be an estimated C1,000 higher or C970 lower.

(b) Warranty claims
The group generally offers three-year warranties for its personal computer products. Management estimates the related provision for future warranty claims based on historical warranty claim information, as well as recent trends that might suggest that past cost information may differ from future claims.

Factors that could impact the estimated claim information include the success of the group's productivity and quality initiatives, as well as parts and labour costs.

Were claims costs to differ by 10% from management's estimates, the warranty provisions would be an estimated C2,000 higher or C1,875 lower.

Critical accounting judgements

1p113   The following critical accounting judgements may be applicable, among many other possible areas not presented in IFRS GAAP plc's consolidated financial statements.

(a) Held-to-maturity investments
The group follows the IAS 39 guidance on classifying non-derivative financial assets with fixed or determinable payments and fixed maturity as held to maturity. This classification requires significant judgement. In making this judgement, the group evaluates its intention and ability to hold such investments to maturity.

If the group fails to keep these investments to maturity other than for specific circumstances explained in IAS 39, it will be required to reclassify the whole class as available for sale. The investments would therefore be measured at fair value not amortised cost.

If the class of held-to-maturity investments is tainted, the fair value would increase by C2,300, with a corresponding entry in the fair value reserve in shareholders' equity.

IFRS GAAP plc 137

(Amounts in C thousands unless otherwise stated)

Appendix IV — Business combinations disclosure under IFRS 3 (revised)

Appendix V presents the acquisition in note 38 in accordance with IFRS 3 (revised) and follows the illustrative example on disclosure provided in IFRS 3 (revised). IFRS 3 (revised) is prospectively applicable for periods beginning on or after 1 July 2009, and may be early adopted from periods beginning on or after 1 June 2007. Local legal or regulatory requirements such as endorsement by the EU may restrict the ability of entities to early adopt. IFRS 3 (revised) is still subject to endorsement by the EU and therefore may not be early adopted by companies domiciled in the EU.

Note – Basis of preparation

Standards early adopted by the group

IAS8p28 IFRS 3 (revised), 'Business combinations' was early adopted by the group in 2008. The revised standard continues to apply the acquisition method to business combinations, with some significant changes. For example, all payments to purchase a business are recorded at fair value at the acquisition date, with contingent payments classified as debt subsequently re-measured through the income statement. There is a choice on an acquisition-by-acquisition basis to measure the non-controlling interest in the acquiree either at fair value or at the non-controlling interest's proportionate share of the acquiree's net assets. All acquisition-related costs should be expensed.

The standard was applied to the acquisition of the controlling interest in Your Shoes Group on 1 March 2008. Contingent consideration of C1,000 has been recognised at fair value at 1 March 2008. The contingent consideration would not have previously been recorded at the date of acquisition, as the probability of the payment to the former owners of Your Shoes Group of 5% of the profit of Your Shoes Group in excess of C7,500 for 2009 (up to a maximum undiscounted amount of C2,500) was less than 50%. Acquisition-related costs of C200 have been recognised in the statement of comprehensive income, which previously would have been included in the consideration for the business combination. Subsequent measurement of the indemnification asset and contingent liability will have no net impact on future earnings. An indemnification asset of C1,000 has been recognised by the group with an equivalent amount deducted from consideration transferred for the business combination. This possible compensation from the selling shareholders of Your Shoes Group would not have previously been recognised as an indemnification asset of the acquirer and would have been adjusted against goodwill once received from the vendor. The group have chosen to recognise the non-controlling interest at fair value of C6,451 for this acquisition rather than the proportionate share of net assets of Your Shoes Group of C4,242 which is also allowed. Previously there was no choice and the non-controlling interest would have been recognised at the proportionate share (30%) of the net assets of Your Shoes Group of C4,242. See note 38 for further details of the business combination which was entered into in the year under review.

As the group has early adopted IFRS 3 (revised) in 2008, it is required to early adopt IAS 27 (revised), 'Consolidated and separate financial statements' at the same time. IAS 27 (revised) requires the effects of all transactions with non-controlling interests to be recorded in equity if there is no change in control and these transactions will no longer result in goodwill or gains and losses. The standard also specifies the accounting when control is lost. Any remaining interest in the entity is re-measured to fair value, and a gain or loss is recognised in profit or loss. There has been no impact of the revised standard on the current period as none of the non-controlling interests have a deficit balance; there have been no transactions whereby an interest in an entity is retained after the loss of control of that entity and there have been no transactions with non-controlling interests.

Note – Accounting policies

1p110 **Consolidation**

27p12 *(a) Subsidiaries*
27p14 Subsidiaries are all entities (including special purpose entities) over which the group has the
27p30 power to govern the financial and operating policies generally accompanying a shareholding of more than one half of the voting rights. The existence and effect of potential voting rights that are currently exercisable or convertible are considered when assessing whether the group controls another entity. Subsidiaries are fully consolidated from the date on which control is transferred to the group. They are de-consolidated from the date that control ceases.

IFRS GAAP plc 138

(Amounts in C thousands unless otherwise stated)

IFRS3p5 IFRS3p37 IFRS3p39 IFRS3p53 IFRS3p18 IFRS3p19	The acquisition method of accounting is used to account for business combinations by the group. The consideration transferred for the acquisition of a subsidiary is the fair values of the assets transferred, the liabilities incurred and the equity interests issued by the group. The consideration transferred includes the fair value of any asset or liability resulting from a contingent consideration arrangement. Acquisition-related costs are expensed as incurred. Identifiable assets acquired and liabilities and contingent liabilities assumed in a business combination are measured initially at their fair values at the acquisition date. On an acquisition-by-acquisition basis, the group recognises any non-controlling interest in the acquiree either at fair value or at the non-controlling interest's proportionate share of the acquiree's net assets.
IFRS3p32 IFRS3p34	The excess of the consideration transferred, the amount of any non-controlling interest in the acquiree and the acquisition-date fair value of any previous equity interest in the acquiree over the fair value of the group's share of the identifiable net assets acquired is recorded as goodwill. If this is less than the fair value of the net assets of the subsidiary acquired in the case of a bargain purchase, the difference is recognised directly in the statement of comprehensive income (note 2.6).
27p20,21	Inter-company transactions, balances and unrealised gains on transactions between group companies are eliminated. Unrealised losses are also eliminated. Accounting policies of subsidiaries have been changed where necessary to ensure consistency with the policies adopted by the group.
27p30,31	*(b) Transactions and non-controlling interests* The group treats transactions with non-controlling interests as transactions with equity owners of the group. For purchases from non-controlling interests, the difference between any consideration paid and the relevant share acquired of the carrying value of net assets of the subsidiary is recorded in equity. Gains or losses on disposals to non-controlling interests are also recorded in equity.
IFRS3pB64(a-d)	On 30 June 2007 the group acquired 15% of the share capital of Your Shoes Group. On 1 March 2008, the group acquired a further 55% of the share capital and obtained the control of Your Shoes Group, a shoe and leather goods retailer operating in the US and most western European countries. As a result of the acquisition, the group is expected to increase its presence in these markets. It also expects to reduce costs through economies of scale.
IFRS3pB64(e)	The goodwill of C6,451 arising from the acquisition is attributable to acquired customer base and economies of scale expected from combining the operations of the group and Your Shoes Group.
IFRS3pB64(k)	None of the goodwill recognised is expected to be deductible for income tax purposes. The following table summarises the consideration paid for Your Shoes Group and the amounts of the assets acquired and liabilities assumed recognised at the acquisition date, as well as the fair value at the acquisition date of the non-controlling interest in Your Shoes Group.

Consideration

	At 1 March 2008	
IFRS3pB64(f)(i)	Cash	4,050
IFRS3pB64(f)(iv)	Equity instruments (3,550 ordinary shares)	10,000
IFRS3pB64(f)(iii); IFRS3pB64(g)(i)	Contingent consideration	1,000
IFRS3pB64(f)	**Total consideration transferred**	**15,050**
	Indemnification asset	(1,000)
IFRS3pB64(p)(i)	**Fair value of equity interest in Your Shoes Group held before the business combination**	**2,000**
		16,050

IFRS GAAP plc 139

(Amounts in C thousands unless otherwise stated)

IFRS3pB64(m)	**Acquisition-related costs** (included in administrative expenses in the statement of comprehensive income for the year ended 31 December 2008)	200
IFRS3pB64(i)	**Recognised amounts of identifiable assets acquired and liabilities assumed**	
	Cash and cash equivalents	300
	Property, plant and equipment (note 6)	67,784
	Trademarks (included in intangibles) (note 7)	2,000
	Licences (included in intangibles) (note 7)	1,000
	Contractual customer relationship (included in intangibles) (note 7)	1,000
	Investment in associates (note 8)	389
	Available-for-sale financial assets (note 10)	473
	Inventories	1,122
	Trade and other receivables	585
	Trade and other payables	(12,461)
	Retirement benefit obligations:	
	– Pensions (note 23)	(1,914)
	– Other post-retirement obligations (note 23)	(725)
	Borrowings	(41,459)
	Contingent liability	(1,000)
	Deferred tax liabilities (note 22)	(1,953)
	Total identifiable net assets	**15,141**
IFRS3pB64(o)(i)	**Non-controlling interest**	(4,542)
	Goodwill (note 7)	5,451
		16,050

IFRS3pB64(f)(iv) The fair value of the 3,550 ordinary shares issued as part of the consideration paid for Your Shoes Group (C10,000) was based on the published share price on 1 March 2008.

IFRS3pB64(f)(iii)
IFRS3pB64(g)
IFRS3B67(b) The contingent consideration arrangement requires the group to pay the former owners of Your Shoes Group 5% of the profit of Your Shoes Group, in excess of C7,500 for 2009, up to a maximum undiscounted amount of C2,500.

The potential undiscounted amount of all future payments that the group could be required to make under this arrangement is between C0 and C2,500.

The fair value of the contingent consideration arrangement of C1,000 was estimated by applying the income approach. The fair value estimates are based on a discount rate of 8% and assumed probability-adjusted profit in Your Shoes Group of C20,000 to C40,000.

As of 31 December 2008, there was an increase of C1,000 recognised in the income statement for the contingent consideration arrangement as the assumed probability-adjusted profit in Your Shoes Group was recalculated to be in the region of C30,000-50,000.

IFRS3pB64(h) The fair value of trade and other receivables is C585 and includes trade receivables with a fair value of C510. The gross contractual amount for trade receivables due is C960, of which C450 is expected to be uncollectible.

IFRS3pB67(a) The fair value of the acquired identifiable intangible assets of C4,000 (including trademarks and licences) is provisional pending receipt of the final valuations for those assets.

IFRS3pB64(j)
B67(c) IAS 37
p84, 85 A contingent liability of C1,000 has been recognised for a pending lawsuit in which the entity is a defendant. The claim has arisen from a customer alleging defects on products supplied to them. It is expected that the courts will have reached a decision on this case by the end of 2010. The potential undiscounted amount of all future payments that the group could be required to make under to make if there was an adverse decision related to the lawsuit is estimated to be between C500 and C1,500. As of 31 December 2008, there has been no change in the amount recognised (except for unwinding of the discount C4) for the liability at 31 March 2008, as there has been no change in the range of outcomes or assumptions used to develop the estimates.

IFRS3pB64(g),
p57 The selling shareholders of Your Shoes Group have contractually agreed to indemnify IFRS GAAP plc for the claim that may become payable in respect of the above-mentioned lawsuit. An indemnification asset of C1,000 has been recognised by the group with an equivalent amount deducted from consideration transferred for the business combination. As is the case with the indemnified liability, there has been no change in the amount recognised for the indemnification asset as at 31 December 2008, as there has been no change in the range of outcomes or assumptions used to develop the estimates.

IFRS GAAP plc   140

(Amounts in C thousands unless otherwise stated)

IFRS3pB64(o) The fair value of the non-controlling interest in Your Shoes Group, an unlisted company, was estimated by applying a market approach and an income approach. The fair value estimates are based on:

(a) an assumed discount rate of 8%;
(b) an assumed terminal value based on a range of terminal EBITDA multiples between three and five times;
(c) long-term sustainable growth rate of 2%;
(d) assumed financial multiples of companies deemed to be similar to Your Shoes Group; and
(e) assumed adjustments because of the lack of control or lack of marketability that market participants would consider when estimating the fair value of the non-controlling interest in Your Shoes Group.

IFRS3pB64(p)(ii) The group recognised a gain of C500 as a result of measuring at fair value its 15% equity interest in Your Shoes Group held before the business combination. The gain is included in other income in the group's statement of comprehensive income for the year ending 31 December 2008.

IFRS3pB64(q)(i) The revenue included in the consolidated statement of comprehensive income since 1 March 2008 contributed by Your Shoes Group was C44,709. Your Shoes Group also contributed profit of C12,762 over the same period.

IFRS3pB64(q)(ii) Had Your Shoes Group been consolidated from 1 January 2008 the consolidated statement of comprehensive income would show revenue of C220,345 and profit of C33,126.

> *IFRS GAAP plc – Illustrative consolidated corporate financial statements 2008* is designed for the information of readers. While every effort has been made to ensure accuracy, information contained in this publication may not be comprehensive, or some information may have been omitted that may be relevant to a particular reader. This publication is not intended to cover all aspects of IFRS, or as a substitute for reading the actual Standards and Interpretations when dealing with specific issues. No responsibility for loss to any person acting or refraining from acting as a result of any material in this publication can be accepted by PricewaterhouseCoopers. Recipients should not act on the basis of this publication without seeking professional advice.

GAAP UK plc — Year ended 31 December 2008

Contents

Directors' report
Statement of directors' responsibilities
Auditors' report on financial statements
Consolidated profit and loss account
Statement of group total recognised gains and losses
Note of group historical cost profits and losses
Reconciliation of movements in group shareholders' funds
Balance sheets
Consolidated cash flow statement
Accounting policies
Notes to the financial statements

GAAP UK plc

Example set of consolidated financial statements

Example annual report under UK GAAP

The example annual report that follows includes the consolidated financial statements of the GAAP UK plc group of companies. The annual report has been prepared to show the disclosures and format that might be expected for a group of its size that prepares its financial statements in accordance with Schedule 4 and Schedule 4A to the Companies Act 1985 as amended by the Companies Act 1989 and subsequent Statutory Instruments. The requirements of Part 15 of the Companies Act 2006 have not been incorporated, as this part is only applicable to financial periods beginning on or after 6 April 2008, except for S417 which applies to the Business Review for periods beginning on or after 1 October 2008.

GAAP UK plc is a fictitious large private company that is incorporated in the UK. It has a number of UK and overseas investments, including subsidiaries and joint ventures. While we acknowledge that GAAP UK plc is not listed and perhaps would not adopt all the following standards, we have followed this course of action to show the disclosures necessary for those who do.

The intention is not to show all conceivable disclosures in this annual report and it should not, therefore, be used as a checklist. Neither is it a substitute for exercising judgement as to the fairness of presentation. These financial statements include many of the disclosure requirements contained in Financial Reporting Standards, Statements of Standard Accounting Practice, Urgent Issues Task Force Abstracts and Company Law in issue at 10 September 2008.

GAAP UK plc has adopted the amendment to FRS 17. Adoption of this amendment is required for accounting periods beginning on or after 6 April 2007.

Because GAAP UK plc is a private company, it is not required to include a directors' remuneration report or corporate governance report. It has not voluntarily included an operating and financial review.

Companies that present a report that purports to be an operating and financial review should comply with the ASB's statement of best practice, 'Reporting statement: Operating and financial review (OFR)'.

References to source material are given in the left hand margin.

The suggested disclosure throughout is intended for guidance only and would not necessarily be applicable to all groups or to all companies. The names of the undertakings included in the annual report are used for illustration only and any resemblance to any existing undertaking is not intended.

Abbreviations

7 Sch 6	=	Schedule [number] to the Companies Act 1985, paragraph number.
CA06 s417	=	Companies Act 2006, section number.
APB 2002/2	=	Auditing Practices Board Bulletin, number
DV	=	Disclosure voluntary
FRS 3 p14	=	Financial Reporting Standard [number], paragraph number.
ISA 720	=	International Standard on Auditing [number], paragraph number.
s 706(2)(a)	=	Companies Act 1985, section number.
SI 1996/189	=	Statutory Instrument [year/number].
SSAP 9 p14	=	Statement of Standard Accounting Practice [number], paragraph number.
UITF 38 p8	=	Urgent Issues Task Force Abstract [number], paragraph number.
Tech 24/03	=	Technical release [number], issued by the Institute of Chartered Accountants in England and Wales.

s 706(2)(a)

Registered no: xxyyzz

GAAP UK plc

Example annual report

for the year ended 31 December 2008

GAAP UK plc   1

s 369

Entities should arrange for the Notice of the AGM and related papers to be sent to shareholders at least 21 working days before the meeting.

2005

GAAP UK plc   2

Directors' report

s 234(2)	**Group directors' report** **for the year ended 31 December 2008**
s 234(1)	The directors present their report and the audited financial statements for the year ended 31 December 2008.

Note: Various matters listed below may be included in the chairman's statement, or the notes to the financial statements provided there is a cross reference in the directors' report to where the matter may be found.

General requirements

s 234ZZA(1) and (2)	*(1) The directors' report for the financial year must state:*

(a) *the names of the persons who, at any time during the financial year, were directors of the company;*
(b) *the principal activities of the company and its subsidiary undertakings included in the consolidation in the course of the year; and*
(c) *the amount (if any) that the directors recommend should be paid by way of dividend.*

s 234ZZA(3)	*(2) The directors' report must also comply with the relevant requirements of Schedule 7.*

Principal activities

s 234ZZA(1)(b), 7 Sch 6(d), s 698(2)	The narrative should cover the principal activities of the company and its subsidiary undertakings and any significant changes to activities in the year. In addition, there should be an indication of the existence of branches (as defined in section 698(2) of the Companies Act 1985) outside the UK.

Review of business

s 234(1)(a)	The report must contain a fair review of the development and performance of the group's business during the year and of its position at the year end.
Best practice	Where non-statutory numbers are disclosed, it should be clear that these differ from the statutory numbers, the equivalent statutory number should be disclosed and there should be a reconciliation between the statutory and non-statutory numbers.

The review of the business should include:

s 234ZZB(1) CA06 s417(3)	*(a) a fair review of the business of the company; and*
	(b) a description of the principal risks and uncertainties facing the company.
s 234ZZB(2) CA06 s417(4)	*The review is required to give a balanced and comprehensive analysis of:*

(a) the development and performance of the business of the company during the financial year; and
(b) the position of the company at the end of the year,
consistent with the size and complexity of the business.

s 234ZZB(3) CA06 s417(6)	*The review must, to the extent necessary for an understanding of the development, performance or position of the business of the company, include:*

(a) analysis using financial key performance indicators; and
(b) where appropriate, analysis using other key performance indicators, including information relating to environmental matters and employee matters.

s 246A(2A) CA06 s417(7)	*Note: For medium-sized companies, where these indicators relate to non-financial information, disclosure is not required.*
s 234ZZB(4) CA06 s417(8)	*The review must, where appropriate, include references to, and additional explanations of, amounts included in the financial statements of the company.*

GAAP UK plc 3

s 246(4)(a) *Note: This disclosure is required within the directors' report of all companies with the exception of small companies, which are exempt.*

Future developments

7 Sch 6(1)(b) The directors' report shall contain an indication of the likely future developments in the company's/group's business.

Results and dividends

See business review above Details of the results should be provided.

s 234ZZA(1)(c) Disclosure of the recommended dividend is required.

Research and development

7 Sch 6(1)(c)
SSAP 13 p30
and 31 ▪ Provide an indication of the group's research and development activities.

Best practice ▪ Comment on the profit and loss account charge for year (which should be separately disclosed in the notes to financial statements).

Donations

7 Sch 3 If the company, or any of its subsidiaries, made any donations to a registered political party or other political organisation in the EU (including the UK) or incurred EU political expenditure exceeding £200 in aggregate in the financial year, disclose:

▪ EU donations – name of political party and total amount given per party, by the company and each subsidiary that has donated or incurred such expenditure individually.
▪ EU political expenditure – total amount incurred in the financial year, by the company and each subsidiary that has donated or incurred such expenditure individually.

7 Sch 4 Total contributions to non-EU political organisations should be disclosed, for the group as a whole in aggregate. (There is no threshold for this disclosure.) If the company, or any of its subsidiaries, have made any contributions to non-EU political parties, disclose the total contributions made by the company and those subsidiaries.

7 Sch 5 If the company, or any of its subsidiaries, has given money in excess of £200 in aggregate for charitable purposes during the year, disclose the total amount given for each such purpose.

Land and buildings

7 Sch 1(2) If significant, indicate the difference between market value and book value of land and buildings for the company or any of its subsidiary undertakings.

Financial instruments

7 Sch 5A(1) and (1A) Where material for the assessment of the assets, liabilities, financial position and profit or loss of the group, the directors' report must contain an indication of:

▪ the financial risk management objectives and policies of the entity, including the policy for hedging each major type of forecasted transaction for which hedge accounting is used; and
▪ the exposure of the entity to price risk, credit risk, liquidity risk and cash flow risk.

Post balance sheet events

7 Sch 6(1)(a),
FRS 21, p19-22 The directors' report must include particulars of any important events affecting the company or group since the year end.

Directors

s 234ZZA(1)(a) Provide the names of all persons who were directors during any part of the period.

GAAP UK plc   4

Best practice	Include changes in directors since the end of the financial year and the dates of any appointments and/or resignations of directors occurring during the financial year.
Best practice	Include information regarding the retirement of directors at the AGM and whether they offer themselves for election.

Qualifying third party indemnity provisions

s309(2)	Disclose whether:

(a) at the time the report is approved any qualifying third party indemnity provision (whether made by the company or otherwise) is in place for the benefit of one or more of the directors; or

(b) at any time during the year any such provision was in force for the benefit of one or more persons who were then directors.

s309(3)	If the company has made a qualifying third party indemnity provision and:

(a) at the time the report is approved any qualifying third party indemnity provision is in place for the benefit of one or more directors of an associated company; or

(b) at any time during the year any such provision was in force for the benefit of one or more persons who were then directors of an associated company,

the report must state that such a provision is (or was) in force.

Employees

7 Sch 11(1)	*The requirements below only apply if the company employed on average 250 or more employees in the UK each week during the financial year.*
7 Sch 11(3)	A statement is required describing the action that has been taken during the period to introduce, maintain or develop arrangements aimed at involving UK employees in the company's affairs. This statement should discuss the group's policy on:

- systematic provision of relevant information to employees;
- regular consultation with employees or their representatives so that the employees' views may be taken into account in making decisions that are likely to affect their interests;
- encouragement of employees' participation in the group's performance by employee share schemes or other means; and
- achieving awareness on the part of all employees of the financial and economic factors affecting the group's performance.

7 Sch 9(3)	A statement should be included as to the policy for giving full and fair consideration to applications for employment that disabled people make to the company, the policy for employment, training, career development and promotion of disabled people and for the continuing employment and training of employees who have become disabled while employed by the company.

Policy and practice on payment of creditors

7 Sch 12(2) and (3)	The company's policy and practice on payment of creditors should be disclosed. The statement must include whether:

7 Sch 12(2)(a)	■ in respect of some, or all, of its suppliers, it is the company's policy to follow any code or standard on payment practice and, if so, the name of the code or standard and the place where information about the code or standard can be obtained; and/or
7 Sch 12(2)(b)	■ in respect of some, or all, of its suppliers, it is the company's policy to settle the terms of payment with those suppliers when agreeing the terms of each transaction and to ensure that these suppliers are made aware of the terms of the payment and to abide by the terms of payment.
7 Sch 12(2)(c)	Where the statement does not cover all suppliers, the policy for the other suppliers needs to be disclosed.
7 Sch 12(3)	The number of creditor days in relation to trade creditors outstanding at the period end needs to be disclosed.

GAAP UK plc   5

Best practice

Note: An additional statement regarding the group's policy and practice and number of days for the company and its UK subsidiaries, whilst not mandatory, is considered best practice.

Purchase of own shares and sales of treasury shares

7 Sch 7,8

Where a company purchases or places a charge on its own shares, there are specific disclosures to be made. These disclosures include the number and nominal value of the shares, percentage of called-up share capital, aggregate consideration paid and the reasons for the purchase. See Schedule 7, paragraph (8) of the Companies Act 1985 for further details.

Statement of disclosure of information to auditors

S 234ZA

This section is applicable unless the directors have taken advantage of the exemption conferred by section 249A(1) or 249AA(1).

The report must contain a statement to the effect that, in the case of each of the persons who are directors at the time when the report is approved under section 234A, the following applies:

(a) so far as the director is aware, there is no relevant audit information of which the company's auditors are unaware; and

(b) he has taken all the steps that he ought to have taken as a director in order to make himself aware of any relevant audit information and to establish that the company's auditors are aware of that information.

Auditors

Best practice (s 384(1))

The auditors, PricewaterhouseCoopers LLP, have indicated their willingness to continue in office and a resolution that they be reappointed will be proposed at the annual general meeting.

s 234A(1)

By order of the board

s 234A(2)

AB Smith
Company Secretary   23 February 2009

Notes:

s 234A(1),(3)

(a) The directors' report has to be signed by the company secretary or a director after it has been approved by the board of directors.

(b) The copy of the directors' report that is delivered to the Registrar of Companies must be manually signed by the company secretary or a director.

GAAP UK plc   6

Statement of directors' responsibilities

The directors are responsible for preparing the annual report and the financial statements in accordance with applicable law and regulations.

ISA 700

Company law requires the directors to prepare financial statements for each financial year. Under that law the directors have elected to prepare the financial statements in accordance with United Kingdom Generally Accepted Accounting Practice (United Kingdom Accounting Standards and applicable law). The financial statements are required by law to give a true and fair view of the state of affairs of the company and group and of the profit or loss of the group for that period.

In preparing those financial statements the directors are required to:

- Select suitable accounting policies and then apply them consistently.
- Make judgements and estimates that are reasonable and prudent.
- State whether applicable accounting standards have been followed, subject to any material departures disclosed and explained in the financial statements.
- Prepare the financial statements on the going concern basis, unless it is inappropriate to presume that the group will continue in business, in which case there should be supporting assumptions or qualifications as necessary. This statement should cover both the parent company and the group as a whole.

Note: The statement by the directors should be made in accordance with what is known to them at the date on which they approve the financial statements; in practice directors will need to perform their work to a date before the approval of the financial statements and update their work as appropriate.

The directors confirm that they have complied with the above requirements in preparing the financial statements.

The directors are responsible for keeping proper accounting records that disclose with reasonable accuracy at any time the financial position of the company and the group and to enable them to ensure that the financial statements comply with the Companies Act 1985. They are also responsible for safeguarding the assets of the company and the group and hence for taking reasonable steps for the prevention and detection of fraud and other irregularities.

Note: Where the financial statements are published on a website, the statement of directors' responsibilities may also include a statement that:

- *the directors are responsible for the maintenance and integrity of the web site; and*
- *legislation in the UK concerning the preparation and dissemination of financial statements may differ from legislation in other jurisdictions.*

By order of the Board

AB Smith
Company Secretary   25 February 2009

GAAP UK plc   7

Auditors' report on financial statements

ISA (UK&I) 700   **Independent auditors' report to the members of GAAP UK plc**

Warning – The audit report is based on the following circumstances. In other circumstances, a different form of report would be needed.

- *Audit of financial statements for period commencing on or after 1 April 2005.*
- *Group and parent company financial statements not presented separately.*
- *UK GAAP used for both group and parent company financial statements.*
- *Company does not meet the Companies Act definition of a quoted company.*
- *Section 230 exemption taken for parent company's own profit and loss account.*

ISA (UK&I) 720 (revised)

APB BUL 2006/6

We have audited the group and parent company financial statements (the 'financial statements') of GAAP UK plc for the year ended 31 December 2008 which comprise the group profit and loss account, the group and company balance sheets, the group cash flow statement, the group statement of total recognised gains and losses and the related notes. These financial statements have been prepared under the accounting policies set out therein.

Respective responsibilities of directors and auditors

The directors' responsibilities for preparing the annual report and the financial statements in accordance with applicable law and United Kingdom Accounting Standards (United Kingdom Generally Accepted Accounting Practice) are set out in the statement of directors' responsibilities.

Our responsibility is to audit the financial statements in accordance with relevant legal and regulatory requirements and International Standards on Auditing (UK and Ireland). This report, including the opinion, has been prepared for and only for the company's members as a body in accordance with Section 235 of the Companies Act 1985 and for no other purpose. We do not, in giving this opinion, accept or assume responsibility for any other purpose or to any other person to whom this report is shown or into whose hands it may come save where expressly agreed by our prior consent in writing.

We report to you our opinion as to whether the financial statements give a true and fair view and are properly prepared in accordance with the Companies Act 1985. We also report to you whether in our opinion the information given in the directors' report is consistent with the financial statements.

In addition, we report to you if, in our opinion, the company has not kept proper accounting records, if we have not received all the information and explanations we require for our audit, or if information specified by law regarding directors' remuneration and other transactions is not disclosed.

We read other information contained in the Annual Report, and consider whether it is consistent with the audited financial statements. This other information comprises only the directors' report. We consider the implications for our report if we become aware of any apparent misstatements or material inconsistencies with the financial information. Our responsibilities do not extend to any other information.

Basis of audit opinion

We conducted our audit in accordance with International Standards on Auditing (UK and Ireland) issued by the Auditing Practices Board. An audit includes examination, on a test basis, of evidence relevant to the amounts and disclosures in the financial statements. It also includes an assessment of the significant estimates and judgments made by the directors in the preparation of the financial statements, and of whether the accounting policies are appropriate to the group's and company's circumstances, consistently applied and adequately disclosed.

We planned and performed our audit so as to obtain all the information and explanations which we considered necessary in order to provide us with sufficient evidence to give reasonable assurance that the financial statements are free from material misstatement, whether caused by fraud or other irregularity or error. In forming our opinion we also evaluated the overall adequacy of the presentation of information in the financial statements.

GAAP UK plc

8

Opinion

In our opinion:

- the financial statements give a true and fair view, in accordance with United Kingdom Generally Accepted Accounting Practice, of the state of the group's and the parent company's affairs as at 31 December 2008 and of the group's profit and cash flows for the year then ended;
- the financial statements have been properly prepared in accordance with the Companies Act 1985; and
- the information given in the directors' report is consistent with the financial statements.

PricewaterhouseCoopers LLP
Chartered Accountants and Registered Auditors
[Location]

[Date]

GAAP UK plc

9

Consolidated profit and loss account

for the year ended 31 December 2008

		Note	2008 £m	2008 £m	2007 £m	2007 £m
FRS 28 p6s 227(3) s 227A(1)(b) 4 Sch Format 1						
4A Sch 19-22 FRS 9 p21	Turnover (including share of joint ventures)					
FRS 3 p14,30 FRS 3 p16	Continuing operations: Existing		532.8		368.8	
FRS 6 p23,28	Acquisitions – Newsub plc – Other		689.8 51.6		– –	
				1,274.2		368.8
FRS 3 p17	Discontinued operations			25.6		117.0
		1		1,299.8		485.8
FRS 9 p21, 27	Less: Share of joint ventures' turnover Continuing operations: – Existing – Acquisitions		(9.1) (29.8)	(38.9)	(9.9) –	(9.9)
4 Sch 8 4 Sch 8	**Group Turnover** Cost of Sales	2 2		1,260.9 (1,083.9)		475.9 (342.4)
4 Sch 8 4 Sch 3(4)	Gross Profit Net operating expenses	2		177.0 (70.8)		133.5 (30.1)
FRS 3 p14,30	Operating profit Continuing operations Acquisitions (after £40.2m (2007: £nil) goodwill amortisation)		82.2		76.3	
FRS 6 p28	– Newsub plc – Other		21.6 0.2		– –	
				104.0		76.3
FRS 3 p17	Discontinued operations			2.2		27.1
FRS 3 p14 4A Sch 21(3)	**Group operating profit** Share of operating profit in joint ventures	2		106.2		103.4
FRS 9 p21, 27	(after £0.9m (2007: £nil) goodwill amortisation)			2.8		1.2
	Total operating profit: group and share of joint ventures	1		109.0		104.6
FRS 3 p20 4 Sch 8	Profit on sale of subsidiary – Discontinued operations Net interest (payable)/receivable	5	6.3		–	
FRS 9 p21, 27	– Group – Joint ventures	3a 3a	(11.3) 0.7	(10.6)	3.6 –	3.6
FRS 17 App (ii) p6 FRS 12 p48	Other finance income	3b		4.0		4.0
4 Sch 3(6) 4 Sch 8, FRS 16 p17	**Profit on ordinary activities before taxation** Tax on profit on ordinary activities	1&4 6		108.7 (82.8)		112.2 (48.8)
4 Sch 8 4A Sch 17(3)(a) FRS 2 p36	**Profit on ordinary activities after taxation** Equity minority interests			25.9 (0.5)		63.4 (0.2)
4 Sch 8	**Profit for the financial year**			25.4		63.2
				2008		2007
FRS 22 p66	Earnings per share expressed in pence per share – Basic – Diluted	9		2.23p 2.22p		7.17p 7.03p
	Earnings per share from continuing operations expressed in pence per share – Basic – Diluted	9		1.55p 1.54p		6.60p 6.48p

GAAP UK plc 10

FRS 3 p27

Statement of group total recognised gains and losses

FRS 28 p6	For the year ended 31 December	Note	2008 £m	2007 £m
FRS 3 p36(a) FRS 9 p21,28	Profit for the financial year			
	– Group		23.8	62.8
	– Joint ventures		1.6	0.4
			25.4	63.2
FRS 3 p36(b), FRS 15 p63	Unrealised surplus on revaluation of properties	26	5.4	1.5
FRS 23 p52(b), FRS 3 p36(b)	Exchange adjustments offset in reserves (translation of overseas sales and foreign investments)	28	(42.5)	34.9
UITF 19 p9 FRS 16 p17	Tax on exchange adjustments offset in reserves	6, 27	3.5	2.8
FRS 17 p57	Actuarial (loss)/gain recognised in the pension scheme	36	(22.2)	2.7
FRS 16 p6	Current tax deductions allocated to actuarial losses		3.6	–
FRS 19 p35 FRS 26 p55(b),	Movement on deferred tax relating to pension asset Movement on AFS investment reserve and other	22, 27	2.8	(0.1)
FRS 29p20a(ii)	reserve	29	(0.7)	(14.5)
FRS 26p102(a)	Movement on hedging reserve	29	7.4	(16.6)
	Total recognised (losses)/gains for the year		**(17.3)**	**73.9**
	Prior year adjustment for adoption of amendment to FRS 17	36	(15.4)	
	Total recognised (losses)/gains since last annual report		**(32.7)**	**73.9**
FRS 9 p21,28	– Group		(34.3)	73.5
FRS 3 p27	– Joint ventures		1.6	0.4
	Total recognised (losses)/gains since last annual report		**(32.7)**	**73.9**

Notes:

FRS 3 p57 (a) *If the group has no recognised gains or losses other than its profit or loss for the period, a statement to this effect should be given immediately below the profit and loss account.*

FRS 9 p28 (b) *Where an associate or joint venture has gains and losses reported in its STRGL, or has such gains and losses when its accounts are restated on to the investor's GAAP, the investor's share of such gains and losses should be included in the investor's consolidated STRGL. The amounts should be shown separately under each heading, if material, either in the statement or in a note referred to in the statement.*

FRS 3 p26

Note of group historical cost profits and losses

For the year ended 31 December	2008 £m	2007 £m
Reported profit on ordinary activities before taxation	108.7	112.2
Realisation of property revaluation gains of previous years	0.1	0.1
Difference between historical cost depreciation charge and the actual depreciation charge of the year calculated on the revalued amount	0.1	–
Historical cost profit on ordinary activities before taxation	**108.9**	**112.3**
Historical cost profit for the year retained after taxation and minority interests	**25.6**	**63.3**

Note: The above note is only required if the difference is material. The difference is unlikely to be material in this example, but is shown for illustrative purposes.

GAAP UK plc
11

FRS 3 p28

Reconciliation of movements in group shareholders' funds

For the year ended 31 December	Note	2008 £m	2007 £m
Profit for the financial year	25.4	63.2	
Dividends	8	(23.7)	(15.7)
Other recognised gains and losses relating to the year (shown in STRGL)		(42.7)	10.7
Proceeds of ordinary shares issued for cash	23	2.6	4.7
Purchase of own shares	27	–	(23.1)
Nominal value of ordinary shares issued for the acquisition of Newsub plc	23	4.8	–
Premium (net of issue expenses) on ordinary shares issued for the acquisition of Newsub plc	29	913.6	–
Goodwill recycled on disposal of subsidiary	34	3.9	–
Adjustment in respect of employee share schemes	27	3.2	1.4
Net change in shareholders' funds		**887.1**	41.2
Opening shareholders' funds as previously reported		**182.4**	139.0
Prior year adjustment for amendment to FRS 17	36	**(15.4)**	(13.2)
Opening shareholders' funds as restated		**167.0**	125.8
Shareholders' funds as at 31 December		**1,054.1**	167.0

2015

GAAP UK plc 12

Balance sheets

Balance sheets at 31 December 2008

			Group		Company	
		Note	**2008** **£m**	£m	**2008** **£m**	2007 £m
Fixed assets						
Intangible assets		10	**1,078.7**	–	–	–
Tangible assets		11	**406.8**	91.3	**11.5**	9.7
Financial assets						
– Derivative financial instruments		21	**12.1**	4.9	–	–
– Available for sale investments		16	**523.1**	410.0	–	–
Investment in subsidiary undertakings		12	–	–	**419.2**	98.5
Interests in joint ventures		12				
– share of gross assets			**105.6**	7.2	–	–
– share of gross liabilities			**(96.7)**	(5.4)	–	–
– goodwill arising on acquisition			**7.6**	–	–	–
			16.5	1.8	–	–
			2,037.2	508.0	**430.7**	108.2
Current assets						
Stock		13	**33.8**	17.0	–	–
Financial assets						
– Derivative financial instruments		21	**8.6**	2.2	–	–
– Current asset investments		15	**25.3**	55.3	–	48.7
– Debtors		17	**290.6**	109.6	**68.3**	101.0
– Cash at bank and in hand			**74.8**	40.5	**7.0**	0.5
			433.1	224.6	**75.3**	150.2
Creditors – Amounts falling due within one year		18	**(401.2)**	(136.7)	**(99.8)**	(68.3)
Net current assets/(liabilities)			**31.9**	87.9	**(24.5)**	81.9
Total assets less current liabilities			**2,069.1**	595.9	**406.2**	190.1
Creditors – Amounts falling due after more than one year		19	**(865.5)**	(427.9)	**(240.5)**	(17.0)
Provisions for liabilities		22	**(163.0)**	(22.2)	**(0.1)**	(0.5)
Net assets excluding pension asset			**1,040.6**	145.8	**165.6**	172.6
Pension asset		36	**15.0**	22.0	–	–
Net assets including pension asset			**1,055.6**	167.8	**165.6**	172.6
Capital and reserves						
Called up share capital		23	**13.8**	8.9	**13.8**	8.9
Share premium account		25	**10.8**	8.3	**10.8**	8.3
Revaluation reserve		26	**7.5**	2.5	**2.3**	0.8
Other reserves		29	**964.2**	5.8	–	–
Profit and loss reserve		27	**57.8**	141.5	**138.7**	154.6
Total shareholders' funds			**1,054.1**	167.0	**165.6**	172.6
Minority interests			**1.5**	0.8	–	–
Capital employed			**1,055.6**	167.8	**165.6**	172.6

Left margin references:

s 227(3)
s 227A(1)(a)
4 Sch Format 1
4A Sch 1(1),
FRS 28 p6
4 Sch 8
4 Sch 8
4 Sch 8
FRS 25 p53, 4 Sch 3(3)
FRS 29p8(a)
4 Sch 8, FRS 29p8(d)
FRS 9 p21
FRS 9 p29
4 Sch 8
FRS 25p53, 4 Sch 3(3)
FRS 29p8(a)
4 Sch 8, FRS 29p8(a)
4 Sch 8, FRS 29p8(c)
4 Sch 8, FRS 29p8
4 Sch 8
4 Sch 8
4 Sch 8
4 Sch 8
4 Sch 8
FRS 17 p47
4 Sch 8
4 Sch 8
4 Sch 8
4 Sch 8
4 Sch 8
4 Sch 8
FRS 2 p35, 4A Sch 17(2)

FRS 21 p17
s 233(1)-(4)

The financial statements on pages 9 to 61 were approved by the board of directors on 25 February 2009 and were signed on its behalf by:

CD Jones
Director

GAAP UK plc   13

FRS 1 p4 **Consolidated cash flow statement for the year ended 31 December 2008**

	Note	2008 £m	2008 £m	2007 £m	2007 £m
Net cash inflow from operating activities	30		**189.4**		116.6
Dividends received from joint ventures			**0.1**		0.2
Returns on investments and servicing of finance					
Interest received		**4.8**		4.1	
Interest paid		**(25.7)**		(1.1)	
Issue costs of new bank loan		**(5.3)**		–	
Interest element of finance lease payments		**(1.0)**		–	
Dividends paid to minority interests		**(0.1)**		(0.1)	
Preference share dividends paid to shareholders		**(0.1)**		(0.1)	
Net cash (outflow)/inflow from returns on investments and servicing of finance			**(27.4)**		2.8
Taxation			**(24.7)**		(37.2)
Capital expenditure and financial investment					
Purchase of tangible fixed assets		**(106.1)**		(34.5)	
Sale of tangible fixed assets		**4.2**		6.7	
Net cash outflow for capital expenditure and financial investment			**(101.9)**		(27.8)
Acquisitions					
Purchase of subsidiary undertakings	34	**(307.2)**		(23.6)	
Net overdrafts acquired with subsidiary undertakings	34	**(15.1)**		–	
Net cash outflow for acquisitions			**(322.3)**		(23.6)
Equity dividends paid to shareholders			**(23.7)**		(15.7)
Net cash (outflow)/inflow before use of liquid resources and financing			**(310.5)**		15.3
Management of liquid resources					
Reduction/(increase) in short-term deposits with banks	31	**91.7**		(21.9)	
Purchase of current asset investments	15	**(100.0)**		(400.0)	
Net cash outflow from management of liquid resources			**(8.3)**		(421.9)
Financing					
Issue of ordinary share capital	23	**2.6**		4.7	
Purchase of own shares		–		(23.1)	
Expenses of share issue to acquire Newsub plc	29	**(1.4)**		–	
Capital element of finance lease payments	31	**(10.8)**		–	
Increase in borrowings	31	**276.5**		421.1	
Net cash inflow from financing			**266.9**		402.7
Decrease in net cash			**(51.9)**		(3.9)
Reconciliation to net (debt)/cash					
Net cash at 1 January	31		**33.2**		39.0
Decrease in net cash			**(51.9)**		(3.9)
Borrowings net of short-term deposits acquired with subsidiaries			**(57.1)**		–
Movement in liquid resources			**8.3**		421.9
Movement in borrowings			**(260.4)**		(421.1)
Other non-cash changes			**(2.1)**		(3.0)
Exchange adjustments			**44.5**		0.3
Net (debt)/cash at 31 December	31		**(285.5)**		33.2

Left margin references:
FRS 1 p48, FRS 1 p7, FRS 1 p7, FRS 1 p7, FRS 1 p14(a), FRS 1 p15(a), FRS 1 p15(b), FRS 1 p15(c), FRS 1 p15(e), FRS 1 p15(d), FRS 1 p7, FRS 1 p7, FRS 1 p21(a), FRS 1 p20(a), FRS 6 p33, FRS 1 p24(a), FRS 1 p24(a), FRS 1 p7, FRS 1 p7,52, FRS 1 p27,28, FRS 1 p28, FRS 1 p7, FRS 1 p30(a), FRS 1 p31(c), FRS 1 p31(d), FRS 1 p31(b), FRS 1 p31(b), FRS 1 p33, FRS 1 p33(c), FRS 1 p33(d)

GAAP UK plc

14

Accounting policies

**Accounting policies
for the year ended 31 December 2008**

4 Sch 36A

These financial statements have been prepared under the historical cost convention, as modified by the revaluation of certain tangible fixed assets, investments and financial instruments in accordance with the Companies Act 1985 and applicable accounting standards. A summary of the more important group accounting policies is set out below, together with an explanation of where changes have been made to previous policies on the adoption of new accounting standards in the year.

s 256

Note: Accounting standards means those issued by bodies prescribed by regulations. The International Accounting Standards Board and the Accounting Standards Board are the only bodies so prescribed. Hence, financial statements drawn up under UK GAAP should only be prepared in accordance with the UK SSAPs and FRSs.

4 Sch 36
FRS 18 p55(a),56

The accounting policies used for dealing with items that are judged material or critical in the context of the company's financial statements should be disclosed.

Where an accounting policy is prescribed by and fully described in an accounting standard, UITF Abstract or companies legislation, a succinct description of the policy should be given. Where an accounting policy is not prescribed by an accounting standard, a UITF Abstract or companies legislation, or an option permitted therein is used, a fuller description should be provided.

FRS 18
p55(b), 57

A description should be given of those estimation techniques adopted that are significant, that is where the range of reasonable amounts is so large that the use of a different amount from within the range could materially affect the view shown by the financial statements.

FRS 18 p58

Where a company falls within the scope of a SORP, the financial statements should state the name of the SORP and whether or not the company has complied with it. Where there is a departure from the SORP, further disclosure is required.

Changes in accounting policies

The group has adopted early the amendment to FRS 17, 'Retirement benefits'. As a result of this, quoted securities held as plan assets in the defined benefit pension scheme are now valued at bid price rather than mid-market value. The effect of this change is that the pension deficit as at 31 December 2007 has increased by £15.4m. Current and prior year profits have been unaffected by this change.

FRS 18 paragraph 55(d) states that where the effect of a change in estimation technique is material, a description of the change and where practicable, the effect on the results for the period should be given.

4A Sch

Consolidation

FRS 6 p21
FRS 2 p23
FRS 9 p20,26
FRS 2 p40
FRS 2 p39
FRS 9 p31(b)

- Basis of consolidation.
- Inclusion of all subsidiaries.
- Equity accounting for associates and gross equity accounting for joint ventures.
- Uniform accounting policies for group.
- Elimination of profits or losses on intra-group transactions.
- Elimination of investor's shares of profits or losses on transactions with amounts and joint ventures.

s 262

Turnover

FRS 5 AppG
UITF 26

- Basis of income recognition and measurement for each principal income stream.
- Barter transactions.

4 Sch 58(1)

Foreign currencies

FRS 23 p23
FRS 23 p44

- Basis of translating foreign currency assets and liabilities.
- Basis of translating results of foreign subsidiaries.
- Treatment of exchange differences arising on the retranslation of opening net investments in subsidiary companies and translation of results (if at an average rate).
- Translation of all other exchange differences.

GAAP UK plc

FRS 23 p53	■ Functional currency if different from presentation currency and reason why.
FRS 23 p54	■ Any change in the functional currency and reason why.
FRS 24 p39(b)	■ Method adopted for dealing with results of foreign subsidiaries operating in hyperinflationary economies.

Capitalisation of finance costs and interest

FRS 15 p31, IAS 18 p56	■ Whether interest is capitalised or not.
	■ If capitalised, basis of capitalisation of interest and other finance costs.

FRS 15   Tangible fixed assets

FRS 18 p55(a), 56	■ Whether carried at cost or revalued amount.
FRS 15 p 42	■ Basis and frequency of revaluations.
UITF 24, UITF 29	■ What is included in cost.
FRS 15 p 100(a)	■ Methods of depreciation (for example, straight line or reducing balance).
FRS 15 p100(b)	■ Useful economic lives/depreciation rates.
FRS 15 p100(d), FRS 18 p55(d)	■ The reason for any change in the depreciation method, useful lives or residual values, if the effect is material.

FRS 10   UITF 27   Goodwill and intangible assets

FRS 10 p52	■ The method used to value intangible assets.
FRS 10 p55	■ The methods and periods of amortisation of goodwill and intangibles and the reasons for choosing those periods.
FRS 10 p71	■ Treatment of goodwill on disposal, including previously eliminated goodwill.
FRS 10 p56,57, FRS 18 p55(a)	■ The reason for any change in the amortisation method or period, if the effect is material.
FRS 10 p58	■ Where the period of amortisation exceeds 20 years, the grounds for rebutting the 20 year presumption.
FRS 10 p59	■ Where goodwill is not amortised, particulars of the departure from the specific requirement of CA85 4 Sch 21, the reasons for it and the effect.
FRS 10 p64	■ Where negative goodwill exceeds the fair values of the non-monetary assets, the source of the excess negative goodwill and the periods in which it is being written back.

Investment properties

SSAP 19 p11	■ Basis of inclusion in the balance sheet.
SSAP 19 p13	■ Treatment of changes in value.

Research and development

SSAP 13 p30	■ Classification of expenditure.
	■ Treatment of expenditure.

FRS 11   Impairment of fixed assets and goodwill

FRS 11 p14	■ Basis for determining impairment write-down, by reference to higher of net realisable value and value-in-use.
FRS 11 p41	■ Use of discounting in determining value-in-use.
FRS 11 p45	■ Basis for using risk-free discount rate and method for adjusting cash flows for risk, where applicable.
FRS 11 p63	■ Treatment of impairment write-down on revalued assets.

SSAP 4 p17   Government grants

SSAP 4 p28(a)	■ Treatment of capital grants.
	■ Treatment of revenue based grants.
	■ Period over which the grants are credited to the profit and loss account.

GAAP UK plc 16

FRS 29 p21	**Accounting for financial assets**
FRS 26 p14, 15, 39, 43, 45-47	■ Basis of recognition and measurements (cost or valuation).
FRS 26 p58	■ Recognition of impairments.
FRS 29 appB5(a)-(f)	■ For financial assets designated as at fair value through profit or loss:

  (i) the nature of the financial assets or financial liabilities the entity has designated as at fair value through profit or loss;
  (ii) the criteria for so designating such financial assets or financial liabilities on initial recognition; and
  (iii) how the entity has satisfied the conditions in paragraph 9, 11A or 12 of FRS 26 for such designation. For instruments designated in accordance with paragraph (b)(i) of the definition of a financial asset or financial liability at fair value through profit or loss in FRS 26, that disclosure includes a narrative description of the circumstances underlying the measurement or recognition inconsistency that would otherwise arise. For instruments designated in accordance with paragraph (b)(ii) of the definition of a financial asset or financial liability at fair value through profit or loss in FRS 26, that disclosure includes a narrative description of how designation at fair value through profit or loss is consistent with the entity's documented risk management or investment strategy.

■ the criteria for designating financial assets as available for sale;
■ when an allowance account is used to reduce the carrying amount of financial assets impaired by credit losses:

  (i) the criteria for determining when the carrying amount of impaired financial assets is reduced directly (or, in the case of a reversal of a write-down, increased directly) and when the allowance account is used; and
  (ii) the criteria for writing off amounts charged to the allowance account against the carrying amount of impaired financial assets.

■ how net gains or net losses on each category of financial instrument are determined, for example, whether the net gains or net losses on items at fair value through profit or loss include interest or dividend income;
■ the criteria the entity uses to determine that there is objective evidence that an impairment loss has occurred;
■ when the terms of financial assets that would otherwise be past due or impaired have been re-negotiated, the accounting policy for financial assets that are the subject of re-negotiated terms;

FRS 29p27(a)	■ methods and, where a valuation technique is used, assumptions applied in determining fair values for each class of financial assets or financial liabilities; and
FRS 26 p9	■ how assets are classified.
FRS 29p21	**Derivative financial instruments and hedging activities**
FRS 18 p14 FRS 29p21	Derivatives are initially accounted for and measured at fair value on the date a derivative contract is entered into and subsequently measured at fair value. The gain or loss on re-measurement is taken to the income statement except where the derivative is a designated cash flow hedging instrument. The accounting treatment of derivatives classified as hedges depends on their designation, which occurs on the date that the derivative contract is committed to. The group designates derivatives as:
FRS 26 p86(a)	■ A hedge of the fair value of an asset or liability ('fair value hedge').
FRS 26 p86(b)	■ A hedge of the income/cost of a highly probable forecasted transaction or commitment ('cash flow hedge').
FRS 26 p86(c)	■ A hedge of a net investment in a foreign operation.
FRS 29p23,24	In order to qualify for hedge accounting, the group is required to document in advance the relationship between the item being hedged and the hedging instrument. The group is also required to document and demonstrate an assessment of the relationship between the hedged item and the hedging instrument, which shows that the hedge will be highly effective on an on-going basis. This effectiveness testing is re-performed at each period end to ensure that the hedge remains highly effective.
FRS 26 p89	Gains or losses on fair value hedges that are regarded as highly effective are recorded in the income statement with the gain or loss on the hedged item attributable to the hedged risk.

GAAP UK plc   17

FRS 26 p95 FRS 26 p97-98	Gains or losses on cash flow hedges that are regarded as highly effective are recognised in equity. Where the forecast transaction results in a financial asset or financial liability, only gains or losses previously recognised in equity are reclassified to profit or loss in the same period as the asset or liability affects profit or loss. Where the forecasted transaction or commitment results in a non-financial asset or a non-financial liability, then any gains or losses previously deferred in equity are included in the cost of the related asset or liability. If the forecasted transaction or commitment results in future income or expenditure, gains or losses deferred in equity are transferred to the income statement in the same period as the underlying income or expenditure. The ineffective portions of the gain or loss on the hedging instrument are recognised in profit or loss.
FRS 26 p101	For the portion of hedges deemed ineffective or transactions that do not qualify for hedge accounting under FRS 26, any change in assets or liabilities is recognised immediately in the income statement. Where a hedge no longer meets the effectiveness criteria, any gains or losses deferred in equity are only transferred to the income statement when the committed or forecasted transaction is recognised in the income statement. However, where an entity applied cash flow hedge accounting for a forecasted or committed transaction that is no longer expected to occur, then the cumulative gain or loss that has been recorded in equity is transferred to the income statement. When a hedging instrument expires or is sold, any cumulative gain or loss existing in equity at that time remains in equity and is recognised when the forecast transaction is ultimately recognised in the income statement.
FRS 26 p102	Where the group hedges net investments in foreign operations through currency borrowings, the gains or losses on the translation of the borrowings are recognised in equity. If the group uses derivatives as the hedging instrument, the effective portion of the hedge is recognised in equity with any ineffective portion being recognised in the income statement. The group has not separated out the interest element of the fair value of the forward currency contract. Gains and losses accumulated in equity are included in the income statement when the foreign operation is disposed of.

Fair value estimation

FRS 29 p27	The fair value of the interest rate swaps and currency swaps is based on the market price of comparable instruments at the balance sheet date if they are publicly traded. The fair value of the forward currency contracts has been determined based on market forward exchange rates at the balance sheet date.
FRS 26 p46 FRS 26 p47	The fair values of short-term deposits, loans and overdrafts with a maturity of less than one year are assumed to approximate to their book values. The fair value of the group's US-dollar bonds has been estimated using quoted market prices for similar instruments. In the case of bank loans and other loans due in more than one year, the fair value of financial liabilities for disclosure purposes is estimated by discounting the future contractual cash flows at the current market interest rate available to the group for similar financial instruments.
	The company's preference shares (shown as debt within these financial statements as they carry a guaranteed dividend and have no residual interest in the equity of the company) are not publicly traded and their fair value is based on the present value of estimated future cash flows, discounted at a rate based on the market rate for a borrowing with similar maturity and credit rating.
SSAP 9 p32	**Stocks, work in progress and long-term contracts**
SSAP 9 p32, 4 Sch 27	■ Basis of amount stated at in the balance sheet (for example, lower of cost and NRV, FIFO). ■ Methods of valuation (for example, average price, FIFO). ■ Basis for inclusion of overheads. ■ Basis of provision for obsolete, slow moving and defective stocks. ■ Method of ascertaining turnover and attributable profit for long-term contracts.
FRS 29p21,	**Trade debtors**
FRS 29app Bp5(d)(f)	■ When an allowance account is used to reduce the carrying amount of financial assets impaired by credit losses: (i) the criteria for determining when the carrying amount of impaired financial assets is reduced directly (or, in the case of a reversal of a write- down, increased directly) and when the allowance account is used; and

GAAP UK plc

(ii) the criteria for writing off amounts charged to the allowance account against the carrying amount of impaired financial assets.

- The criteria the entity uses to determine that there is objective evidence that an impairment loss has occurred.

FRS 26 p43, 46(a), 59

- When a financial asset or financial liability is recognised initially, an entity shall measure it at its fair value plus, in the case of a financial asset or financial liability not at fair value through profit or loss, transaction costs that are directly attributable to the acquisition or issue of the financial asset or financial liability.

FRS 29p21 **Cash and cash equivalents**

FRS 29p21 **Trade creditors**

FRS 26p43, 47

- When a financial liability is recognised initially, an entity shall measure it at its fair value plus, in the case of a financial asset or financial liability not at fair value through profit or loss, transaction costs that are directly attributable to the acquisition or issue of the financial asset or financial liability.

- After initial recognition, an entity shall measure all financial liabilities at amortised cost using the effective interest method.

FRS 29p21 **Borrowings**

FRS 26p43, 47
FRS 25p18(a), 28,
33, FRS 29p27(a)

- When a financial liability is recognised initially, an entity shall measure it at its fair value plus, in the case of a financial asset or financial liability not at fair value through profit or loss, transaction costs that are directly attributable to the acquisition or issue of the financial asset or financial liability.
- After initial recognition, an entity shall measure all financial liabilities at amortised cost using the effective interest method.
- The substance of a financial instrument, rather than its legal form, governs its classification on the entity's balance sheet.
- The issuer of a non-derivative financial instrument shall evaluate the terms of the financial instrument to determine whether it contains both a liability and an equity component. Such components shall be classified separately as financial liabilities, financial assets or equity instruments in accordance with paragraph 15 of FRS 25.

Own equity instruments

- If an entity reacquires its own equity instruments, those instruments ('treasury shares') shall be deducted from equity. No gain or loss shall be recognised in profit or loss on the purchase, sale, issue or cancellation of an entity's own equity instruments. Such treasury shares may be acquired and held by the entity or by other members of the consolidated group. Consideration paid or received shall be recognised directly in equity.
- The methods and, when a valuation technique is used, the assumptions applied in determining fair values of each class of financial assets or financial liabilities. For example, if applicable, an entity discloses information about the assumptions relating to prepayment rates, rates of estimated credit losses, and interest rates or discount rates.

Leases

SSAP 21 p57 As lessee:

- Basis of recognition of fixed assets held under finance leases in the balance sheet.
- Depreciation policy for assets held under finance leases.
- Treatment of the interest element of finance lease rental obligations.
- Treatment of payments for operating leases.

UITF 28 p14
- Treatment of incentives to take on operating leases (for example, rent free periods).

SSAP 21 p60 As lessor:

- Policy for operating leases.
- Policy for finance leases.
- Policy for finance lease income.
- Treatment of the costs of assets acquired for the purpose of letting under finance lease.

UITF 28 p15
- Treatment of lease incentives.

GAAP UK plc

Leases include hire purchase contracts which have characteristics similar to operating or finance leases.

FRS 12	**Provisions**
FRS 12 p14	■ Basis of accounting for each class of provision.
	■ Extent of use of discounting.

FRS 17, UITF 35	**Pensions and post retirement benefits**
	■ Type of scheme – defined contribution or defined benefit.
	■ For defined benefit schemes – valuation frequency and method.
	■ Method of charging to profit and loss account.
	■ Treatment of actuarial gains and losses for defined benefit schemes.
	■ Funding policy.

FRS 16 FRS 19 UITF 19 FRS 19 p61	**Taxation including deferred tax**
	■ Basis of charge for taxation.
	■ Policy adopted for providing for deferred taxation.
	■ Policy adopted regarding discounting.

FRS 20 p44 46, 50 UITF 32 UITF 25 UITF 38	**Share-based payment**
	■ Basis of accounting.
	■ Basis of accounting for employee share ownership plans (ESOPs).
	■ Basis of recognition and measurement of the cost of share-based payments.
	■ Basis of accounting for employer NICs on employee share schemes.

FRS 29 p21	**Share capital**

FRS 25 p33	**Treasury shares**
	■ Basis of accounting.

Financial risk management

Financial risk factors

FRS 29 p31   The group's activities expose it to a variety of financial risks: market risk (including currency risk, fair value interest rate risk, cash flow interest rate risk and price risk), credit risk and liquidity risk. The group's overall risk management programme focuses on the unpredictability of financial markets and seeks to minimise potential adverse effects on the group's financial performance. The group uses derivative financial instruments to hedge certain risk exposures.

Risk management is carried out by a central treasury department (group treasury) under policies approved by the Board of Directors. Group treasury identifies, evaluates and hedges financial risks in close co-operation with the group's operating units. The Board provides written principles for overall risk management, as well as written policies covering specific areas, such as foreign exchange risk, interest rate risk, credit risk, use of derivative financial instruments and non-derivative financial instruments, and investment of excess liquidity.

(a) Market risk

(i) Foreign exchange risk

FRS 29 p33(a)   The group operates internationally and is exposed to foreign exchange risk arising from various currency exposures, primarily with respect to the US dollar and the euro. Foreign exchange risk arises from future commercial transactions, recognised assets and liabilities and net investments in foreign operations.

FRS 29 p33(b),
FRS 29 p22(c)   The management has set up a policy to require group companies to manage their foreign exchange risk against their functional currency. The group companies are required to hedge their entire foreign exchange risk exposure with the group treasury. To manage their foreign exchange risk arising from future commercial transactions and recognised assets and liabilities, entities in the group use forward contracts, transacted with group treasury. Foreign exchange

GAAP UK plc

20

risk arises when future commercial transactions or recognised assets or liabilities are denominated in a currency that is not the entity's functional currency.

FRS 26 p73

The Group treasury's risk management policy is to hedge between 75% and 100% of anticipated cash flows (mainly export sales and purchase of inventory) in each major foreign currency for the subsequent 12 months. Approximately 90% (2007: 95%) of projected sales in each major currency qualify as 'highly probable' forecast transactions for hedge accounting purposes.

FRS 29 p33(a)(b)
FRS 29 p22(c)

For segment reporting purposes, each subsidiary designates contracts with group treasury as fair value hedges or cash flow hedges, as appropriate. External foreign exchange contracts are designated at group level as hedges of foreign exchange risk on specific assets, liabilities or future transactions on a gross basis.

FRS 29 p40, IG36

The group has certain investments in foreign operations, whose net assets are exposed to foreign currency translation risk. Currency exposure arising from the net assets of the group's foreign operations is managed primarily through borrowings denominated in the relevant foreign currencies.

At 31 December 2008, if the pound had weakened/strengthened by 11% against the euro with all other variables held constant, post-tax profit for the year would have been £251,000 (2007: £220,000) higher/lower, mainly as a result of foreign exchange gains/losses on translation of euro-denominated trade receivables, financial assets at fair value through profit or loss and debt securities classified as available for sale. Equity would have been £1,913,000 (2007: £932,000) lower/higher, arising mainly from foreign exchange losses/gains on translation of euro-denominated borrowings designated as a hedge of the net investment in subsidiaries. The impact on equity in net investment hedges is netted by a corresponding credit/charge resulting from the translation of the hedged net investment. Equity is more sensitive to movement in pound/euro exchange rate in 2008 than 2007 because of the increased amount of euro-denominated borrowings designated as a hedge of the net investment and anticipated cash flows hedged in a cash flow hedge.

At 31 December 2008, if the pound had weakened/strengthened by 4% against the US dollar with all other variables held constant, post-tax profit for the year would have been £135,000 (2007: £172,000) lower/higher, mainly as a result of foreign exchange gains/losses on translation of US dollar-denominated trade receivables, financial assets at fair value through profit or loss, debt securities classified as available for sale and foreign exchange losses/gains on translation of US dollar-denominated borrowings.

(ii) Price risk

FRS 29 p33(a)(b)

The group is exposed to equity securities price risk because of investments held by the group and classified on the consolidated balance sheet either as available for sale or at fair value through profit or loss. The group is not exposed to commodity price risk. To manage its price risk arising from investments in equity securities, the group diversifies its portfolio. Diversification of the portfolio is done in accordance with the limits set by the group.

The group's equity investments are publicly traded and are included in the FTSE-100.

FRS 29 p40, IG36

The table below summarises the impact of increases/decreases of the FTSE 100 on the group's post-tax profit for the year and on equity. The analysis is based on the assumption that the equity indexes had increased/decreased by 5% with all other variables held constant and all the group's equity instruments moved according to the historical correlation with the index:

Index	Impact on post-tax profit £m		Impact on equity £m	
	2008	2007	2008	2007
FTSE-100 UK	6	3	16	15

Post-tax profit for the year would increase/decrease as a result of gains/losses on equity securities classified as at fair value through profit or loss. Equity would increase/decrease as a result of gains/losses on equity securities classified as available for sale.

(b) Credit risk

FRS 29 p33(a)(b)
FRS 29 p34(a)

Credit risk is managed on a group basis. Credit risk arises from cash and cash equivalents, derivative financial instruments and deposits with banks and financial institutions, as well as credit exposures to wholesale and retail customers, including outstanding receivables and committed transactions. For banks and financial institutions, only independently rated parties with a minimum rating of 'A' are accepted. If wholesale customers are independently rated,

GAAP UK plc   21

these ratings are used. Otherwise, if there is no independent rating, risk control assesses the credit quality of the customer taking into account its financial position, past experience and other factors. Individual risk limits are set based on internal or external ratings in accordance with limits set by the Board. The utilisation of credit limits is regularly monitored. Sales to retail customers are settled in cash or using major credit cards.

The below table shows the credit rating and the utilisation of the credit facilities of the six major counterparties at the balance sheet date.

FRS 29 p36(c)

Counterparty	Rating	31 December 2008 Credit facility £m	Utilised £m	31 December 2007 Credit facility £m	Utilised £m
Bank A	AAA	750	739	450	414
Bank B	AA	60	53	30	25
Bank C	A	40	34	20	17
		850	826	500	456
Wholesaler Q	A	64	26	62	9
Wholesaler T	BBB	18	17	31	2
Wholesaler Z	BB	9	4	11	1
		91	47	104	12

No credit limits were exceeded during the reporting period, and management does not expect any losses from non-performance by these counterparties.

(c) Liquidity risk

FRS 29 p33,
39(b)
FRS 29 p34(a)

Prudent liquidity risk management includes maintaining sufficient cash and marketable securities, the availability of funding from an adequate amount of committed credit facilities and the ability to close out market positions. Due to the dynamic nature of the underlying businesses, Group Treasury maintains flexibility in funding by maintaining availability under committed credit lines.

Management monitors the Group's liquidity reserves defined as follows:

Liquidity reserve as of 31 December 2008

	December 2008 £m	September 2008 £m	June 2008 £m	March 2008 £m	December 2007 £m
Cash at bank and on hand	74.8	84.7	106.1	73.5	40.5
Unused portion of committed long-term credit lines	212.0	207.0	196.0	224.0	253.0
Liquidity reserve	286.8	291.7	302.1	297.5	293.5

Management also monitors the rolling forecasts of the group's liquidity reserve on the basis of expected cash flows. This is generally carried out at local level in the operating companies of the group in accordance with practice and limits set by the group. These limits vary by location to take into account the liquidity of the market in which the entity operates. In addition, the group's liquidity management policy involves projecting cashflows in major currencies and considering the level of liquid assets necessary to meet these; monitoring balance sheet liquidity ratios against internal and external regulatory requirements; and maintaining debt financing plans.

FRS 29 p39(a)

The table below analyses the group's financial liabilities that will be settled on a net basis into relevant maturity groupings based on the remaining period at the balance sheet to the contractual maturity date. The amounts disclosed in the table are the contractual undiscounted cash flows. Balances due within 12 months equal their carrying balances, as the impact of discounting is not significant.

GAAP UK plc

At 31 December 2008	Less than 1 month £m	Between 1 and 3 months £m	Between 3 and 12 months £m	Between 1 and 2 years £m	Between 2 and 5 years £m	Over 5 years £m
Bank borrowings	11.5	21.9	54.2	188.4	192.6	642.0
Trade and other payables	103.6	41.1	154.2	50.2	–	–
At 31 December 2007						
Bank borrowings	11.7	8.7	21.2	164.1	74.3	219.6
Trade and other payables	31.2	25.2	27.9	5.0	–	–

FRS 29 p39(a)
AppxB15

The table below analyses the group's derivative financial instruments that will be settled on a gross basis into relevant maturity groupings based on the remaining period at the balance sheet to the contractual maturity date. The amounts disclosed in the table are the contractual undiscounted cash flows. Balances due within 12 months equal their carrying balances, as the impact of discounting is not significant.

At 31 December 2008	Less than 1 month £m	Between 1 and 3 months £m	Between 3 and 12 months £m	Between 1 and 2 years £m	Between 2 and 5 years £m	Over 5 Years £m
Forward foreign exchange contracts – Cash flow hedges:						
– Outflow	940.1	836.7	1,082.7	–	–	–
– Inflow	942.3	835.2	1,086.4	–	–	–
At 31 December 2007						
Forward foreign exchange contracts – Cash flow hedges:						
– Outflow	287.1	321.4	198.2	–	–	–
– Inflow	287.2	323.2	195.2	–	–	–

(d) Cash flow and fair value interest rate risk

FRS 29 p33(a)

As the group has no significant interest-bearing assets, the group's income and operating cash flows are substantially independent of changes in market interest rates.

FRS 29 p33(a)(b)
FRS 29 p22(c)

The group's interest rate risk arises from long-term borrowings. Borrowings issued at variable rates expose the group to cash flow interest rate risk. Borrowings issued at fixed rates expose the group to fair value interest rate risk. Group policy is to maintain approximately 60% of its borrowings in fixed rate instruments. During 2008 and 2007, the group's borrowings at variable rate were denominated in the pound and the euro.

FRS 29 p22(b)(c)

The group analyses its interest rate exposure on a dynamic basis. Various scenarios are simulated taking into consideration refinancing, renewal of existing positions, alternative financing and hedging. Based on these scenarios, the group calculates the impact on profit and loss of a defined interest rate shift. For each simulation, the same interest rate shift is used for all currencies. The scenarios are run only for liabilities that represent the major interest bearing positions.

FRS 29 p22(b)(c)

Based on the simulations performed, the impact on profit or loss of a 10 basis point shift would be a maximum increase of £41,000 (2007: £37,000) or decrease of £34,000 (2007: £29,000), respectively. The simulation is done on a quarterly basis to verify that the maximum loss potential is within the limit given by the management.

FRS 29 p22(b)(c)

Based on the various scenarios, the group manages its cash flow interest rate risk by using floating-to-fixed interest rate swaps. Such interest rate swaps have the economic effect of

GAAP UK plc 23

converting borrowings from floating rates to fixed rates. Generally, the group raises long-term borrowings at floating rates and swaps them into fixed rates that are lower than those available if the group borrowed at fixed rates directly. Under the interest rate swaps, the group agrees with other parties to exchange, at specified intervals (primarily quarterly), the difference between fixed contract rates and floating-rate interest amounts calculated by reference to the agreed notional amounts.

FRS 29 p40
IG36

Occasionally the group also enters into fixed-to-floating interest rate swaps to hedge the fair value interest rate risk arising where it has borrowed at fixed rates in excess of the 60% target.

At 31 December 2008, if interest rates on pound-denominated borrowings at that date had been 10 basis points higher/lower with all other variables held constant, post-tax profit for the year would have been £22,000 (2007: £21,000) lower/higher, mainly as a result of higher/lower interest expense on floating rate borrowings; equity would have been £5,000 (2007: £3,000) lower/higher mainly as a result of a decrease/increase in the fair value of fixed rate financial assets classified as available for sale. At 31 December 2008, if interest rates on UK pound-denominated borrowings at that date had been 50 basis points higher/lower with all other variables held constant, post-tax profit for the year would have been £57,000 (2007: £38,000) lower/higher, mainly as a result of higher/lower interest expense on floating rate borrowings; equity would have been £6,000 (2007: £4,000) lower/higher mainly as a result of a decrease/increase in the fair value of fixed rate financial assets classified as available for sale.

1p124(a)(b) IG5 **Capital risk management**

The group's objectives when managing capital are to safeguard the group's ability to continue as a going concern in order to provide returns for shareholders and benefits for other stakeholders and to maintain an optimal capital structure to reduce the cost of capital.

In order to maintain or adjust the capital structure, the group may adjust the amount of dividends paid to shareholders, return capital to shareholders, issue new shares or sell assets to reduce debt.

Consistent with others in the industry, the group monitors capital on the basis of the gearing ratio. This ratio is calculated as net debt divided by total capital. Net debt is calculated as total borrowings (including borrowings and trade and other payables, as shown in the consolidated balance sheet) less cash and cash equivalents. Total capital is calculated as equity, as shown in the consolidated balance sheet, plus net debt.

During 2008, the group's strategy, which was unchanged from 2007, was to maintain a gearing ratio over 40% and a BB credit rating. The gearing ratios at 31 December 2008 and at 31 December 2007 were as follows:

	2008 £m	2007 £m
Total borrowings	908.7	459.6
Less: cash at banks and in hand	(74.8)	(40.5)
Net debt	833.9	419.1
Total equity	1,055.6	167.8
Total capital	1,889.5	586.9
Gearing ratio	**44%**	71%

The decrease in the gearing ratio during 2008 resulted primarily from the issue of shares for the acquisition of Newsub (see note 34).

Fair value estimation

FRS 29 p27

The fair value of financial instruments traded in active markets (such as trading and available-for-sale securities) is based on quoted market prices at the balance sheet date. The quoted market price used for financial assets held by the group is the current bid price.

FRS 29 p29(a)
FRS 29 p27(a)

The fair value of financial instruments that are not traded in an active market (for example, over-the-counter derivatives) is determined by using valuation techniques. The group uses a variety of methods and makes assumptions that are based on market conditions existing at each balance sheet date. Quoted market prices or dealer quotes for similar instruments are used for long-term debt. Other techniques, such as estimated discounted cash flows, are used to determine fair value for the remaining financial instruments. The fair value of interest rate swaps

GAAP UK plc 24

is calculated as the present value of the estimated future cash flows. The fair value of forward foreign exchange contracts is determined using quoted forward exchange rates at the balance sheet date.

The carrying value less impairment provision of trade receivables and payables are assumed to approximate their fair values. The fair value of financial liabilities for disclosure purposes is estimated by discounting the future contractual cash flows at the current market interest rate that is available to the group for similar financial instruments.

GAAP UK plc   25

Notes to the financial statements

Notes to the financial statements for the year ended 31 December 2008

SSAP 25 p35-48 **1 Group segmental reporting**

		Turnover		Profit before tax	
		2008	2007	**2008**	2007 (c)
		£m	£m	**£m**	£m
4 Sch 55(2)	**Geographical analysis**				
	UK	**576.9**	207.2	**34.6**	39.7
	Continental Europe				
FRS 9 p21, 27	– Group	**243.1**	98.8	**28.8**	28.8
SSAP 25 p36	– Joint ventures (a)	**38.9**	9.9	**2.8**	1.2
	North America	**344.7**	91.6	**11.0**	10.4
	Asia Pacific and Africa	**96.2**	78.3	**31.8**	24.5
		1,299.8	485.8	**109.0**	104.6
	Profit on sale of subsidiary – UK			**6.3**	–
SSAP 25 p34	Net finance (cost)/income			**(6.6)**	7.6
	Total				
	– Group (b)	**1,260.9**	475.9	**105.2**	111.0
FRS 9 p21, 27	**– Joint ventures**	**38.9**	9.9	**3.5**	1.2
		1,299.8	485.8	**108.7**	112.2
4 Sch 55(1)(a)	**Business analysis**				
	Food products	**404.4**	175.1	**38.8**	37.7
	Personnel services	**125.7**	3.3	**(15.4)**	0.3
	Retail services	**113.8**	113.3	**35.8**	36.2
	Distribution services				
FRS 9 p21	– Group	**259.3**	11.9	**15.9**	4.6
SSAP 25 p36	– Joint ventures (a)	**38.9**	9.9	**2.8**	1.2
	Property services	**154.3**	84.9	**18.8**	18.0
	Healthcare	**203.4**	87.4	**12.3**	6.6
		1,299.8	485.8	**109.0**	104.6

SSAP 25 p34   Analyses by business are based on the group's management structure. Turnover between segments is immaterial. Geographical analysis is based on the country in which the order is received. It would not be materially different if based on the country in which the customer is located

SSAP 25 p36   *Notes:*
(a) The group's share of the profit before taxation and net assets of its joint ventures and associates, should be separately disclosed on a segmental basis if any exceed 20% of the relevant total.
(b) Where non-statutory profit measures are shown, the statutory profit measure should be also shown.
(c) There was no goodwill amortisation in 2007 as the group has until 2008 made no acquisitions in the years following the adoption of FRS 10 where advantage was taken of the transitional provisions in not reinstating previous goodwill eliminated against reserves.

GAAP UK plc   26

	Net assets	2008 £m	2007 £m
SSAP 25 p34(c)	**Geographical analysis**		
	UK	**465.3**	77.1
	Continental Europe		
FRS 9 p21, 27,	– Group	**354.0**	34.5
SSAP 25 p26	– Joint ventures	**16.5**	1.8
	North America	**505.7**	17.0
	Asia Pacific and Africa	**29.9**	20.2
		1,371.4	150.6
SSAP 25 p37	Central	**518.1**	439.3
	Net debt excluding liquid resources (note 32)	**(833.9)**	(422.1)
	Total		
FRS 9 p21, 27	**– Group**	**1,039.1**	166.0
	– Joint ventures	**16.5**	1.8
		1,055.6	167.8
SSAP 25 p34(c)	**Business analysis**		
	Food products	**199.2**	62.2
	Personnel service	**644.7**	0.1
	Retail services	**16.0**	33.2
	Distribution services		
FRS 9 p21	– Group	**420.1**	46.1
SSAP 25 p26	– Joint ventures	**16.5**	1.8
	Property services	**37.3**	10.1
	Healthcare	**37.6**	(2.9)
		1,371.4	150.6
SSAP 25 p37	Central	**518.1**	439.3
	Net debt excluding liquid resources (note 32)	**(833.9)**	(422.1)
	Total		
	– Group	**1,039.1**	166.0
	– Joint ventures	**16.5**	1.8
		1,055.6	167.8

SSAP 25 p37 Central net assets comprise assets, partially offset by liabilities, that cannot practicably be divided between the segments. These liabilities and assets are:

	2008 £m	2007 £m
AFS investment	**539.0**	410.0
Other central current assets	**39.3**	68.7
Corporation tax payable	**(60.2)**	(29.4)
	518.1	439.3

GAAP UK plc   27

FRS 3 p15,53   The above business analyses of turnover, profit before tax and net assets in 2008 includes
FRS 6 p28   contributions from Newsub plc:

Geographical analysis

	Turnover £m	Profit £m	Net operating assets £m
UK	300.6	12.7	57.2
Continental Europe			
– Group	120.2	5.6	24.8
– Joint ventures	29.8	1.1	6.6
North America	234.0	4.7	20.1
Asia Pacific and Africa	5.2	0.3	21.7
	689.8	24.4	130.4
Net interest (including £0.7m in joint ventures)	–	(17.4)	–
Total			
– Group	660.0	7.3	123.8
– Joint ventures	29.8	1.5	6.6

Business analysis

	Turnover £m	Profit £m	Net operating assets £m
Food products	214.7	14.0	31.1
Personnel services	121.7	(8.4)	18.1
Distribution services			
– Group	190.9	10.1	75.4
– Joint ventures	29.8	2.2	6.6
Property services	66.9	(0.7)	0.4
Healthcare	65.8	7.2	(1.2)
	689.8	24.4	130.4
Net interest (including £0.7m in joint ventures)		(17.4)	
Total			
– Group	660.0	7.3	123.8
– Joint ventures	29.8	1.5	6.6

FRS 3 p53   The segmental analysis of turnover, profit before tax and net assets for the UK and Food
              Products includes £25.6m (2007: £117.0m) turnover, £2.2m (2007: £6.2m) profit before tax and
              £5.3m of net assets at 31 December 2007 in respect of H Limited which was sold during the year.

GAAP UK plc

2 Cost of sales, gross profit, distribution costs and administrative expenses

		Continuing £m	Acquisitions £m	Discontinued £m	2008 Total £m	Continuing £m	Discontinued £m	2007 Total £m
FRS 3 p14	Turnover	523.7	711.6	25.6	**1,260.9**	358.9	117.0	475.9
	Cost of sales	408.4	613.5	(18.3)	**(1,040.2)**	(259.5)	(82.9)	(342.4)
	Exceptional cost of sales	–	3.5	–	**(3.5)**	–	–	–
FRS 10 App 1 p16	Goodwill amortisation	–	40.2	–	**(40.2)**	–	–	–
	Total cost of sales	408.4	657.2	(18.3)	**(1,083.9)**	(259.5)	(82.9)	(342.4)
	Gross profit	115.3	54.4	7.3	**177.0**	99.4	34.1	133.5
4 Sch 8	Distribution costs	9.1	4.7	–	**13.8**	–	–	–
4 Sch 8	Administrative expenses	26.5	18.8	5.1	**50.4**	25.1	7.0	32.1
FRS 6 p31	Exceptional acquisition reorganisation costs	–	9.1	–	**9.1**	–	–	–
4 Sch 8	Total administrative expenses	35.6	32.6	5.1	**73.3**	25.1	7.0	32.1
4 Sch 8	Less: other operating income – Royalties	(2.5)	–	–	**(2.5)**	(2.0)	–	(2.0)
	Net operating expenses	33.1	32.6	5.1	**70.8**	23.1	7.0	30.1
	Group operating profit	82.2	21.8	2.2	**106.2**	76.3	27.1	103.4

GAAP UK plc 29

3(a) Interest and similar items

		2008 £m	2007 £m
4 Sch 53(2)(a)	Interest payable on bank loans and overdrafts	(16.4)	(1.3)
	Amortisation of issue costs of bank loan	(1.1)	–
4 Sch 53(2)(b)	Interest payable on other loans	(5.2)	(0.1)
SSAP 21 p53	Interest payable on finance leases	(1.2)	–
	Preference share dividends paid: 7p per £1 share	(0.1)	–
	Group interest and similar charges payable	(24.0)	(1.4)
FRS 9 p21	Share of joint venture interest payable	(0.5)	–
	Total interest and similar charges payable	(24.5)	(1.4)
4 Sch 8	Group interest receivable	12.7	5.0
FRS 9 p21, 27	Share of joint venture interest receivable	1.2	–
4 Sch 8, FRS 29 p20(b)	Total interest receivable	13.9	5.0
	Net interest (payable)/receivable and similar items	(10.6)	3.6

4 Sch 26(3)(b), FRS 15 p31 *Note: If the group capitalises interest or other finance cost into assets, the total finance cost for the year should be shown in the above table and the amount capitalised shown as a deduction in arriving at the net amount shown on the face of the profit and loss account. In addition the rate of capitalisation should be given.*

3(b) Other finance income

		2008 £m	2007 £m
FRS 12 p48	Unwinding of discounts in provisions (note 22)	(0.4)	–
FRS 17 App(ii) p6	Other finance income (note 36)	4.4	4.0
		4.0	4.0

4 Profit on ordinary activities before taxation

		2008 £m	2007 £m
	Profit before taxation is stated after charging/(crediting):		
4 Sch 8	Staff costs (note 35)	626.9	237.0
FRS 15 p100	Depreciation of tangible fixed assets		
	– Owned assets	68.5	22.9
SSAP 21 p50	– Under finance leases	2.6	–
	Amortisation of goodwill		
FRS 10 p53	– Subsidiaries	40.2	–
FRS 9 p27	– Joint ventures	0.9	–
FRS 3 p19	Loss/(profit) on disposal of fixed assets	6.6	(1.3)
SSAP 21 p55	Hire of machinery and equipment	12.2	1.2
SSAP 21 p55	Other operating lease rentals	5.2	5.6
FRS 29 p20(e)	Trade debtors impairment	21.8	18.4
FRS 3 p19	Costs of product remediation (see below)	3.5	–
FRS 6 p31, 4 Sch 57(3), FRS 3 p19	Costs incurred in reorganising acquired businesses (see below)	9.1	–
FRS 23 p 52(a)	Net exchange differences on foreign currency borrowings less deposits	5.4	2.3
4 Sch 45A(2)(i)	Net fair value gains on open forward foreign exchange contracts	4.1	–

2033

GAAP UK plc 30

Tech 06/06 **Services provided by the company's auditor and its associates**

SI 2005/2417 During the year the group (including its overseas subsidiaries) obtained the following services from the company's auditor and its associates:

	2008 £m	2007 £m
Fees payable to company auditor for the audit of parent company and consolidated accounts	0.7	0.6
Fees payable to the company's auditor and its associates for other services:		
The audit of company's subsidiaries pursuant to legislation	0.9	0.5
Other services pursuant to legislation	0.3	–
Tax services	0.1	0.1
	2.0	1.2

	2008 £m	2007 £m
Fees in respect of the GAAP UK plc pension scheme:		
Audit	0.2	0.2
Other services pursuant to legislation	0.1	–
	0.3	0.2

Exceptional items

4 Sch 57(3)
FRS 3 p19
During the year, a few batches of one of the group's food products were found to have been contaminated with small pieces of glass. As a precaution the group recalled all batches of this product made within six weeks of the contamination being discovered. The exceptional charge to cost of sales represents the cost of correcting the defective machinery, replacing the withdrawn product and meeting product liability claims.

FRS 3 p46
FRS 6 p31
The costs of £9.1m incurred in reorganising the businesses of Newsub plc arise from the integration and streamlining of the food products and health care divisions within the group's existing businesses. These costs relate to the project identified and controlled by management as part of the integration programme set up at the time of Newsub plc's acquisition.

5 Profit on sale of subsidiary

Discontinued operations	2008 £m	2007 £m
Gain on disposal of subsidiary net tangible assets (note 34c)	10.2	–
FRS 10 p71(c)(ii) Goodwill previously eliminated against reserves (note 34c)	(3.9)	–
FRS 3 p20 **Profit on sale of subsidiary**	6.3	–
4 Sch 54(2) FRS 3 p20 **Taxation**	0.7	–

FRS 3 p24
4 Sch 57(3)
On 1 December 2008, the group sold H Limited, a wholly-owned subsidiary, for £15.7m in cash. The consideration is due to be received in March 2009. H Limited was the group's only poultry product manufacturing operation and the disposal completed the exit from these activities. As a result of the material change in the nature and focus of the group's operations that this disposal represented, it has been treated as a discontinued operation in the profit and loss account.

6 Tax on profit on ordinary activities

Analysis of charge in period

		2008 £m	2007 £m
	Current tax		
4 Sch 54(3)	**United Kingdom**		
FRS 16 p17(a)	Corporation tax at 28.5% (2007: 30%)	**20.2**	31.5
FRS 16 p17	Double tax relief	**(0.9)**	(13.1)
		19.3	18.4
	Foreign tax		
FRS 16 p17(b)	Corporation taxes	**22.8**	18.5
	Other current tax		
FRS 16 p17	Adjustment in respect of prior period tax charge	**1.6**	5.3
FRS 9 p21	Share of joint ventures	**1.9**	0.8
	Total current tax	**45.6**	43.0
	Deferred tax		
FRS 19 p60(a)(i)	Origination and reversal of timing differences:		
	– UK	**18.1**	3.0
	– Foreign tax	**19.1**	3.3
	Impact of change in UK tax rate	–	(0.5)
FRS 19 p60	Total deferred tax	**37.2**	5.8
	Tax on profit on ordinary activities	**82.8**	48.8

FRS 16 p17 **Tax on recognised gains and losses not included in the profit and loss account (note 27)**

	2008 £m	2007 £m
UK corporation tax at 28.5% (2007: 30%)		
Current tax credit allocated to actuarial losses	**3.6**	–
Current tax credit/(charge) on exchange movements offset in reserves	**3.5**	2.8
Impact of change in tax rate on deferred tax relating to pension scheme	–	0.7
Other deferred tax movement relating to pension scheme	**2.8**	(0.8)
	9.9	2.7

FRS 19 p64(a) The tax for the period is higher (2007: higher) than the standard effective rate of corporation tax in the UK for the year ended 31 December 2008 of 28.5% (2007: 30%). The differences are explained below:

	2008 £m	2007 £m
Profit on ordinary activities before tax	**108.7**	112.2
Profit on ordinary activities multiplied by standard rate of corporation tax in the UK of 28.5% (2007: 30%)	**31.0**	33.7
Effects of:		
Adjustments to tax charge in respect of prior periods	**1.6**	5.3
Adjustment in respect of foreign tax rates	**6.4**	5.9
Pension cost charge in excess of pension cost relief	–	1.3
Capital allowances in excess of depreciation	**(40.4)**	(4.8)
Other short-term timing differences	**3.2**	(2.3)
Expenses not deductible for tax purposes	**43.8**	3.9
Total current tax	**45.6**	43.0

Factors that may affect future tax charges:

The standard rate of corporation tax in the UK changed from 30% to 28% with effect from 1 April 2008. Accordingly, the company's profits for this accounting period are taxed at an effective rate of 28.5% and will be taxed at 28% in the future.

GAAP UK plc   32

Based on current capital investment plans, the group expects to continue to be able to claim capital allowances in excess of depreciation in future years at a similar level to the current year.

7 Profits of holding company

s 230(1)(b),(4) Of the profit for the financial year, a profit of £9.2m (2007: profit of £11.9m) is dealt with in the accounts of GAAP UK plc. The directors have taken advantage of the exemption available under section 230 of the Companies Act 1985 and not presented a profit and loss account for the company alone.

8 Dividends

	2008 £m	2007 £m
Equity – Ordinary		
Final paid: 1.54p (2007: 1.17p) per 1p share	**13.4**	10.3
Interim paid: 1.17p (2007: 0.62p) per 1p share	**10.3**	5.4
	23.7	15.7

FRS 21 p12, 13 In addition, the directors are proposing a final dividend in respect of the financial year ending 31 December 2008 of 1.81p per share which will absorb an estimated £24.8m of shareholders' funds. It will be paid on 1 June 2009 to shareholders who are on the register of members at 12 May 2008.

UITF 38 p10(f) Dividends amounting to £491,700 (2007: £356,400) in respect of the company's shares held by an employee share trust have been deducted in arriving at the aggregate of dividends paid.

UITF 38 p10(f) *Note: The deduction of dividends received on own shares held in an ESOP trust should be disclosed on the face of the profit and loss account where the amount is material.*

9 Earnings per share

FRS 22 p10
FRS 22 p20 Basic earnings per share is calculated by dividing the earnings attributable to ordinary shareholders by the weighted average number of ordinary shares outstanding during the year, excluding those held in the employee share trust (note 27), which are treated as cancelled.

FRS 22 p31 For diluted earnings per share, the weighted average number of ordinary shares in issue is adjusted to assume conversion of all dilutive potential ordinary shares. The group has two classes of dilutive potential ordinary shares: those share options granted to employees where the exercise price is less than the average market price of the company's ordinary shares during the year, and the contingently issuable shares under the group's long-term incentive plan. At 31 December 2008, the performance criteria for the vesting of the awards under the incentive scheme had not been met and consequently the shares in question are excluded from the diluted EPS calculation.

FRS 22 p70(a)
FRS 22 p70(b) Reconciliations of the earnings and weighted average number of shares used in the calculations are set out below.

	2008 Number of shares (millions)	2007 Number of shares (millions)
FRS 22 p70(b) Weighted average ordinary shares in issue	**1,137.8**	881.6
FRS 22 p70(b) Options	**5.0**	17.2
FRS 22 p70(b) Diluted number of shares	**1,142.8**	898.8

GAAP UK plc

33

	Continuing	**2008** **Discontinued**	**Total**	Continuing	2007 Discontinued	Total
FRS 22 p70(a) **Earnings (£m)**	**17.6**	**7.8**	**25.4**	58.2	5.0	63.2
Earnings per share						
– Basic (p)	**1.55**	**0.68**	**2.23**	6.6	0.57	7.17
– Diluted (p)	**1.54**	**0.68**	**2.22**	6.48	0.55	7.03

10 Intangible fixed assets

		Goodwill £m
4 Sch 8	**Group**	
4 Sch 42(1)	**Cost**	
FRS 10 p53(a)	At 1 January 2008	–
FRS 10 p53(c)	Additions (note 34)	1,151.5
	Exchange adjustments	(32.6)
FRS 10 p53(a)	**At 31 December 2008**	**1,118.9**
4 Sch 42(3)	**Accumulated amortisation**	
FRS 10 p53(b)	At 1 January 2008	–
FRS 10 p53(c)	Charge for the year	40.2
FRS 10 p53(b)	**At 31 December 2008**	**40.2**
FRS 10 p53(d)	**Net book amount at 31 December 2008**	**1,078.7**
FRS 10 p53(d)	Net book amount at 31 December 2007	–

11 Tangible fixed assets

	Group	**Land and buildings short leasehold £m**	**Land and buildings freehold and long leasehold £m**	**Fit-out, plant and equipment £m**	**Vehicles and office equipment £m**	**Total £m**
4 Sch 8						
4 Sch 42(3)	**Cost or valuation**					
FRS 15 p100(e)	At 1 January 2008	–	20.7	85.2	77.2	183.1
FRS 15 p100(g)	Exchange adjustments	–	(3.2)	(14.7)	(9.3)	(27.2)
	Additions at cost	1.2	10.9	54.3	30.4	96.8
	Acquisitions	4.2	64.7	181.6	61.9	312.4
	Surplus on revaluation	–	3.1	–	–	3.1
	Disposals	–	(0.2)	(27.5)	(24.8)	(52.5)
FRS 15 p100(e)	**At 31 December 2008**	**5.4**	**96.0**	**278.9**	**135.4**	**515.7**

GAAP UK plc

	Land and buildings short leasehold £m	Land and buildings freehold and long leasehold £m	Fit-out, plant and equipment £m	Vehicles and office equipment £m	Total £m
4 Sch 42(1) **Accumulated depreciation**					
FRS 15 p100(f) At 1 January 2008	–	2.4	52.8	36.6	91.8
FRS 15 p100(g) Exchange adjustments	–	(0.3)	(5.5)	(4.2)	(10.0)
FRS 15 p100(c) Charge for the year	2.0	4.4	39.5	25.2	71.1
Revaluation	–	(2.3)	–	–	(2.3)
Disposals	–	(0.2)	(24.6)	(16.9)	(41.7)
FRS 15 p100(f) **At 31 December 2008**	**2.0**	**4.0**	**62.2**	**40.7**	**108.9**
FRS 15 p100(g) **Net book amount at 31 December 2008**	**3.4**	**92.0**	**216.7**	**94.7**	**406.8**
FRS 15 p100(g) Net book amount at 31 December 2007	–	18.3	32.4	40.6	91.3

SSAP 21 p49,50   Assets held under finance leases, capitalised and included in tangible fixed assets:

	2008 £m	2007 £m
Cost	**21.2**	–
Accumulated depreciation	**(2.6)**	–
Net book amount	**18.6**	–

4 Sch 26(3)(b)
FRS 15 p31(b),
(c), (e)

Note: If the group capitalises finance costs directly attributable to tangible fixed assets, the amount added in the year and the cumulative total of such interest included at the balance sheet date should be disclosed. In addition, disclosure of the rate of capitalisation is required.

GAAP UK plc

	Land and buildings short leasehold £m	Land and buildings freehold and long leasehold £m	Total £m
Company			

4 Sch 42(1)	**Cost or valuation**			
FRS 15 p100(e)	At 1 January 2008	–	10.9	10.9
FRS 15 p100(g)	Additions at cost	0.1	0.6	0.7
	Surplus on revaluation	–	1.1	1.1
	Disposals	–	(0.3)	(0.3)
FRS 15 p100(e)	**At 31 December 2008**	**0.1**	**12.3**	**12.4**
4 Sch 42(3)	**Accumulated depreciation**			
FRS 15 p100(f)	At 1 January 2008	–	1.2	1.2
FRS 15 p100(g)	Charge for year	–	0.3	0.3
	Revaluation	–	(0.4)	(0.4)
	Disposals	–	(0.2)	(0.2)
FRS 15 p100(f)	**At 31 December 2008**	–	**0.9**	**0.9**
FRS 15 p100(g)	**Net book amount at 31 December 2008**	**0.1**	**11.4**	**11.5**
FRS 15 p100(g)	Net book amount at 31 December 2007	–	9.7	9.7

4 Sch 33(2)
4 Sch 43(a),
FRS 15
p74(a)(ii)(iii)

The group's freehold properties and long leasehold properties were revalued at 30 November 2008, on the basis of existing use value by independent qualified valuers. The valuations were undertaken in accordance with the Appraisal and Valuation Manual of the Royal Institution of Chartered Surveyors in the United Kingdom by Surveyor & Son, a firm of independent Chartered Surveyors and overseas by valuers having equivalent professional qualifications.

FRS 15 p74(a)(i), (v)

FRS 15 p74(a)(i) These valuations have been incorporated into the financial statements and the resulting revaluation adjustments have been taken to the revaluation reserve. The revaluations during the year ended 31 December 2008 resulted in a revaluation surplus of £5.4m (note 26).

FRS 19 p15 No deferred tax is provided on timing differences arising from the revaluation of fixed assets unless, by the balance sheet date, a binding commitment to sell the asset has been entered into and it is unlikely that any gain will be rolled over.

		Group		Company	
		2008 £m	2007 £m	2008 £m	2007 £m
4 Sch 44	**Analysis of net book value of land and buildings – freehold and long leasehold**				
	Freehold	**87.1**	18.3	**10.8**	9.7
4 Sch 83	Leasehold: (over 50 years unexpired)	**4.9**	–	**0.6**	–
		92.0	18.3	**11.4**	9.7

If the revalued assets were stated on the historical cost basis, the amounts would be:

Freehold and long leasehold land and buildings

		Group		Company	
		2008 £m	2007 £m	2008 £m	2007 £m
	At cost	**88.8**	17.1	**10.5**	9.1
	Aggregate depreciation	**(4.3)**	(1.3)	**(0.5)**	(0.2)
4 Sch 33(3),(4), FRS 15 p74(a)(iv)	Net book value based on historical cost	**84.5**	15.8	**10.0**	8.9

GAAP UK plc

4 Sch 8, FRS 29
p29(b), 4 Sch 42(1)

12 Investments in subsidiaries and joint ventures

	Group 2008 £m	2007 £m	Company 2008 £m	2007 £m
Shares in group undertakings				
At 1 January	–	–	98.5	95.0
Additions in year	–	–	320.7	3.5
At 31 December	**–**	**–**	**419.2**	**98.5**

4A Sch 21(2) **Interests in joint ventures**

	Group 2008 £m	2007 £m	Company 2008 £m	2007 £m
At 1 January				
(FRS 9 p29) – Net assets	**1.8**	1.5	–	–
– Goodwill	–	–	–	–
	1.8	1.5	–	–
Exchange adjustments	**(0.9)**	(0.1)	–	–
Additions				
– Net assets	**5.5**	–	–	–
– Goodwill	**8.5**	–	–	–
Share of profits retained	**2.5**	0.4	–	–
At 31 December				
(FRS 9 p29) **– Net assets**	**8.9**	1.8	–	–
– Goodwill	**8.5**	–	–	–
	17.4	1.8	–	–
Accumulated amortisation of goodwill				
At 1 January	–	–	–	–
Charge for the year	**(0.9)**	–	–	–
At 31 December	**(0.9)**	–	–	–
Net book amount at 31 December				
– Net assets	**8.9**	1.8	–	–
(FRS 9 p29) – Goodwill	**7.6**	–	–	–
Total fixed asset investments	**16.5**	1.8	419.2	98.5

FRS 9 p57,58   *Note: Further disclosures are required for associates and joint ventures if the 15% and/or 25% thresholds are exceeded.*

s 231(5),(6)   Investments in group undertakings are stated at cost. As permitted by section 133 of the Companies Act 1985, where the relief afforded under section 131 of the Companies Act 1985 applies, cost is the aggregate of the nominal value of the relevant number of the company's shares and the fair value of any other consideration given to acquire the share capital of the subsidiary undertakings. The directors consider that to give full particulars of all subsidiary undertakings would lead to a statement of excessive length. A list of principal subsidiary undertakings and joint ventures is given on page xx. A full list of subsidiary undertakings and joint ventures, at 31 December 2008, will be annexed to the company's next annual return.

FRS 10 p55   The goodwill arising on the joint ventures acquired with Newsub plc is being amortised on a straight-line basis over five years. This is the period over which the directors estimate that values of the underlying businesses are expected to exceed the values of the underlying assets.

GAAP UK plc

4 Sch 8	**13 Stock**				

		Group		Company	
		2008 £m	2007 £m	**2008** £m	2007 £m
	Stock and work in progress				
	Raw materials	**6.1**	4.3	–	–
SSAP 9 p27	Work in progress	**3.0**	0.8	–	–
4 Sch 8	Finished products	**24.7**	11.9	–	–
		33.8	17.0	–	–

4 Sch 27(3),(4) *Note: If there is a material difference between the balance sheet amount of stock and its replacement cost, the latter amount should be disclosed.*

FRS 29 p6 **14 Financial instruments by category**

The accounting policies for financial instruments on pages 16 to 17 have been applied to the line items below:

Group	Loans and receivables £m	Assets at fair value through profit and loss £m	Derivatives used for hedging £m	Available for sale £m	Total £m
Assets at 31 December 2008					
Available-for-sale investments	–	–	–	523.1	523.1
Derivative financial instruments	–	4.9	15.8	–	20.7
Current asset investments	25.3	–	–	–	25.3
Debtors	290.6	–	–	–	290.6
Cash at bank and in hand	74.8	–	–	–	74.8
	390.7	**4.9**	**15.8**	**523.1**	**934.5**
Assets at 31 December 2007					
Available-for-sale investments	–	–	–	410.0	410.0
Derivative financial instruments	–	3.1	4.0	–	7.1
Current asset investments	55.3	–	–	–	55.3
Debtors	109.6	–	–	–	109.6
Cash at bank and in hand	40.5	–	–	–	40.5
	205.4	**3.1**	**4.0**	**410.0**	**622.5**

GAAP UK plc   38

Group	Liabilities at fair value through profit and loss £m	Derivatives used for hedging £m	Other financial liabilities £m	Total £m
Liabilities at 31 December 2008				
Borrowings	–	–	908.7	908.7
Derivative financial instruments	13.6	2.2	–	15.8
	13.6	**2.2**	**908.7**	**924.5**
Liabilities at 31 December 2007				
Borrowings	–	–	459.6	459.6
Derivative financial instruments	13.8	3.3	–	17.1
	13.8	**3.3**	**459.6**	**476.7**

Company
All financial assets of the company were categorised as loans and receivables at both 31 December 2008 and 31 December 2007. All financial liabilities of the company were categorised as other financial liabilities at both 31 December 2008 and 31 December 2007.

4 Sch 8, FRS 29 p29(b)
15 Current asset investments

	Group 2008 £m	2007 £m	Company 2008 £m	2007 £m
Short-term deposits	**25.3**	55.3	–	48.7

FRS 29 p6
Short-term deposits are with major UK banks. The credit risk associated with these investments is considered to be low.

FRS 29p8(d), 25
16 Available-for-sale investments

	Group 2008 £m	2007 £m	Company 2008 £m	2007 £m
At 1 January	**410.0**	12.8	–	–
Exchange differences (note 29)	**21.4**	1.2	–	–
Additions	**100.0**	400.0	–	–
Disposals	**(2.0)**	–		
Revaluation surplus/(deficit) transfer to equity (note 29)	**6.3**	(4.0)		
At 31 December	**523.1**	410.0	–	–

4 Sch 34E (against Revaluation surplus row)

FRS 29 p16
There were no impairment provisions on the available-for-sale investments in 2008 or 2007.

GAAP UK plc 39

4 Sch 23-25,
FRS 29p27(b),
31, 34(c) Available-for-sale financial assets include the following:

	2008 £m	2007 £m
Listed securities:		
– Equity securities – UK	396.8	334.9
– Equity securities – Europe	78.4	32.1
– Debentures with fixed interest of 6.5% and maturity date of 12 August 2009*	39.2	21.1
Unlisted securities:		
– Debt securities traded on inactive markets	24.6	11.9
	539.0	400.0

* Effective interest rate was 7.3%

FRS 29 p27(a) The fair values of unlisted securities are based on cash flows discounted using a rate based on the market interest rate and the risk premium specific to the unlisted securities (2008: 6%; 2007: 5.8%).

FRS 29 p36(a) The maximum exposure to credit risk at the reporting date is the fair value of the derivatives assets in the balance sheet.

5 Sch 23-25 *Additional disclosures are required if either the entity owns more than 20% of an investment which is not treated as an associate, joint venture or subsidiary or the investment represents more than 20% of the entity or group net assets, including name, shares held, aggregate capital and reserves and profit for most recent year end.*

4 Sch 33(3),(4) If the revalued assets were stated on the historical cost basis, the amounts would be:

	2008 £m	2007 £m
Listed securities:		
– Equity securities — UK	384.8	334.9
– Equity securities — Europe	58.4	32.1
– Debentures with fixed interest of 6.5% and maturity date of 12 August 2010	35.2	21.1
Unlisted securities:		
– Debt securities	21.6	11.9
	500.0	400.0

4 Sch 8 **17 Debtors**

	Group 2008 £m	Group 2007 £m	Company 2008 £m	Company 2007 £m
Amounts falling due within one year:				
Trade debtors	230.2	100.6	–	–
Less: Provision for impairment of receivables	(8.0)	(7.0)	–	–
	222.2	93.6	–	–
Amounts owed by group undertakings	–	–	67.1	55.4
Amounts owed by joint ventures (*all trading balances*)	1.3	1.5	–	–
Amount due on sale of subsidiary (Note 34(c))	15.7	–	–	–
Other debtors (see below)	39.4	5.8	–	–
Prepayments and accrued income	12.0	8.7	–	–
Dividends due from group undertakings	–	–	1.2	45.6
	290.6	109.6	68.3	101.0

Row labels: FRS 29p36 (Trade debtors); FRS 9 p55 (Amounts owed by joint ventures); 4 Sch 8 Note 6 (Prepayments and accrued income)

GAAP UK plc

FRS 29p25, 29(a)	The carrying amount of debtors is a reasonable approximation to fair value.
4 Sch 8	*Note: The amount falling due after more than one year must be shown separately for each item included within debtors.*
UITF 4 p3	*Debtors due after one year must be disclosed separately on the face of the balance sheet if material to net current assets.*
6 Sch 29(a)(b)	Other debtors at 31 December 2008 include £7,000 in respect of loans to two officers of the company.
6 Sch 22(2)(b) 6 Sch 22(2)(d)	Included in other debtors at 31 December 2008 is a bridging loan to Mr G Wallace, the marketing director. The loan was made prior to his appointment as a director and is unsecured, does not carry interest and is repayable on demand. The loan started and ended the year at £60,000 (2007: £60,000). This was also the maximum amount during the year.
FRS 29 p37(b)	As of 31 December 2008, trade debtors with a carrying value of £10m (2007: £9.2m) were impaired and provided for. The amount of the provision was £8.0m as of 31 December 2008 (2007: £7.0m). The ageing of these debtors is as follows:

	2008 £m	2007 £m
3 to 6 months past due	8.5	7.3
Over 6 months past due	1.5	1.9
	10.0	9.2

FRS 29 p37(b)	The debtors determined as individually impaired were mainly wholesalers, which are in unexpected difficult economic situations and it was assessed that not all of the debtor balance may be recovered.
FRS 29 p37(a) FRS 29 p36	Trade debtors that are less than three months past their due date are not considered impaired. As of 31 December 2008, trade debtors of carrying value of £7.0m (2007: £5.8m) were past their due date but not impaired. These are balances from a number of independent customers and there is no history of defaults for these customers recently. The ageing of the trade debtors, which are past due but not impaired is the following:

	2008 £m	2007 £m
Up to 3 months past due	2.6	2.2
3 to 6 months past due	0.9	0.7
Over 6 months past due	3.5	2.9

FRS 29 p31	Concentration of credit risk with respect to trade receivables is limited due to the group's customer base being large and unrelated. Due to this, management believe there is no further credit risk provision required in excess of normal provision for doubtful receivables.
FRS 29 p36(c))	The credit quality of trade debtors that are neither past due nor impaired is assessed by reference to external credit ratings where available. Where no external credit rating is available, historical information about counterparty default rates is used.

Trade debtors that are neither past due nor impaired are shown by their credit risk below.

	2008 £m	2007 £m
Counterparties with external credit rating:		
A	56.7	20.3
BB	17.0	4.8
BBB	40.9	7.3
	114.6	32.4
Counterparties with no external credit rating:		
New customers (less than 6 months)	23.4	13.9
Existing customers with no defaults in the past	49.5	26.7
Existing customers with some defaults in the past	25.7	12.6
	98.6	53.2
Total neither past due nor impaired	**213.2**	85.6

GAAP UK plc

FRS 29 p36(d)   None of those trade debtors that are neither past due nor impaired have had their terms re-negotiated.

FRS 29 p31, 34(c)   The carrying amounts of the group's debtors are denominated in the following currencies:

	2008 £m	2007 £m
Pounds	210.6	78.7
Euros	19.6	9.7
US dollars	50.4	15.2
Other currencies	10.0	6.0
	290.6	109.6

FRS 29 p16   Movements on the provision for impairment of trade debtors are as follows:

	2008 £m	2007 £m
At 1 January	7.0	6.0
Provision for debtors impairment	22.3	18.6
Debtors written off during the year as uncollectible	(20.8)	(17.4)
Unused amounts reversed	(0.5)	(0.2)
At 31 December	8.0	7.0

FRS 29 p20(e) appears beside "Provision for debtors impairment" row.

FRS 29 p16   The other classes within debtors do not contain impaired assets.

FRS 29 p36(a)   The maximum exposure to credit risk at the reporting date is the fair value of each class of debtor mentioned above. The company does not hold any collateral as security.

4 Sch 8, FRS 29 p8(f)   **18 Creditors – Amounts falling due within one year**

	Group 2008 £m	Group 2007 £m	Company 2008 £m	Company 2007 £m
Bank and other borrowings (note 20)	92.2	41.7	53.4	43.6
Trade creditors	55.7	15.3	–	–
Amounts owed to group undertakings	–	–	45.0	24.7
Amounts owed to joint ventures (all trading balances)	2.4	1.8	–	–
Corporation tax	60.2	29.4	1.4	–
Other tax and social security payable	38.7	20.5	–	–
Other creditors	45.7	7.4	–	–
Derivative financial instruments (note 21)	10.1	(10.7)	–	–
Accruals and deferred income	96.2	9.9	–	–
	401.2	136.7	99.8	68.3

FRS 9 p55 appears beside "Amounts owed to joint ventures" row. 4 Sch 8 Note 9 appears beside "Corporation tax" row. 4 Sch 8 Note 10 appears beside "Other creditors" row. FRS 29 p8(e) appears beside "Derivative financial instruments" row. FRS 12 p11(b) appears beside "Accruals and deferred income" row.

FRS 9 p55   *Note: Amounts owed to (or owing from) an associate or joint venture should be analysed between loans and trading balances, if applicable.*

GAAP UK plc

4 Sch 8

19 Creditors – Amounts falling due after more than one year

	Group 2008 £m	Group 2007 £m	Company 2008 £m	Company 2007 £m
Bank and other borrowings (note 20)	**816.5**	417.9	**240.5**	17.0
Deferred consideration for acquisitions	**0.8**	0.6	–	–
Derivative financial instruments (note 21)	**5.7**	6.4	–	–
Other creditors	**42.5**	3.0	–	–
	865.6	427.9	**240.5**	17.0

FRS 29 p8(e) *(rows: Derivative financial instruments)*

FRS 9 p55 *Note: Amounts owed to (or owing from) an associate or joint venture should be analysed between loans and trading balances, if applicable.*

20 Bank and other borrowings

	Group 2008 £m	Group 2007 £m	Company 2008 £m	Company 2007 £m
Due within one year or on demand:				
Bank loans and overdrafts				
Secured (a)	**21.2**	–	–	–
Unsecured (b)	**66.4**	41.6	**53.4**	43.6
	87.6	41.6	**53.4**	43.6
Unsecured debenture loans due within one year (c)	**1.3**	0.1	–	–
Finance lease obligations	**3.3**	–	–	–
	92.2	41.7	**53.4**	43.6
Due after more than one year				
Bank loans:				
Secured (a)	**0.1**	–	–	–
Unsecured (b)	**738.6**	414.0	**237.5**	14.0
	738.7	414.0	**237.5**	14.0
Debenture loans (d)	**65.0**	–	–	–
Other unsecured loans	–	0.9	–	–
Finance lease obligations	**9.8**	–	–	–
Cumulative preference shares of £1 each 2,000,000 shares	**3.0**	3.0	**3.0**	3.0
	816.5	417.9	**240.5**	17.0
Total borrowings	**908.7**	459.6	**293.9**	60.6

4 Sch 48(4) *(rows: Secured (a))*
4 Sch 48(4) *(rows: Bank loans Secured (a))*
SSAP 21 p51 *(rows: Finance lease obligations)*
4 Sch 48(4) *(Total borrowings / notes below)*

4 Sch 48(4)

(a) The secured bank loans and overdrafts are secured by a fixed charge over the group's freehold property in Exeter and by floating charges over the remaining assets of GAAP UK plc.

(b) Group and company unsecured bank loans are stated net of unamortised issue costs of £4.2m (2007: £nil). The company incurred total issue costs of £5.3m in respect of the five year committed multi-option facility entered into in June 2008 under which amounts have been drawn down to fund the acquisition of Newsub plc. These costs together with the interest expense are allocated to the profit and loss account over the five year term of the facility. Interest is calculated using the effective interest rate method.

(c) Debenture loans represents 6½% unsecured loan stock, which is redeemable at par on 1 July 2011. Debenture loans issued during the year are stated at net proceeds.

(d) The debenture loans represent US$110m 7% bonds due 2010.

GAAP UK plc

4 Sch 48(2)   Bank loans are denominated in a number of currencies and bear interest based on LIBOR or foreign equivalents or government bond rates appropriate to the country in which the borrowing is incurred. In June 2008, as part of the interest rate management strategy the company entered into one interest rate swap (2007: nil) for a notional principal amount of £100m maturing in 2012. Under this swap, the company receives interest on a variable basis and pays interest fixed at a rate of 8.8%.

The group's borrowing limit at 31 December 2008 calculated in accordance with the Articles of Association was £973m (2007: £331m).

FRS 29 p31   The exposure of the group's borrowings to interest rate changes and the contractual repricing dates at the balance sheet are as follows.

	2008 £m	2007 £m
6 months or less	85.1	40.0
6-12 months	3.8	1.7
1-5 years	457.1	62.3
Over 5 years	362.7	355.6
	908.7	459.6

FRS 29 p25   The carrying amounts and fair value of the borrowings due after more than one year are as follows:

	Group carrying amount		Group fair value	
	2008 £m	2007 £m	2008 £m	2007 £m
Bank borrowings	738.7	417.9	730.2	411.7
Preference shares	3.0	–	2.9	–
Debentures and other loans	74.8	–	73.9	–
	816.5	417.9	807.0	411.7

	Company 2008		Company 2007	
	Book value £m	Fair value £m	Book value £m	Fair value £m
Long-term borrowings	(237.5)	(205.6)	(14.0)	(12.6)
Preference shares	(3.0)	(2.9)	(3.0)	(2.9)
	(240.5)	(208.5)	(17.0)	(15.5)

FRS 29 p27(a)   The fair values are based on cash flows discounted using a rate based on the borrowing rate of 7.5% (2007: 7.2%).

FRS 29 p25   The carrying amounts of short-term borrowings approximate their fair value.

FRS 29 p31, 34(c)   The carrying amounts of the group's borrowings are denominated in the following currencies:

	2008 £m	2007 £m
Pounds	762.4	364.8
US dollars	71.3	8.1
Euros	53.4	54.0
Other currencies	21.6	32.7
	908.7	459.6

GAAP UK plc

Borrowing facilities

DV FRS 29
p50(a)

The group has the following undrawn committed borrowing facilities available at 31 December 2008 in respect of which all conditions precedent had been met at that date:

	Floating rate £m	Fixed rate £m	2008 Total £m
Expiring within 1 year	110.5	–	110.5
Expiring between 1 and 2 years	199.1	323.5	522.6
Expiring in more than 2 years	100.0	–	100.0
	409.6	**323.5**	**733.1**

The facilities expiring within one year are annual facilities subject to review at various dates during 2009. The other facilities have been arranged to help finance the proposed expansion of the group's activities into Continental Europe. All these facilities incur commitment fees at market rates.

Where a company has issued convertible debt, that debt should be shown separately from other liabilities. Where such convertible debt is not shown separately on the face of the balance sheet but instead is shown separately in the notes, the relevant caption for liabilities on the face of the balance sheet should state that convertible debt is included.

Preference share capital

Group and company

Authorised, issued and fully paid	Shares	2008 £m
7% cumulative preference shares of £1 each at 1 January	2,000,000	3.0
At 31 December	2,000,000	3.0

FRS 25 p 15
FRS 25 p 18(a)
4 Sch 38(2)

The 7% cumulative preference shares, which do not carry any voting rights, were issued in 2000 at £1.50 per share and are redeemable at £1.50 at the option of the shareholders on 1 June 2011. Shareholders are entitled to receive dividends at 7% per annum on the par value of these shares on a cumulative basis; these dividends are payable on 22 December each year. On winding up, the preference shareholders rank above ordinary shareholders and are entitled to receive £1 per share and any dividends accrued but unpaid in respect of their shares. In the event that dividends on the preference share are in arrears for six months or more, holders of the preference shares become entitled to vote at general meetings of members.

SSAP 21 p 51, 52 The minimum lease payments under finance leases fall due as follows:

	2008 £m	2007 £m
Less than one year	3.3	4.4
Later than one year but not more than two	3.7	2.0
In more than two years but not more than five years	6.1	1.0
	13.1	**7.4**
Future finance charges on finance leases	–	–
Present value of finance lease liabilities	13.1	7.4

SSAP 21 p53 (row: Future finance charges on finance leases)

GAAP UK plc

Maturity of financial liabilities

The maturity profile of the carrying amount of the group's liabilities, at 31 December was as follows:

	Debt £m	Finance leases £m	Other financial liabilities £m	2008 Total £m	2007 Total £m
Less than one year	88.9	3.3	–	**92.2**	41.7
In more than one year but not more than two years	94.0	3.7	–	**97.7**	10.0
In more than two years but not more than five years	347.0	6.1	–	**353.1**	52.3
In more than five years	362.7	–	3.0	**365.7**	355.6
	892.6	13.1	3.0	**908.7**	459.6

Company	2008 £m	2007 £m
Between two and five years	237.5	205.5
In more than five years	3.0	3.0

	2008 £m	2007 £m
Amounts repayable otherwise than by instalment after more than 5 years	250.0	–

21 Derivative financial instruments

	2008		2007	
	Assets £m	Liabilities £m	Assets £m	Liabilities £m
At 31 December				
Interest rate swaps	4.9	(7.9)	3.1	(7.4)
Cross-currency swap – net investment hedge	7.2	–	1.8	–
Forward foreign currency contracts – cash flow hedge	8.6	(2.2)	2.2	(3.3)
Embedded derivative – operating lease renewal option	–	(5.7)	–	(6.4)
	20.7	(15.8)	7.1	(17.1)
Current portion	8.6	(10.1)	2.2	(10.7)
Non Current portion	12.1	(5.7)	4.9	(6.4)

In accordance with FRS 26, 'Financial instruments: Recognition and measurement', GAAP UK plc has reviewed all contracts for embedded derivatives that are required to be separately accounted for if they do not meet certain requirements set out in the standard. In relation to the group head office there is a renewal clause that determines the rent the group will pay from 2008 to 2017 based on a measure of the performance of construction companies as recorded in the London Stock Exchange. This is not cancellable or alterable without the payment of a significant penalty, which the directors believe would not be in the interests of the shareholders to pay. As at 1 January 2008, the fair value of this embedded derivative was a liability of £3.7m. This derivative is fair valued based on discounted future cash flows with gains and losses passing through the profit and loss account as hedge accounting is not available. Amounts recorded in the profit and loss account are shown below:

GAAP UK plc

46

	2008 £m	2007 £m
Gain/(loss) in profit and loss	0.7	(2.7)

FRS 29 p24(b,c)   The ineffective portion recognised in the profit or loss that arose from cash flow hedges was not material in either 2008 or 2007. There was no ineffectiveness to be recorded from net investment in foreign operation hedges.

FRS 29p23(a)
4 Sch 45A
(2)(b)(i)   The net fair value gains at 31 December 2008 on open forward foreign exchange contracts that hedge the foreign currency risk of anticipated future sales are £4.1m (2007: £2.3m). These will be transferred to the income statement when the forecast sales occur over the next four months. There were no derivatives outstanding at the balance sheet date that were designated as fair value hedges.

Interest rate swaps

FRS 29p31   The notional principal amount of the outstanding interest rate swap contracts at 31 December 2008 was £100m (2007: £87m).

FRS 29p23(a),22   At 31 December 2008 the fixed interest rates vary from 3.3% to 8.8% and floating rates are 6.5% (LIBOR plus 275 basis points), 3.9% (US PRIME plus 215 basis points) and 4.5% (EUROBOR plus 200 basis points).

Hedge of net investment in foreign entity

FRS 29p22
4 Sch 34(c)   The group has both dollar- and euro- denominated borrowings which it has designated as a hedge of the net investment in its subsidiaries in the US and France. The fair value of the dollar borrowings at 31 December 2008 was £130.0m (2007: £120m) and the euro borrowings £32.1m (2007: £27.1m)

FRS 29p31   **Fair values of non-derivative financial assets and financial liabilities**

Where market values are not available, fair values of financial assets and financial liabilities have been calculated by discounting expected future cash flows at prevailing interest rates and by applying year end exchange rates. The carrying amounts of short-term borrowings approximate to book value.

GAAP UK plc

4 Sch 8   **22 Provisions for liabilities**

Group	Vacant properties £m	Restructuring £m	Environment £m	Deferred tax £m	Total £m
FRS 12 p89(a), 4 Sch 46(2)(a) At 1 January 2008 as previously reported	5.7	2.7	–	13.8	22.2
FRS 6 p32 On acquisition (note 34)	68.1	3.8	18.3	22.5	112.7
Exchange adjustments	(2.0)	(0.4)	–	–	(2.4)
FRS 12 p89(b) Charged to profit and loss account	–	13.1	–	–	13.1
Utilised in year					
FRS 12 p89(c) – Existing	(0.5)	(15.2)	–	–	(15.7)
FRS 6 p32 – Acquired	(3.8)	(0.7)	–	–	(4.5)
FRS 12 p89(e) Amortisation of discount	0.3	–	0.1	–	0.4
FRS 19 p61 (c), 4 Sch 46(2)(b) Transfer from/to profit and loss account	–	–	–	37.2	37.2
4 Sch 46(2)(a), FRS 12 p89(a) **At 31 December 2008**	**67.8**	**3.3**	**18.4**	**73.5**	**163.0**

Company					
4 Sch 46(2)(a) At 1 January 2008	–	–	–	0.5	0.5
FRS 19 p61(c) Sch 4 46(2)(b) Transfer from/to profit and loss account	–	–	–	(0.4)	(0.4)
At 31 December 2008	**–**	**–**	**–**	**0.1**	**0.1**

Vacant properties

FRS 12 p90(a), (b)
Prior to the acquisition of Newsub plc, the group's vacant leasehold properties comprised the old Food Product's divisional head office in Swindon and a disused warehouse in Cleveland, Ohio. Full provision had been made for the residual lease commitments, together with other outgoings for the remaining period of the leases, which at 31 December 2008 is approximately 12 years. It is not expected that these premises will be sub-let.

FRS 12 p90(b)
With the acquisition of Newsub plc, the group has inherited a substantial number of vacant and partly sub-let leasehold properties arising from the significant downsizing and retrenchment undertaken by Newsub plc in the early part of the decade. The properties are primarily located in London and Bradford in the UK, and Los Angeles in the US. Provision has been made for the residual lease commitments, together with other outgoings, after taking into account existing sub-tenant arrangements. It is not assumed that the properties will be able to be sub-let beyond the periods in the present sub-lease agreements. This has resulted in increasing the provision already made by Newsub plc to bring its provisioning policy in line with the group's and has been reflected as a fair value adjustment. Investigations are still being made as to the extent that there might be other contractual arrangements separate from the sub-lease agreements that enable the sub-lessees to terminate their leases early. Should the investigations prove this to be the case, it may be necessary to increase the amount of the provision. In determining the provision for Newsub plc's properties, the cash flows have been discounted on a pre-tax basis using appropriate government bond rates.

GAAP UK plc

Maturity profile of provisions	2008 £m	2007 £m
Within 1 year	8.4	0.5
Between 1 and 2 years	16.8	1.0
Between 2 and 5 years	13.8	1.0
Over 5 years	28.8	3.2
	67.8	5.7

FRS 12 p90 **Restructuring**

FRS 12 p90(b) The £3.8m provision in 2008 arises in respect of a re-organisation commenced by Newsub plc in November 2007 of its healthcare activities. The restructuring of the healthcare activities involves the loss of 125 jobs at two factories and the closure of the site at Newark, New Jersey. Agreement had been reached in October 2007 with the local union representatives that specified the number of staff involved and quantified the amounts payable to those made redundant and customers and suppliers of the Newark site were informed in early November 2007. The associated impairment charge for the write-down of the property and other fixed assets at the Newark site was recognised in Newsub plc's financial statements for its year ended 31 March 2008, prior to the acquisition. As indicated in note 34, the level of provision at the date of Newsub plc's acquisition was reviewed and considered insufficient to cover the costs envisaged in the plans drawn up by Newsub plc's management. Consequently, an adjustment was made as part of the fair value exercise. The provision is expected to be fully utilised during the first half of 2009.

FRS 12 p90 A group company, UK GAAP Limited, announced on 11 December 2008 a rationalisation of product processes at two of its factories. A provision of £0.1m has been raised in respect of the redundancies that will occur over the next few months.

FRS 12 p90 **Environmental**

As part of the group's normal acquisition review procedures, Environmental Appraisers, Inc of San Francisco have been commissioned to ascertain the extent of land contamination of Newsub plc's operational sites in the US. The interim report received from the appraisers indicates that four sites require remediation to deal with chemical spills that have occurred over the last decade. A provisional estimate of the cost of the remediation has been made as part of the fair value exercise on the acquisition of Newsub plc (note 34). It is expected that the decontamination work will take three years to complete. In determining the provision, the cash flows have been discounted on a pre-tax basis using appropriate US Treasury bill rates.

Deferred tax

	Group 2008 £m	2007 £m	Company 2008 £m	2007 £m
FRS 19 p61 **Provision for deferred tax comprises:**				
Accelerated capital allowances	96.5	10.8	0.1	0.6
Short-term timing differences	(23.0)	3.0	–	(0.1)
Deferred tax provision	73.5	13.8	0.1	0.5
Deferred tax liability on pension asset (note 36)	5.8	8.6	–	–
Provision at end of year including deferred tax on pension asset	79.3	22.4	0.1	0.5

Deferred tax liability relating to pension surplus	2008 £m	2007 £m
1 January	8.6	9.8
Deferred tax charged/(credited) to profit and loss account	–	(1.3)
Deferred tax charged/(credited) to the statement of total recognised gains and losses:		
– on actuarial loss	(2.8)	0.8
– change in tax rate	–	(0.7)
31 December	5.8	8.6

The deferred tax asset of £5.8m (2007: £8.6m) has been deducted in ariving at the net pension surplus on the balance sheet.

GAAP UK plc   49

Factors that may affect future tax charges

FRS 19 p64   Based on current capital investment plans, the group expects to continue to be able to claim capital allowances in excess of depreciation in future years at a similar level to the current year.

FRS 19 p64(b)   No provision has been made for deferred tax on gains recognised on revaluing property to its market value or on the sale of properties where potentially taxable gains have been rolled over into replacement assets. Such tax would become payable only if the property were sold without it being possible to claim rollover relief. The total amount unprovided for is £5.8m. At present it is not envisaged that any such tax will become payable in the foreseeable future.

No deferred tax is recognised on the unremitted earnings of overseas subsidiaries, associates and joint ventures. As the earnings are continually reinvested by the group, no tax is expected to be payable on them in the foreseeable future. If tax were to be recognised a provision of approximately £50m (2007: £40m) would have been required.

During the year, as a result of the change in the UK corporation tax rates from 30% to 28% that was substantively enacted on 26 June 2007 and effective from 1 April 2008, deferred tax balances have been remeasured. This has resulted in a credit to the 2007 profit and loss account of £500,000 (see note 6) and a credit to the 2007 STRGL of £700,000 (see note 6).

23 Called up share capital

		Group and company	
4 Sch 38(1)(a)	**Authorised**	**2008**	2007
		£m	£m
	1,720,000,000 (2005 – 1,170,000,000) ordinary shares of 1p each	**17.2**	11.7

		2008	2007
4 Sch 38(1)(b)	**Allotted, called up and fully paid**	**£m**	£m
4 Sch 38(1)(b)	**Ordinary shares of 1p each**		
4 Sch 8 Note 12	At 1 January – 887,125,690	8.9	8.8
4 Sch 39(b)(c)	Allotted under share option schemes (10,008,001 shares)	0.1	0.1
4 Sch 39(b)(c)	Allotted on acquisition of Newsub plc (486,586,318 shares)	4.8	–
	At 31 December – 1,383,898,437 shares*	**13.8**	8.9

4 Sch 39(b)(c)   * Included in the total are 178,428 1p ordinary shares allotted to directors under the group's long-term incentive plan (2007: 148,447 1p ordinary shares) with a nominal value of £1,784 (2007: £1,484).

4 Sch 39(c)   The value of the shares allotted on the acquisition of Newsub plc was £933.6m and the consideration received for the shares allotted under the share option schemes during 2008 was £2.6m (2007: £4.7m). The shares allotted on the acquisition of Newsub plc did not rank for the interim dividend paid on 27 August 2008. Issue expenses of £1.4m arising on the allotment of the shares on the acquisition of Newsub plc have been charged to other reserves.

The 7% cumulative preference shares, which do not carry any voting rights, were issued in 2003 at £1.50 per share and are redeemable at £1.50 at the option of the shareholders on 1 June 2012. Shareholders are entitled to receive dividends at 7% per annum on the par value of these shares on a cumulative basis; these dividends are payable on 22 December each year. On winding up, the preference shareholders rank above ordinary shareholders and are entitled to receive £1 per share and any dividends accrued but unpaid in respect of their shares. In the event that dividends on the preference share are in arrears for six months or more, holders of the preference shares become entitled to vote at general meetings of members.

Potential issues of ordinary shares

4 Sch 40(1)   Certain senior executives hold options to subscribe for shares in the company at prices ranging
FRS 20 p45(d)   from 26.0p to 223.5p under the share option schemes approved by shareholders in October 2000 and September 2007. Options on 10,008,001 shares were exercised in 2008 and 70,300 options lapsed. The number of shares subject to options, the periods in which they were granted and the periods in which they may be exercised are given below:

GAAP UK plc

50

Year of grant	Exercise price (pence)	Exercise period	2008 **Numbers**	2007 Numbers
2000	26.00	2003 – 2009	**197,777**	10,205,778
2002	50.00	2007 – 2011	**1,152,500**	1,152,500
2004	136.25	2008 – 2013	**3,182,866**	3,182,866
2007	185.75	2008 – 2014	**7,451,486**	7,451,486
2008	223.50	2009 – 2015	**8,630,316**	–
			20,614,945	21,992,630

4 Sch 40(1)   Under the group's long-term incentive plan for executive directors and former directors, such individuals hold rights over ordinary shares which may result in the issue of up to 466,439 1p ordinary shares by 2008.

24 Share-based payments

FRS 20 p45(a)   The Executive Share Option Plan (ESOP) was introduced in January 2007. Under the ESOP the remuneration committee can grant options over shares in the company to employees of the group. Options are granted with a fixed exercise price equal to the market price of the shares under option at the date of grant. The contractual life of an option is 10 years. Awards under the ESOP are generally reserved for employees at senior management level and above; and 107 employees are currently eligible to participate in this group. There are no reload features. The company has made annual grants on 1 January each year since January 2007. Options granted under the ESOP will become exercisable on the third anniversary of the date of grant, subject to the growth in earnings per share over that period exceeding an average of inflation plus 3% (for

FRS 20 p47(a)(i) awards in January 2007 and January 2008, 4%). Exercise of an option is subject to continued employment. Options were valued using the Black-Scholes option-pricing model. No performance conditions were included in the fair value calculations. The fair value per option granted and the assumptions used in the calculation are as follows:

FRS 20 p46		01 Jan 2008	01 Jan 2007
	Grant date		
	Share price at grant date	£2.235	£1.8575
	Exercise price	£2.235	£1.8575
	Number of employees	107	85
	Shares under option	8,630,316	7,451,486
	Vesting period (years)	3	3
	Expected volatility	40%	40%
	Option life (years)	10	10
	Expected life (years)	5	5
	Risk free rate	4.80%	4.80%
	Expected dividends expressed as a dividend yield	2.50%	2.50%
	Fair value per option	£0.73	£0.85

FRS 20 p47(a)(ii) The expected volatility is based on historical volatility over the last three years. The expected life is the average expected period to exercise. The risk free rate of return is the yield on zero-coupon UK government bonds of a term consistent with the assumed option life. A reconciliation of option movements over the year to 31 December 2008 is shown below:

		2008		2007	
		Number (000)	Weighted average exercise price	Number (000)	Weighted average exercise price
FRS 20 p45(b)(i)	Outstanding at 1 January	21,993	£0.97	21,698	£0.49
FRS 20 p45(b)(ii)	Granted	8,630	£2.23	7,541	£1.86
FRS 20 p45(b)(iii)	Forfeited	–	–	(6,112)	£0.46
FRS 20 p45(b)(iv)	Exercised	(10,008)	£0.26	(1,134)	£0.50
FRS 20 p45(b)(vi)	Outstanding at 31 December	20,615	£1.85	21,993	£0.97
FRS 20 p45(b)(vii)	Exercisable at 31 December	1,350	£0.46	10,206	£0.26

FRS 20 p47(a) The weighted average fair value of options granted in the year was £6.3m (2007: £6.4m).

FRS 20 p45(d)

Range of exercise prices	2008 Weighted average exercise price	2008 Number of shares ('000)	2008 Weighted average remaining life: Expected	2008 Weighted average remaining life: Contractual	2007 Weighted average exercise price	2007 Number of shares ('000)	2007 Weighted average remaining life: Expected	2007 Weighted average remaining life: Contractual
£0.00 – £1.50	£1.37	4,246	1.5	7.0	£0.35	10,254	2.2	7.7
£1.50 – £2.50	£1.97	16,369	2.8	8.8	£1.58	11,739	3.3	9.3

FRS 20 p45(c),50,51(a) The weighted average share price during the period for options exercised over the year was £0.46 (2007: £0.26). The total charge for the year relating to employee share-based payment plans was £3.2m (2007: £1.4m), all of which related to equity-settled share-based payment transactions. After deferred tax, the total charge was £1.8m (2007: £2.2m).

25 Share premium account

	Group and Company	2008 £m	2007 £m
4 Sch 46	At 1 January	8.3	3.7
	Premium on shares issued during the year under the share option schemes	2.5	4.6
	At 31 December	**10.8**	8.3

26 Revaluation reserve

		Group £m	Company £m
4 Sch 46	At 1 January 2008	2.5	0.8
	Exchange adjustments	(0.2)	–
FRS 29 20(a)(ii)	Revaluation in year	5.4	1.5
	Transfer to profit and loss account	(0.2)	–
	At 31 December 2008	**7.5**	2.3

27 Profit and loss reserve

		Group £m	Company £m
	At 1 January 2008	141.5	154.6
	Net exchange adjustments	(80.4)	(1.4)
UITF 19 p9	Tax on exchange adjustments	3.5	–
	Profit for the year	25.4	9.2
	Dividend	(23.7)	(23.7)
	Adjustment in respect of employee share schemes	3.2	–
	Goodwill recycled on disposal of subsidiary	3.9	–
4 Sch 46(2)(b)	Transfer from revaluation reserve (note 26)	0.2	–
	Actuarial (loss)/gain on pension scheme (note 36)	(22.2)	–
	Current tax deductions allocated to actuarial losses	3.6	–
	Movement on deferred tax relating to pension asset	2.8	–
	At 31 December 2008	**57.8**	138.7

4A Sch 14
FRS 10 p71(a)(ii) Cumulative goodwill relating to acquisitions made prior to 1998, which has been eliminated against reserves, amounts to £172.2m (2007: £176.1m).

FRS 2 p53 The reserves of subsidiary undertakings have generally been retained to finance their businesses. The ability to distribute £0.7m (2007: £1.2m) of consolidated retained profits of the group is restricted by exchange controls in certain countries.

GAAP UK plc   52

Included in net exchange adjustments are exchange gains of £16.9m (2007: £2.4m) arising on borrowings denominated in, or swapped into, foreign currencies designated as hedges of net investments overseas.

FRS 17 p90   The profit and loss reserve includes £15.0m (2007: £22.0m), stated after deferred taxation of £5.8m (2007: £8.6m) in respect of pension scheme assets of the group pension fund.

UITF 38 p11(b)   The GAAP UK plc ESOP Trust ('the Trust') holds 16,500,000 (2007: 16,500,000) shares with a
UITF 38 p11(a)   cost of £23,100,000 (2007: £23,100,000) and a market value at 31 December 2008 of £36,135,000 (2007: £28,380,000). These shares were acquired in April 2007 by the Trust in the open market. The Trust used funds provided by GAAP UK plc to meet the group's obligations under the senior executive share option scheme. Share options are granted to employees at the discretion of GAAP UK plc and shares are awarded to employees by the trust in accordance with the wishes of GAAP UK plc.

UITF 38 p11(c)   All shares in the Trust are held to satisfy the group's obligation in respect of share options granted.

28 Reconciliation of exchange differences recognised through the statement of total recognised gains and losses

	Note	2008 £m	2007 £m
Opening balance of cumulative exchange difference		**8.9**	(26.0)
Exchange adjustments on intangibles	10	**32.6**	26.3
Exchange adjustments on plant, property and equipment	11	**27.2**	24.1
Exchange adjustments on plant, property and equipment accumulated depreciation	11	**(10.0)**	(9.0)
Exchange adjustments on interests in joint ventures	12	**0.9**	1.5
Exchange adjustments on AFS investment	16	**(21.4)**	(1.2)
Exchange adjustments on provisions	21	**(2.4)**	(1.0)
Exchange adjustments on overseas subsidiaries		**(69.4)**	(5.8)
Closing balance of cumulative exchange differences		**(33.6)**	8.9

FRS 23 p52(b) appears beside this table.

29 Other reserves

	Merger reserve £m	Other reserve £m	AFS Revn reserve £m	Hedging reserve £m	Total £m
As at 1 January 2008	–	0.2	5.6	–	5.8
Shares issued on acquisition of Newsub plc	933.6	–	–	–	933.6
Issue expenses	(1.4)	–	–	–	(1.4)
Exchange adjustments	(1.9)	21.4	19.5	–	
Net revaluation to AFS investments	–	–	(6.3)	–	(6.3)
Net movement on foreign currency cash flow hedge	–	–	–	4.5	4.5
Net movement on cross currency net investment hedge	–	–	–	5.0	5.0
Movement on other reserve	–	5.6	–	–	5.6
Net movement on interest rate swap	–	–	–	(2.1)	(2.1)
As at 31 December 2008	932.2	3.9	20.7	7.4	964.2

4 Sch 46, 34E, 34F / 4 Sch 45A (2)(b)(ii) / FRS 29 p20(a)(ii) appear beside this table.

GAAP UK plc

53

30 Cash flow from operating activities

FRS 1 p12 Reconciliation of operating profit to net cash inflow from operating activities:

	Group	
Continuing operations	**2008** **£m**	2007 £m
Operating profit	**104.0**	76.3
Depreciation charge (net of profit on disposals)	**77.7**	15.5
Goodwill amortisation	**40.2**	–
Difference between pension charge and cash contributions	**(8.0)**	9.3
(Increase) in stocks	**(2.7)**	(3.3)
Decrease/(increase) in debtors	**15.0**	(3.1)
(Decrease) in creditors	**(47.5)**	(13.5)
Other non-cash changes	**3.2**	1.7
Net cash inflow from continuing operations	**181.9**	82.9
Discontinued operations		
Operating profit	**2.2**	27.1
Depreciation charge	**5.8**	6.2
Decrease in stock	**1.0**	2.0
(Increase) in debtors	**(3.8)**	(4.9)
Increase in creditors	**2.3**	3.3
Net cash inflow from discontinued operations	**7.5**	33.7
Total net cash inflow from operating activities	**189.4**	116.6

31 Reconciliation in net debt

	As at 1 Jan 2008 £m	Cash flow £m	Acquisition (excluding Cash and over- drafts) £m	Other non- cash changes £m	Exchange movements £m	At 31 Dec 2008 £m
Cash in hand and at bank	40.5	40.1	–	–	(5.8)	**74.8**
Overdrafts	–	(92.0)	–	–	5.0	**(87.0)**
Debt due after 1 year	(417.9)	(328.3)	(65.8)	(1.1)	9.4	**(803.7)**
Debt due within 1 year	(41.7)	57.1	(17.5)	–	0.2	**(1.9)**
Finance leases due after 1 year	–	–	(17.8)	8.0	–	**(9.8)**
Finance leases due within 1 year	–	10.8	(6.1)	(8.0)	–	**(3.3)**
Liquid resources	455.3	8.3	50.1	(1.0)	35.7	**548.4**
Preference shares	(3.0)	–	–	–	–	**(3.0)**
	33.2	**(304.0)**	**(57.1)**	**(2.1)**	**44.5**	**(285.5)**

FRS 1 p33 appears alongside the table rows.

FRS 1 p26 Liquid resources comprise short-term deposits with banks which mature within 12 months of the date of inception and current asset investments that are traded in an active market.

Non-cash charges comprise amortisation of issue costs relating to debt issues and transfers between categories of finance leases.

GAAP UK plc 54

Movement in borrowings

	£m	£m
Debt due within 1 year:		
Repayment of part of bank loan	–	(57.1)
Debt due after 1 year:	–	–
New secured bank loan	321.2	–
New unsecured bank loan	100.0	–
Repayment of part of bank loan	(87.6)	333.6
Increase in borrowings	–	276.5
Issue costs of new bank loan	–	(5.3)
	–	271.2
Capital element of finance lease payment	–	(10.8)
Cash inflow	–	**260.4**

32 Cash flow relating to exceptional items

FRS 1 p37

Operating cash flows include under continuing operations an outflow of £8.5m which relates to the reorganisation costs of £9.1m incurred in integrating Newsub plc. The balance of £0.6m was paid in January 2008. In addition, operating cash flows from continuing operations includes an outflow of £3.5m in respect of product remediation costs.

33 Major non-cash transactions

FRS 1 p46

Part of the consideration for the purchase of Newsub plc comprised shares. Further details of the acquisition are set out in note 34.

34 Acquisitions and disposals

(a) Acquisition of Newsub plc

4A Sch 13(2)
FRS 6 p21

The group purchased three companies during the year for a total consideration of £1,239.4m, of which £1,234.7m was in respect of the acquisition on 30 June 2008 of Newsub plc. The total adjustments required to the book values of the assets and liabilities of the companies acquired in order to present the net assets of those companies at fair values in accordance with group accounting principles were £106.2m, of which £105.5m related to Newsub plc, details of which are set out together with the resultant amount of goodwill arising. All of these purchases have been accounted for as acquisitions.

FRS 6 p29
FRS 1 p45

Newsub plc contributed £77.0m to the group's net operating cash flows, paid £17.4m in respect of interest, £8.6m in respect of taxation and utilised £63.4m for capital expenditure.

FRS 6 p35

In its last financial year to 31 March 2008, Newsub plc made a profit after tax and minority interests of £56.6m. For the period since that date to the date of acquisition, Newsub plc management accounts show:

	£m
FRS 6 p36,83 Turnover	94.3
Operating profit	4.0
Profit before taxation	2.9
Taxation and minority interests	(1.2)
Profit attributable to shareholders	1.7
Exchange adjustments	(0.3)
Total recognised gains for the period	1.4

GAAP UK plc   55

4A Sch 13(5)	Newsub plc acquisition	Book value £m	Revaluations £m	Consistency of accounting policy £m	Other £m	Provisional fair value £m
FRS 6 p25	Intangible fixed assets	7.9	–	(7.9)	–	–
	Tangible fixed assets	330.5	(18.1)	–	–	312.4
	Investments in joint ventures	17.5	(1.9)	(1.6)	–	14.0
	Stock	15.3	(1.7)	–	–	13.6
	Debtors	206.9	6.9	(0.3)	–	213.5
	Creditors	(244.2)	–	(3.4)	(30.9)	(278.5)
	Provisions					
	– Vacant property	(13.9)	–	(54.2)	–	(68.1)
	– Environmental	–	–	–	(18.3)	(18.3)
	– Pre-acquisition restructuring	(1.0)	–	–	(2.8)	(3.8)
	Taxation					
	– Current	(6.2)	–	–	–	(6.2)
	– Deferred	(53.9)	–	–	31.4	(22.5)
	Cash	10.3	–	–	–	10.3
	Overdrafts	(25.7)	–	–	–	(25.7)
	Loans net of deposits	(54.0)	(3.1)	–	–	(57.1)
		189.5	(17.9)	(67.4)	(20.6)	83.6
	Minority interests	(0.8)	0.4	–	–	(0.4)
	Net assets acquired	188.7	(17.5)	(67.4)	(20.6)	83.2
	Goodwill					1,151.5
	Consideration					1,234.7
4A Sch 13(3) FRS 6 p24	**Consideration satisfied by:** Shares issued (net of issue costs of £1.4m)					932.2
FRS 1 p45	Cash					302.5
						1,234.7

FRS 6 p25
4A Sch 13(5)
FRS 6 p27

The book values of the assets and liabilities have been taken from the management accounts of Newsub plc at 30 June 2008 (the date of acquisition) at actual exchange rates on that date. The fair value adjustments contain some provisional amounts, as indicated below, which will be finalised in the 2009 financial statements when the detailed acquisition investigation has been completed.

Revaluation adjustments in respect of tangible fixed assets comprise the valuations of certain freehold properties.

Revaluations of investments and stock reflect the write-down to estimated realisable value. The revaluation adjustment to debtors includes a revision to the bad debt provision to reflect an adjustment for an amount distributed in respect of a customer in receivership.

The revaluation of loans relates to an adjustment of £3.1m in order to reflect current market rate of interest on the Newsub plc US$ bond. Other adjustments to creditors of £30.9m relate to liabilities that were not fully reflected in the balance sheet of Newsub plc at the date of acquisition. These include adjustments to increase the creditor amounts for certain insurance and legal claims to reflect their final settlement shortly after 30 June 2008.

The fair value adjustment for alignment of accounting policies reflects the restatement of assets and liabilities in accordance with the group's policies including: the removal of capitalised in-store marketing costs (£7.9m); provision for the group's share of deferred consideration payable by an associated company for the acquisition of a business (£1.6m); establishing a creditor for outstanding holiday pay entitlement of employees and the alignment of general bad debt provisioning policy.

A provisional adjustment (£18.3m) has been made for the remediation of Newsub plc operational sites in the US. The final report from Environment Appraisers, Inc. will not be available until April 2009 and further provision may be required.

GAAP UK plc 56

The book values of the net assets acquired included provisions for reorganisation and restructuring costs amounting to £1.0m. These provisions were established by Newsub plc in November 2008 and relate to an irrevocable reorganisation commenced by Newsub plc management before the acquisition. However on review at the time of acquisition, the provisions were considered to be insufficient to cover the expected costs and have been increased by £2.8m.

The adjustment in respect of vacant property is discussed in note 22.

No deferred tax has been recognised on fair value adjustments on non-monetary fixed assets as there is no intention to sell the assets concerned. However, the book value of deferred tax liability of £53.9m was reduced by a net deferred asset of £31.4m in respect of various fair value adjustments arising on the acquisition in accordance with FRS 19.

(b) Other acquisitions	£m
Book value of net assets acquired (includes £0.3m cash)	0.2
Fair value adjustments	(0.7)
Goodwill	5.2
Consideration satisfied by cash	4.7

FRS 6 p21
4A Sch 13(2)

Co Limited and Sub SA were acquired by GAAPsub Ltd on 6 May 2008 and 12 July 2008 respectively. Fair value adjustments of £0.7m were made to align accounting policies in respect of fixed assets (£0.2m), stock (£0.2m) and creditors (£0.3m).

4A Sch 15

(c) Disposal of H Limited	£m
Tangible fixed assets	1.4
Stocks	2.5
Debtors	6.5
Creditors	(4.9)
Goodwill previously written off to reserves	3.9
	9.4
Profit on disposal (Note 5)	6.3
Deferred cash consideration	15.7

FRS 2 p47
FRS 10 p71(c)(ii)
FRS 10 p54
FRS 1 p45

FRS 1 p45

H Limited contributed £7.5m to the net operating cash flows, paid £0.8m in respect of net returns on investments and servicing of finance and £0.9m in respect of taxation.

35 Employees and directors

4 Sch 56(4)

Staff costs for the group during the year	2008 £m	2007 £m
Wages and salaries	544.3	203.7
Social security costs	62.0	22.3
Other pension costs current service cost (note 36)	17.2	9.3
Defined contribution pension cost	0.2	–
Cost of employee share schemes (note 24)	3.2	1.7
	626.9	237.0

FRS 20 p51(a)

4 Sch 56(1),(2)
4 Sch 56(3)
S 231A

Average monthly number of people (including executive directors) employed by the group		
By business group		
Food products	18,630	7,602
Personnel services	5,789	138
Retail services	5,241	4,758
Distribution services	13,735	915
Property services	7,107	3,565
Health care	9,368	3,499
	59,870	20,477

Note: If GAAP UK plc (the parent company) had employees, the above disclosures would be required for the company as well as the group.

GAAP UK plc

57

s 232 (1)	**Directors**	**2008**	2007
		£'000	£'000
6 Sch 1(1)(a)	Aggregate emoluments	**753**	574
6 Sch 1(1)(b)	Aggregate gains made on the exercise of share options	**231**	157
6 Sch 1(1)(c)	Aggregate amounts receivable under long-term incentive schemes	**318**	239
6 Sch 1(1)(d)	Company contributions to money purchase pension schemes	**72**	–
		1,374	970

6 Sch 1(1)(e) Two directors (2007: nil) have retirement benefits accruing under money purchase pension schemes. In addition, retirement benefits are accruing to five (2007: five) directors under the company's defined benefit pension scheme.

	Highest paid director	**2008**	2007
		£	£
6 Sch 2(1)	Aggregate emoluments, gains on share options exercised and benefits under long-term incentive schemes	**200,000**	180,000
6 Sch 2(2)(a) (b)	Defined benefit scheme:		
	– Accrued pension at end of year	**30,000**	25,000
	– Accrued lump sum at end of year	**60,000**	50,000

6 Sch 2(3)(a) and (b) The highest paid director exercised share options during the year and received shares under the executive long-term incentive scheme.

6 Sch 15(c), 16(c) *Note: Details should be given of all transactions or arrangements with the company or any subsidiary of it in which a person who was a director of the company or its holding company had a material interest.*

6 Sch 7 *Note: Details should be given of any excess retirement benefits of directors and past directors.*
6 Sch 8(l) *Note: Details should be given of the aggregate of compensation paid to directors or past directors for loss of office, including retirement.*

6 Sch 9 *Note: Details should be given of the aggregate of any consideration paid to or receivable by third parties for making available the services of any person while a director. This includes benefits other than in cash.*

36 Pension commitments

FRS 17 p77(a)
4 Sch 50(4) The group has established a number of pension schemes around the world covering many of its employees. The principal funds are those in the UK: the GAAP UK plc staff pension plan, the UK GAAP Ltd pension scheme and the Newsub plc pension plan. The GAAP UK Plc staff pension plan and the UK GAAP Ltd pension scheme are funded schemes of the defined benefit type with assets held in separate trustee administered funds. The Newsub plc pension plan and schemes outside the UK are predominantly of the money purchase type.

FRS 17 p77(a) The most recent actuarial valuations of the GAAP UK plc staff pension plan and the UK GAAP Ltd pension scheme were at 31 December 2008. The valuations of both schemes used the projected unit method and were carried out by Actuary & Actuary, professionally qualified actuaries. The principal assumptions for both plans made by the actuaries were:

		2008	2007
		%	%
FRS 17 p77(m)	Rate of increase in pensionable salaries	**4.0**	6.0
FRS 17 p77(m)	Rate of increase in pensions in payment and deferred pensions	**3.0**	4.0
FRS 17 p77(m)	Discount rate	**5.2**	5.2
FRS 17 p77(m)	Inflation assumption	**2.6**	2.5

FRS 17 p77(m) The mortality assumptions used in the group's actuarial valuations have been amended to assume that pensioners have a longer life expectancy. The mortality assumptions used in the valuation of the defined benefit pension liabilities of the group's UK plans are summarised in the table below and have been selected to reflect the characteristics and experience of the membership of those plans. This has been done by adjusting standard mortality tables which reflect recent research into mortality experience in the UK (PA 92 tables combined with the 2002 short cohort improvement factors) and the US (UP-94 tables using projection scale AA). In

GAAP UK plc   58

addition, the UK assumptions have been further adjusted to reflect the latest available trend information, which indicates that mortality relating, in particular, to blue collar workers may not be improving as quickly as indicated by the standard tables. Accordingly, based on an analysis of the mix of blue and white-collar workers in the group's plan, the UK assumptions have been adjusted (using a scaling factor of 118.75%) to reflect a lower level of longevity amongst the blue collar membership.

	UK		US	
	2008 **years**	2007 years	**2008** **years**	2007 years
Longevity at age 65 for current pensioners				
– Men	**19.7**	18.4	**17.7**	17.7
– Women	**22.4**	21.3	**20.6**	20.6
Longevity at age 65 for future pensioners				
– Men	**20.4**	19.3	**18.5**	17.7
– Women	**23.1**	22.3	**21.0**	20.6

The assets of the schemes and the weighted average expected rate of return were:

		Long-term rate of return expected 31 December 2008 %	Value at 31 December 2008 £m	Long-term rate of return expected 31 December 2007 %	As restated Value at 31 December 2007 £m
FRS 17 p77(i)	Equities	**8.7**	**140.6**	8.4	116.6
FRS 17 p77(i)	Bonds	**5.6**	**94.2**	5.6	81.0
	Total market value of assets		**234.8**		197.6
	Present value of scheme liabilities		**(214.0)**		(167.0)
FRS 17 p77(e)	Surplus in the scheme		**20.8**		30.6
	Related deferred tax liability		**(5.8)**		(8.6)
FRS 17 p77(e)	**Net pension asset**		**15.0**		22.0

FRS 17 p77(b)   **Reconciliation of present value of scheme liabilities**

	2008 £m	2007 £m
1 January	**167.0**	136.9
Current service cost	**17.2**	8.3
Past service cost	**–**	1.0
Interest cost	**10.0**	7.8
Benefits paid	**(49.5)**	(32.7)
Actuarial loss	**69.3**	45.7
31 December	**214.0**	167.0

Best Practice   **Sensitivity analysis of scheme liabilities**

The sensitivity of the present value of scheme liabilities to changes in the principle assumptions used is set out below.

	Change in assumption	Impact on scheme liabilities
Discount rate	Increase/decrease by 1%	Increase/decrease by 9.5%
Rate of inflation	Increase/decrease by 1%	Increase/decrease by 4.5%
Rate of increase in salaries	Increase/decrease by 1%	Increase/decrease by 4.0%
Rate of increase in pensions in payment	Increase/decrease by 1%	Increase/decrease by 3.5%
Mortality	Increase by 1 year	Increase by 5.0%

GAAP UK plc

FRS 17 p77(d)   **Reconciliation of fair value of scheme assets**

	2008 £'000	As restated 2007 £'000
1 January	197.6	170.1
Expected return on scheme assets	14.4	11.8
Actuarial gains	47.1	48.4
Benefits paid	(49.5)	(32.7)
Contributions paid by employer	25.2	–
31 December	234.8	197.6

FRS 17 p77(j)   Scheme assets do not include any of GAAP UK plc's own financial instruments, or any property occupied by GAAP UK plc.

FRS 17 p77(k)   The expected return on scheme assets is determined by considering the expected returns available on the assets underlying the current investment policy. Expected yields on fixed interest investments are based on gross redemption yields as at the balance sheet date. Expected returns on equity investments reflect long-term real rates of return experienced in the respective markets.

FRS 17 p77(l)   The actual return on scheme assets in the year was £61.5m (2006: £61.0m).

FRS 17 p77(f)   **The amounts recognised in the profit or loss account are as follows:**

	2008 £m	2007 £m
Current service cost	17.2	8.3
Past service cost	–	1.0
Expected return on pension scheme assets	(14.4)	(11.8)
Interest on pension scheme liabilities	10.0	7.8
Total charge	**12.8**	**5.3**

£12.6m (2006: £6.3m) of the current service cost is included within cost of sales, and £4.6m (2006: £2.0m) is included within administrative expenses.

FRS 17 p77(o)

Amounts for current period and previous four periods	2008	2007	2006	2005	2004
Defined benefit obligation	(214.0)	(167.0)	(136.9)	(120.0)	(115.8)
Plan assets	234.8	197.6	170.1	165.0	156.7
Surplus/(Deficit)	20.8	30.6	33.2	45.0	40.9
Experience adjustments on plan assets: Amount (£m)	47.1	48.4	40.6	40.4	20.6
Experience adjustments on plan liabilities: Amount (£m)	(12.3)	(14.7)	(15.9)	2.9	5.2

FRS 17 p77(g)

Total actuarial gains and losses recognised in statement of total recognised gains and losses: Amount (£m)	(22.2)	2.7	7.8	6.3	(3.8)

FRS 17p75   The Newsub plc pension plan is a defined contribution plan. The contributions made to the plan from the date of acquisition were £242,000. (2007: £nil). At the end of the year, contributions of £21,000 (2007: £nil), representing the unpaid contributions for December 2008, were outstanding.

GAAP UK plc has no employees (the members of the group defined benefit scheme are or were employed by subsidiaries of GAAP UK plc) and, consequently, no defined benefit scheme disclosures are given for the company.

FRS 17 p77(p)   The valuation at 31 December 2008 showed a decrease in the surplus from £30.6m to £20.8m. Improvements in benefits of £1m were made in 2007 and no additional improvements in benefits

GAAP UK plc

were made in 2008. From 1 January 2008 contributions were made to the pension scheme at a rate of 5% of pensionable salaries. It has been agreed with the trustees that contributions will remain at that level for the next three years.

37 Operating lease commitments

At 31 December 2008 the group has lease agreements in respect of properties, vehicles, plant and equipment, for which the payments extend over a number of years.

| | | 2008 | 2007 | |
| | | Vehicles, plant and equipment | | Vehicles, plant and equipment |
	Property £m	£m	Property £m	£m
SSAP 21 p56 **Annual commitments under non-cancellable operating leases expiring:**				
Within one year	**1.1**	**0.6**	0.3	0.3
Within two to five years	**6.1**	**3.5**	1.0	2.5
After five years	**6.9**	**0.5**	0.6	1.2
	14.1	**4.6**	1.9	4.0

38 Contingent liabilities

FRS 12 p91
4 Sch 59A
FRS 9 p53

The company has guaranteed bank and other borrowings of subsidiary undertakings and, jointly with its co-investors, of joint ventures amounting to £2.7m (2007: £0.4m) and £3.7m (2007: £0.7m) respectively.

4 Sch 50(2)
FRS 12 p91

At 31 December 2008, the group was in dispute with one of its food suppliers over surcharges invoiced above the original contracted price for specialist ingredients. The directors are strongly resisting the payment of the surcharges and it is unlikely that the outcome of this dispute will have a material effect on the group's financial position.

39 Capital and other financial commitments

| | Share of joint ventures | | Group | | Company | |
FRS 9 p53	2008 £m	2007 £m	2008 £m	2007 £m	2008 £m	2007 £m
4 Sch 50(3) Contracts placed for future capital expenditure not provided in the financial statements	**2.1**	0.7	**12.9**	2.4	**0.1**	0.1
SSAP 21 p54 Commitments under finance leases entered into, but not yet provided for	**1.0**	–	**6.7**	–	–	–

40 Other related-party transactions

FRS 8 p6,19
FRS 9 p55

During the year the group purchased food products from two joint ventures, Lawrence AG and Michel Stuart AG to the value of £19.5m (2007: £16.7m). At 31 December 2008 £2.4m (2007: £1.8m) was payable in respect of these purchases. During the year the group sold healthcare products totalling £11.2m (2007: £13.4m) to Italia Health SpA, a joint venture. At 31 December 2008 the outstanding balances receivable from Italia Health SpA were £1.3m (2007: £1.5m).

s 346(5)
6 Sch PartII
FRS 8 p6

Mrs S James, wife of Mr F James, a main board director and managing director of the healthcare division, owns the entire share capital of CPS Inter Ltd. The nature of the business of the healthcare division necessitates the exporting of products to Saudi Arabia. CPS Inter Ltd acts as an export agency on behalf of a group subsidiary company, GAAPhealth Ltd. Throughout the year, CPS Inter Ltd has traded under the same terms as those available to other customers in the ordinary course of business. The value of export work performed during the year ended 31 December 2008 for GAAPhealth Ltd amounted to £9.7m (2007: £8.4m). The amount owed to CPS Inter Ltd at the year end amounted to £0.9m (2007: £0.8m).

GAAP UK plc 61

41 Post balance sheet events

FRS 21 p21,
4 Sch 12(b)

On 15 February 2008, the company completed the purchase of Millennium Resources, Inc for a total consideration of £75.1m. The company operates in North America providing healthcare services. At the date of acquisition it had estimated net assets of US$40m (£25m).

s 231

42 Principal subsidiaries, joint ventures and associates

Subsidiary undertakings

5 Sch 15

Particulars of subsidiary undertaking:

5 Sch 16

(a) Name.
(b) Country of incorporation, if incorporated outside Great Britain.
(c) If unincorporated, address of principal place of business.

5 Sch 15(4)
5 Sch 15(5)

(d) Description and proportion of the nominal value of the shares of each class distinguishing between shares held by the parent undertaking and those held by the group.
(e) State whether or not included in the consolidation and explain if not.

FRS 2 p34

(f) The specific definition of subsidiary undertaking which makes the undertaking a subsidiary – this need not be given if the reason is that the parent holds a majority of the voting rights and the proportion of shares and voting rights held are the same.

FRS 2 p33

(g) Where a subsidiary undertaking is consolidated on the basis of a participating interest with actual dominant influence, the basis of dominant influence should be disclosed.
(h) Proportion of voting rights held by group.
(i) Indication of nature of business.

Joint ventures and associates

For joint ventures and associates included in the group accounts, give:

5 Sch 22
FRS 9 p52

(a) Name.
(b) Country of incorporation, if incorporated outside Great Britain.
(c) If unincorporated, address of principal place of business.

FRS 9 p52(a)

(d) The identity and proportion of each class of shares held by the parent company and by the group, indicating any special rights or constraints attaching to them.

FRS 9 p52(c)
FRS 9 p52(b)

(e) Indication of nature of business.
(f) The accounting period or date of the financial statements used if they differ from the group's.

FRS 9 p56

Note: An explanation must be given to each case where either of the following presumptions is rebutted:
(a) An investor holding 20% or more of the voting rights has significant influence.
(b) An investor holding 20% or more of the shares of another entity has a participating interest.

FRS 9 p53

Note: Disclosure should be made of any notes or matters that should have been noted had the investor's accounting policies been applied, that are material to understanding the effect on the investor of its investments, particularly in respect of contingent liabilities and capital commitments.

UK GAAP Limited — Year ended 31 December 2008

Contents

Example set of company financial statements

The example annual report that follows includes the financial statements of UK GAAP Limited, a wholly-owned private subsidiary company. Although UK GAAP Limited meets the size criteria for a medium-sized company, it is ineligible due to its ultimate parent company, GAAP UK plc, being a plc, and therefore it does not qualify as a medium-sized company.

UK GAAP Limited is a fictitious company. The annual report has been prepared for illustrative purposes only and shows the disclosures and formats that might be expected for a company of its size that prepares its financial statements in accordance with Schedule 4 to the Companies Act 1985 as amended by the Companies Act 1989 and subsequent statutory instruments. The requirements of Part 15 of the Companies Act 2006 have not been incorporated, as this part is only applicable to financial periods beginning on or after 6 April 2008, except for S417 which applies to the Business Review for periods beginning on or after 1 October 2008. The intention is not to show all conceivable disclosures and this annual report should not, therefore, be used as a checklist. The suggested disclosures are not necessarily applicable for all private companies. These financial statements include many of the disclosure requirements contained in current Financial Reporting Standards, Statements of Standard Accounting Practice, Urgent Issues Task Force Abstracts and Company Law, current at 30 September 2008. Proposals included in exposure drafts at that date are not yet standard practice and have, therefore, not been reflected in these financial statements.

These illustrative financial statements do not cover (amongst other items):

- Discontinued activities.

- Exceptional items.

- ESOP and similar share-based payment schemes where the entity's employees are recipients.

- Long-term contracts.

- Government grants.

- Investment properties.
- Sophisticated capital instruments.
- Impairment of fixed assets.
- Acquisition of a business.
- A cash flow statement.
- Share-based payment

UK GAAP Limited does not apply the fair value accounting rules and therefore has not adopted FRS 23, FRS 26, FRS 29 or paragraphs 51 to 95 of FRS 25.

The GAAP UK plc example accounts are consolidated financial statements for a group of companies that include many of these items.

UK GAAP Limited

Contents

UK GAAP Ltd

1

Directors' report

Directors' report for the year ended 31 December 2008

The directors present their report and the audited financial statements of the company for the year ended 31 December 2008.

Principal activities
The company's principal activity during the year was the manufacture and sale of processed foods and bakery products.

All of the company's product areas continued to expand during the year but, because of difficult trading conditions, suffered a fall in profitability.

At the year end the company was in a strong position to take advantage of suitable expansion opportunities that may arise.

Business review
The review should cover the following:

(a) a fair review of the company's business; and
(b) a description of the principal risks and uncertainties facing the company.

The review required is a balanced and comprehensive analysis of:

(a) the development and performance of the company's business during the financial year; and
(b) the company's position at the end of that year, consistent with the business size and complexity.

The review must, to the extent necessary for an understanding of the development, performance or position of the business, include:

(a) analysis using financial key performance indicators; and
(b) where appropriate, analysis using other key performance indicators, including information relating to environmental matters and employee matters.

Notes:

(a) Section 234ZZB of the Companies Act requires this disclosure within the directors' report of all companies with the exception of small companies which are exempt.

(b) For medium-sized companies, where these indicators relate to non-financial information, disclosure is not required.

The review must, where appropriate, include references to, and additional explanations of, amounts included in the annual accounts of the company.

Future developments

An indication should be given of the likely future developments in the business of the company.

Financial risk management

The company's operations expose it to a variety of financial risks that include the effects of changes in debt market prices, credit risk, liquidity risk and interest rate risk. The company has in place a risk management programme that seeks to limit the adverse effects on the financial performance of the company by monitoring levels of debt finance and the related finance costs.

In order to ensure stability of cash out flows and hence manage interest rate risk, the company has a policy of maintaining 100 per cent of its debt (2007: 100 per cent) at fixed rate. Further to this the company seeks to minimise the risk of uncertain funding in its operations by borrowing within a spread of maturity periods. Given the size and nature of operations, the company's policy is to operate with 50 per cent of its debt being repayable within one year. At the year end, 52 per cent (2007: 43 per cent) of debt was repayable within one year. The company does not use derivative financial instruments to manage interest rate costs and as such, no hedge accounting is applied.

UK GAAP Ltd   2

Given the size of the company, the directors have not delegated the responsibility of monitoring financial risk management to a sub-committee of the board. The policies set by the board of directors are implemented by the company's finance department. The department has a policy and procedures manual that sets out specific guidelines to manage interest rate risk, credit risk and circumstances where it would be appropriate to use financial instruments to manage these.

Price risk

The company is exposed to commodity price risk as a result of its operations. However, given the size of the company's operations, the costs of managing exposure to commodity price risk exceed any potential benefits. The directors will revisit the appropriateness of this policy should the company's operations change in size or nature. The company has no exposure to equity securities price risk as it holds no listed or other equity investments.

Credit risk

The company has implemented policies that require appropriate credit checks on potential customers before sales are made. Where debt finance is utilised, this is subject to pre-approval by the board of directors and such approval is limited to financial institutions with an AA rating or better. The amount of exposure to any individual counterparty is subject to a limit, which is reassessed annually by the board.

Liquidity risk

The company actively maintains a mixture of long-term and short-term debt finance that is designed to ensure the company has sufficient available funds for operations and planned expansions.

Interest rate cash flow risk

The company has both interest bearing assets and interest bearing liabilities. Interest bearing assets include only government securities and cash balances, all of which earn interest at fixed rate. The company has a policy of maintaining debt at fixed rate to ensure certainty of future interest cash flows. The directors will revisit the appropriateness of this policy should the company's operations change in size or nature.

Note: This disclosure is required by Schedule 7(5A) of the Companies Act 1985. It is not required where such information is not material for the assessment of the entity's assets, liabilities, financial position and profit or loss. In addition, an exemption from making these disclosures is available to small companies.

Results and dividends

The company's profit for the financial year is £243,000 (2007: £519,000). An interim dividend of 3.51p (2007: 2.57p) per ordinary share, amounting to £71,000 (2007: £52,000) was paid on 1 September 2008. A final dividend of 5.0p (2007: 3.32p) per ordinary share amounting to £102,000 (2007: £67,000) is proposed and, if approved, will be paid on 6 April 2009. The company also paid a preference dividend amounting to £2,625 (2007: £2,625). The aggregate dividends on the ordinary shares recognised as an expense during the year amounts to £138,000 (2007: £52,000) excluding proposed dividends that have yet to be approved by the balance sheet date.

Directors
The directors who held office during the year are given below:

C D Jones   (Chairman)
E F Logan (resigned 6 July 2008)
J F King   (Company Secretary)
I D Davies (appointed 31 July 2008)

UK GAAP Ltd

Qualifying third party indemnity provisions

The directors' report should disclose whether:

(a) at the time the report is approved any qualifying third party indemnity provision (whether made by the company or otherwise)is in place for the benefit of one or more of the directors; or

(b) at any time during the year any such provision was in force for the benefit of one or more persons who were then directors.

If the company has made a qualifying third party indemnity provision and:

(a) at the time the report is approved any qualifying third party indemnity provision is in place for the benefit of one or more directors of an associated company; or

(b) at any time during the year any such provision was in force for the benefit of one or more persons who were then directors of an associated company, the report must state that such a provision is (or was) in force.

Research and development

The company is currently undertaking research and development into a new form of processed food based on soya beans.

Differences between market and balance sheet value of land

In the opinion of the directors, the difference between the market value and balance sheet value of land is not significant.

Note: For the purpose of this disclosure, 'land' includes the buildings and other structures. Where there is a significant difference, it should be shown with such degree of precision as is practicable.

Post balance sheet events

Particulars of any important events affecting the reporting entity that have occurred since the end of the financial year must be disclosed.

Purchase of own shares and sale of treasury shares

Where the company has an interest in its own shares, the directors' report should disclose the number and nominal value of shares purchased and the percentage of the called-up share capital which those shares represent. The aggregate consideration paid and the reason for the purchase should also be given.

Employees

Applications for employment by disabled persons are always fully considered, bearing in mind the respective aptitudes and abilities of the applicant concerned. In the event of members of staff becoming disabled every effort is made to ensure that their employment with the company continues and the appropriate training is arranged. It is the policy of the company that the training, career development and promotion of a disabled person should, as far as possible, be identical to that of a person who does not suffer from a disability.

Note: This disclosure is required if the average number of employees during the year and working within the UK exceeds 250.

Consultation with employees or their representatives has continued at all levels, with the aim of ensuring that their views are taken into account when decisions are made that are likely to affect their interests and that all employees are aware of the financial and economic performance of their business units and of the company as a whole. Communication with all employees continues through the in-house newspaper and newsletters, briefing groups and the distribution of the annual report.

Note: This disclosure is required if the average number of employees during the year and working within the UK exceeds 250.

UK GAAP Ltd   4

Policy and practice on payment of creditors

The company is a registered supporter of the Better Payment Practice Group's 'Better Payment Practice Code' to which it subscribes when dealing with all of its suppliers. Copies of the Better Payment Practice Group's code are available from the Department of Trade & Industry. Trade creditors at the year end represented 34 days (2007: 34 days) of purchases. It is the company's policy in respect of all suppliers to agree payment terms in advance of the supply of goods and to adhere to those payment terms.

Note: This disclosure is required for any company that was at any time within the financial year a public company or a large private subsidiary of a plc. Large private companies are those that exceed the limits in section 247(3) of the Companies Act 1985.

Statement of directors' responsibilities

The directors are responsible for preparing the annual report and the financial statements in accordance with applicable law and regulations.

Company law requires the directors to prepare financial statements for each financial year. Under that law the directors have elected to prepare the financial statements in accordance with United Kingdom Generally Accepted Accounting Practice (United Kingdom Accounting Standards and applicable law). The financial statements are required by law to give a true and fair view of the state of affairs of the company and of the profit or loss of the company for that period.

In preparing those financial statements, the directors are required to:

- select suitable accounting policies and then apply them consistently;
- make judgements and estimates that are reasonable and prudent[1];
- state whether applicable UK Accounting Standards have been followed, subject to any material departures disclosed and explained in the financial statements[2]; and
- prepare the financial statements on the going concern basis unless it is inappropriate to presume that the company will continue in business[3], in which case there should be supporting assumptions or qualifications as necessary.

The directors confirm that they have complied with the above requirements in preparing the financial statements.

The directors are responsible for keeping proper accounting records that disclose with reasonable accuracy at any time the financial position of the company and enable them to ensure that the financial statements comply with the Companies Act 1985. They are also responsible for safeguarding the assets of the company and hence for taking reasonable steps for the prevention and detection of fraud and other irregularities.

Auditors and disclosure of information to auditors

Note: Section 234ZA of the Companies Act requires this disclosure within the directors' report. This section is applicable unless the directors have taken advantage of the exemption conferred by section 249A(1) or 249AA(1). The report must contain a statement to the effect that, in the case of each of the persons who are directors at the time when the report is approved, the following applies:

- *so far as the director is aware, there is no relevant audit information of which the company's auditors are unaware; and*
- *he has taken all the steps that he ought to have taken as a director in order to make himself aware of any relevant audit information and to establish that the company's auditors are aware of that information.*

Auditors

The auditors, PricewaterhouseCoopers LLP, have indicated their willingness to continue in office and a resolution concerning their re-appointment will be proposed at the Annual General Meeting.

By order of the Board

J F King
Secretary   29 February 2009

---

[1] Paragraph 12 of Part II of Schedule 4 to CA 1985 requires that the amount of any item *"shall be determined on a prudent basis"*.

[2] This bullet does not apply to small and medium-sized companies as defined by CA 1985.

[3] Included where no separate statement on going concern is made by the directors.

UK GAAP Ltd

5

Auditors' report

Independent auditors' report to the members of UK GAAP Limited

Warning – *Although this audit report was current at the date of going to press, it may not be the most up-to-date version. Therefore, it should not be used without checking that it is the appropriate version.*

We have audited the financial statements of UK GAAP Ltd for the year ended 31 December 2008 which comprise the profit and loss account, the balance sheet, the statement of total recognised gains and losses and the related notes. These financial statements have been prepared under the accounting policies set out therein.

Respective responsibilities of directors and auditors

The directors' responsibilities for preparing the financial statements in accordance with applicable law and United Kingdom Accounting Standards (United Kingdom Generally Accepted Accounting Practice) are set out in the Statement of directors' responsibilities.

Our responsibility is to audit the financial statements in accordance with relevant legal and regulatory requirements and International Standards on Auditing (UK and Ireland). This report, including the opinion, has been prepared for and only for the company's members as a body in accordance with Section 235 of the Companies Act 1985 and for no other purpose. We do not, in giving this opinion, accept or assume responsibility for any other purpose or to any other person to whom this report is shown or into whose hands it may come save where expressly agreed by our prior consent in writing.

We report to you our opinion as to whether the financial statements give a true and fair view and are properly prepared in accordance with the Companies Act 1985. We report to you whether in our opinion the information given in the directors' report is consistent with the financial statements.

In addition we also report to you if, in our opinion, the company has not kept proper accounting records, if we have not received all the information and explanations we require for our audit, or if information specified by law regarding directors' remuneration and transactions is not disclosed.

We read the directors' report and consider the implications for our report if we become aware of any apparent misstatements within it.

Basis of audit opinion

We conducted our audit in accordance with International Standards on Auditing (UK and Ireland) issued by the Auditing Practices Board. An audit includes examination, on a test basis of evidence relevant to the amounts and disclosures in the financial statements. It also includes an assessment of the significant estimates and judgements made by the directors in the preparation of the financial statements, and of whether the accounting policies are appropriate to the company's circumstances, consistently applied and adequately disclosed.

We planned and performed our audit so as to obtain all the information and explanations which we considered necessary in order to provide us with sufficient evidence to give reasonable assurance that the financial statements are free from material misstatement, whether caused by fraud or other irregularity or error. In forming our opinion we also evaluated the overall adequacy of the presentation of information in the financial statements.

Opinion

In our opinion:

■ the financial statements give a true and fair view, in accordance with United Kingdom Generally Accepted Accounting Practice of the state of the company's affairs as at 31 December 2008 and of its profit for the year then ended;
■ the financial statements have been properly prepared in accordance with the Companies Act 1985; and
■ the information given in the directors' report is consistent with the financial statements.

UK GAAP Ltd   6

PricewaterhouseCoopers LLP

Chartered Accountants and Registered Auditors
London
24 February 2009

Notes:

- Where the financial statements are published on the company's web site, include these notes unless the statement of directors' responsibilities clearly:

  - states the directors' responsibility for the maintenance and integrity of the web site; and

  - refers to the fact that uncertainty regarding legal requirements is compounded as information published on the internet is accessible in many countries with different legal requirements relating to the preparation and dissemination of financial statements.

"a) The maintenance and integrity of the [name of entity] web site is the responsibility of the directors; the work carried out by the auditors does not involve consideration of these matters and, accordingly, the auditors accept no responsibility for any changes that may have occurred to the financial statements since they were initially presented on the web site.

b) Legislation in the United Kingdom governing the preparation and dissemination of financial statements may differ from legislation in other jurisdictions."

UK GAAP Ltd

7

Profit and loss account

Profit and loss account for the year ended 31 December 2008

Continuing operations	Note	£'000	2008 £'000	£'000	2007 £'000
Turnover			11,275		10,010
Cost of sales			(8,734)		(7,305)
Gross profit			2,541		2,705
Administrative expenses			(1,536)		(1,220)
Selling & distribution expenses			(434)		(590)
Other operating income			13		11
Operating profit	4		584		906
Income from fixed asset investments			17		9
Profit on ordinary activities before interest and taxation			601		915
Interest receivable and similar income		21		13	
Interest payable and similar charges	7	(166)		(97)	
Other finance income	23	45		94	
			(100)		10
Profit on ordinary activities before taxation			501		925
Tax on profit on ordinary activities	8		(258)		(406)
Profit for the financial year			243		519

Note: The above presentation of the profit and loss account follows format 1 as outlined in Schedule 4 of the Companies Act 1985. Alternatively a company may present its profit and loss account such that expenses are classified by type using, for example, format 2. An example of presentation of expenses by type in line with format 2 using the above profit and loss account balances is shown below:

Continuing operations	£'000	2008 £'000	£'000	2007 £'000
Turnover		11,275		10,010
Change in stocks of finished goods and work in progress		76		74
Own work capitalised		11		9
Other operating income		13		11
		11,375		10,104
Raw materials and consumables	(6,519)		(5,537)	
Other external charges	(293)		(278)	
Staff costs	(3,277)		(2,921)	
Depreciation	(202)		(200)	
Other operating charges	(500)		(262)	
		(10,791)		(9,198)
Operating profit		584		906

UK GAAP Ltd   8

Statement of total recognised gains and losses for the year ended 31 December 2008

		2008 £'000	2007 £'000
Profit for the financial year		**243**	519
Actuarial losses on pension scheme	23	**(131)**	(124)
Current tax deductions allocated to actuarial losses		**17**	35
Movement on deferred tax relating to pension deficit	18	**22**	2
Total recognised gains and losses relating to the year		**151**	432
Prior year adjustment for adoption of amendment to FRS 17	23	**(40)**	
Total recognised gains and losses since last annual report		**191**	432

There are no material differences between the profit on ordinary activities before taxation and the retained profit for the year stated above and their historical cost equivalents.

UK GAAP Ltd   9

Balance sheet

Balance sheet as at 31 December 2008

	Note	2008 £'000	2008 £'000	2007 £'000	2007 £'000
Fixed assets					
Tangible assets	10	2,385		2,031	
Investments	11	56		76	
			2,441		2,107
Current assets					
Stock	12	1,908		1,779	
Debtors (including £205,000 (2007: £56,000) due after one year)*	13	2,015		1,509	
Investments	14	50		125	
Cash at bank and in hand		91		159	
			4,064		3,572
Creditors – Amounts falling due within one year	15		(2,232)		(1,959)
Net current assets			1,832		1,613
Total assets less current liabilities			4,273		3,720
Creditors – Amounts falling due after more than one year	16		(794)		(524)
Provisions for liabilities and charges	18		(234)		(48)
Net assets excluding pension deficit			3,245		3,148
Pension deficit	23		(150)		(93)
Net assets including pension deficit			3,095		3,055
Capital and reserves					
Called up share capital	19		508		505
Share premium account	20		144		120
Revaluation reserve	20		172		177
Profit and loss reserve	20		2,271		2,253
Total shareholders' funds	21		3,095		3,055

Notes:
Debtors due after one year must be disclosed separately if material compared to net current assets.

The financial statements on pages 7 to 22 were approved by the board of directors on 24 February 2009 and were signed on its behalf by:

C D Jones
Director

UK GAAP Ltd   10

Notes to the financial statements

Notes to the financial statements for the year ended 31 December 2008

1 Accounting policies

These financial statements are prepared on the going concern basis, under the historical cost convention, as modified by the revaluation of certain tangible fixed assets and in accordance with the Companies Act 1985 and applicable accounting standards. The principal accounting policies are set out below.

Note: A description of each of the accounting policies that is material in the context of the entity's financial statements should be disclosed. The policies must be the most appropriate. Where an accounting policy is prescribed by and fully described in an accounting standard, UITF abstract or companies legislation a succinct description of the policy should be given. Where an accounting policy is not prescribed by an accounting standard, a UITF abstract or companies legislation, or an entity uses an option therein, a further description should be provided. In addition there should be a description of those estimation techniques adopted that are significant (those where the range of reasonable amounts is so large that the use of a different amount from within the range could materially affect the view shown by the financial statements). The list of areas where companies might reasonably be expected to disclose accounting policies is not exhaustive.

- *Capital instruments.*
- *Deferred taxation.*
- *Depreciation and amortisation.*
- *Finance costs.*
- *Financial instruments.*
- *Fixed assets.*
- *Foreign currencies.*
- *Goodwill and intangible assets.*
- *Government grants.*
- *Impairment and provisions.*
- *Interest capitalisation.*

- *Investment properties.*
- *Leases.*
- *Long-term contracts.*
- *Pensions.*
- *Post-retirement benefits.*
- *Provisions.*
- *Research and development.*
- *Revaluation of fixed assets.*
- *Stocks and work in progress.*
- *Revenue recognition.*

Change in accounting policy

The company has adopted the amendment to FRS 17, 'Retirement benefits'. As a result of this quoted securities held as plan assets in the defined benefit pension scheme are now valued at bid price rather than mid-market value. The effect of this change is that the value of plan assets at 31 December 2007 has been restated from £6,875,000 to £6,841,000, a decrease of £34,000, resulting in an increase of the pension deficit of £34,000. Current and prior year profit have been unaffected by this change.

2 Cash flow statement and related party disclosures

The company is a wholly-owned subsidiary of GAAP UK plc and is included in the consolidated financial statements of GAAP UK plc, which are publicly available. Consequently, the company has taken advantage of the exemption from preparing a cash flow statement under the terms of FRS 1. The company is also exempt under the terms of FRS 8 from disclosing related party transactions with entities that are part of the GAAP UK plc group or investees of the GAAP UK plc group. For details of other related party transactions see note 26.

3 Segmental reporting

The company's activities consist solely of the processing and sale of food in the United Kingdom.

Note: SSAP 25 disclosures are not required for a private company subsidiary where disclosures consistent with SSAP 25 are given in the financial statements of its parent. Where the parent reports under IFRS and presents information in accordance with IAS 14, this will only be sufficient to enable the subsidiary to qualify for this exemption where the parent's IAS 14 disclosures are compliant with SSAP 25. However, the SSAP 25 disclosures are not required for a private company that is smaller than ten times the medium-sized thresholds as defined in section 247 of the Companies Act 1985.

UK GAAP Limited — Year ended 31 December 2008

UK GAAP Ltd

11

4 Operating profit

	2008 £'000	2007 £'000
Operating profit is stated after charging		
Wages and salaries	2,661	2,391
Social security costs	515	436
Other pension costs (note 23)	101	94
Staff costs	**3,277**	**2,921**
Depreciation of tangible fixed assets		
– owned assets	159	158
– leased assets	43	42
Operating lease charges		
– plant and machinery	42	34
– other	55	48
Own work capitalised	11	9
Research and development — current year	15	18
Services provided by the company's auditor		
Fees payable for the audit	13	13
Fees payable for other services — tax compliance	5	5

Notes:

(a) Disclosure of research and development expenditure charged in the profit and loss account is not required for private companies that are smaller than ten times the medium-sized thresholds as defined in section 247 of the Companies Act 1985.

(b) Disclosure of auditors' remuneration for other services is not required for companies that are small or medium-sized as defined in section 247 of the Companies Act 1985, as amended from time to time by statutory instrument.

5 Directors' emoluments

	2008 £'000	2007 £'000
Aggregate emoluments	210	206
Aggregate amounts (excluding shares) receivable under long-term incentive schemes	5	7
Sums paid to third parties for directors' services	2	–

Retirement benefits are accruing to three (2007: two) directors under a defined benefit scheme.

Notes:

(a) If the company has a defined contribution scheme, a separate figure is to be disclosed showing the aggregate value of any company contributions paid or treated as paid to a pension scheme in respect of money purchase benefits. The number of directors to whom retirement benefits are accruing under each of money purchase and defined benefit schemes must also be disclosed.

(b) For unlisted companies the net value of assets received or receivable under a long-term incentive scheme excludes shares and, hence, such companies must disclose the number of directors entitled to shares under a long-term incentive scheme, if applicable.

(c) The aggregate amount of excess retirement benefits and the aggregate amount of compensation for loss of office must also be disclosed, where applicable.

Highest paid director

	2008 £'000	2007 £'000
Total amount of emoluments and amounts (excluding shares) receivable under long-term incentive schemes	75	70
Defined benefit pension scheme:		
Accrued pension at end of year	38	36

UK GAAP Ltd   12

Note: Where the highest paid director exercised any share options, and where any shares under a long-term incentive scheme were receivable by him, these facts must be disclosed (Companies Act 1985 6 Sch 2(3)). Where he is a member of a defined contribution scheme, the amount of company contributions in respect of him must be disclosed.

6 Employee information

The average monthly number of persons (including executive directors) employed by the company during the year was:

By activity	2008	2007
Production	166	170
Selling and distribution	32	30
Administration	55	55
	253	255

7 Interest payable and similar charges

	2008 £'000	2007 £'000
Interest payable on overdrafts and bank loans	109	33
Interest payable on other loans	18	23
Preference share dividend paid: 3.5p (2007:3.5p) per £1 share	3	3
Finance lease interest	36	38
	166	97

8 Taxation on the profit for the year

	2008 £'000	2007 £'000
Current tax:		
UK corporation tax on profits of the period	211	339
Adjustment in respect of previous periods	25	36
Total current tax	236	375
Deferred tax:		
Origination and reversal of timing differences	22	29
Change in tax rate – impact on deferred tax liabilities	–	(2)
Change in tax rate – impact of deferred tax asset	–	4
Total deferred tax (note 18)	22	31
Tax on profit on ordinary activities	258	406

The tax assessed for the period is higher (2007: higher) than the standard effective rate of corporation tax in the UK for the year ended 31 December 2008 of 28.5% (2007: 30%). The differences are explained below:

	2008 £'000	2007 £'000
Profit on ordinary activities before tax	501	925
Profit on ordinary activities multiplied by standard rate in the UK 28.5% (2007: 30%)	143	278
Effects of:		
Expenses not deductible for tax purposes	90	90
Accelerated capital allowances and other timing differences	(22)	(29)
Adjustments to tax charge in respect of previous period	25	36
Current tax charge for the period	236	375

UK GAAP Ltd 13

Factors affecting current and future tax charges

The standard rate of Corporation Tax in the UK changed from 30% to 28% with effect from 1 April 2008. Accordingly, the company's profits for this accounting period are taxed at an effective rate of 28.5% and will be taxed at 28% in the future.

Based on current capital investment plans, the company expects to continue to be able to claim capital allowances in excess of depreciation in future years at a similar level to the current year.

No provision has been made for deferred tax on gains recognised on revaluing property to its market value. Such tax would become payable only if the property was sold without it being possible to claim rollover relief. The total amount unprovided for is £53,100 (2007: £53,100).

Deferred tax liabilities have not been discounted.

9 Dividends

	2008 £'000	2007 £'000
Equity -Ordinary		
Interim paid: 3.51p (2007: 2.57p) per £0.25 share	71	52
Final paid (2007): 3.32p per £0.25 share	67	–
	138	52

The directors have proposed a final dividend for the year ended 31 December 2008 of 5.0p per share that is a total of £102,000. This dividend has not been accounted for within the current year financial statements as it has yet to be approved.

10 Tangible assets

	Land and buildings £'000	Plant and machinery £'000	Total £'000
Cost or valuation			
At 1 January 2008	1,291	1,561	2,852
Additions	246	426	672
Disposals	(24)	(106)	(130)
At 31 December 2008	**1,513**	**1,881**	**3,394**
Accumulated depreciation			
At 1 January 2008	211	610	821
Charge for the year	45	157	202
Disposals	(6)	(8)	(14)
At 31 December 2008	**250**	**759**	**1,009**
Net book amount			
At 31 December 2008	**1,263**	**1,122**	**2,385**
At 31 December 2007	1,080	951	2,031

Analysis of land and buildings

	2008 £000	2007 £000
Analysis of land and buildings at cost or valuation		
At cost	1,224	1,002
At valuation	289	289
	1,513	1,291

On first time adoption of FRS 15, 'Tangible fixed assets', in the financial statements for the year ended 31 December 2001, the company took advantage of the transitional arrangements available and retained the book amounts at that date of the land and buildings that had previously been revalued in accordance with the company's accounting policies. The land and

UK GAAP Ltd   14

buildings concerned were independently valued on an existing use basis by Surveyor & Son on 31 December 2000 and are carried at their valuation at that date of £289,000.

	2008 £'000	2007 £'000
The net book amount of land and buildings comprises		
Freehold	1,216	1,031
Long leaseholds	36	37
Short leaseholds	11	12
	1,263	1,080

If land and buildings had not been revalued, they would have been included at the following amounts:

	Land and Buildings 2008 £'000	2007 £'000
Cost	1,326	1,104
Aggregate depreciation	(235)	(201)
Net book amount	1,091	903

	2008 £'000	2007 £'000
Assets held under finance leases and capitalised in plant and machinery		
Cost	349	396
Aggregate depreciation	(116)	(132)
Net book amount	233	264

11 Fixed asset investments

	£'000
At 1 January 2008	76
Disposals	(20)
At 31 December 2008	**56**

Investments comprise equity shares in a trade investment with a cost of £56,000 (2007: £76,000). These are listed on the London Stock Exchange and had a market value of £145,000 (2007: £170,000) at 31 December 2008.

12 Stock

	2008 £'000	2007 £'000
Raw materials and consumables	873	820
Work in progress	209	182
Finished goods and goods for resale	826	777
	1,908	1,779

£200,000 (2007: £100,000) of finished goods included above are consignment stocks that are held on a sale or return basis from the manufacturer. Title to these stocks passes at the earlier of when they are sold or nine months from delivery date. On delivery a deposit of 30% is payable. The balance is included in trade creditors and bears interest at LIBOR plus 1¾% and becomes payable when title passes.

UK GAAP Ltd 15

The replacement cost of stocks exceeds balance sheet values as follows

	2008 £'000	2007 £'000
Raw materials and consumables	40	19

13 Debtors

	2008 £'000	2007 £'000
Trade debtors	1,533	1,067
Amounts owed by group undertakings	389	367
Other debtors	32	21
Prepayments and accrued income	61	54
	2,015	1,509

Trade debtors include £205,000 (2007: £56,000) falling due after more than one year. Amounts owed by group undertakings are unsecured, interest free, have no fixed date of repayment and are repayable on demand.

14 Current asset investments

	2008 £'000	2007 £'000
Government securities	50	125

The market value of the government securities is not materially different from their carrying amount.

15 Creditors – Amounts falling due within one year

	2008 £'000	2007 £'000
Debenture loans (Note 17)	349	12
Bank loans and overdrafts (Note 17)	388	319
Trade creditors	876	1,005
Amounts due to group undertakings	241	180
Finance leases (Note 17)	27	31
Taxation and social security	243	291
Other creditors	15	12
Accruals and deferred income	93	109
	2,232	1,959

Amounts due to group undertakings are unsecured, interest free and repayable on demand.

16 Creditors – Amounts falling due after more than one year

	2008 £'000	2007 £'000
Debenture loans (Note 17)	175	107
Bank loans (Note 17)	166	52
Finance leases (Note 17)	283	250
Cumulative preference shares of £1 each — 75,000 (Note 17)	75	75
Other creditors	95	40
	794	524

UK GAAP Ltd

17 Loans and other borrowings

	2008 £'000	2007 £'000
7% unsecured loan stock 2008/2009	349	12
10% unsecured loan stock 2014/2015	175	107
Bank loans and overdrafts	554	371
Finance leases	310	281
Cumulative preference shares of £1 each – 75,000	75	75
	1,463	846

Maturity of financial liabilities

	2008 £'000	2007 £'000
In one year or less, or on demand	764	362
In more than one year, but not more than two years	218	102
In more than two years, but not more than five years	211	168
In more than five years	270	214
	1,463	846

Note: The maturity time bandings are derived from paragraph 67 of FRS 25. This disclosure is suggested best practice for those companies that are not applying the disclosure requirements of FRS 25 as the equivalent disclosure requirements in FRS 4 have been deleted.

The 7% unsecured loan stock 2008/2009 is redeemable at par between 1 January 2008 and 31 December 2009. The 10% unsecured loan stock 2014/2015 is redeemable at par between 1 January 2014 and 31 December 2015.

Included in the bank loans is an amount of £300,000 which is payable in two annual instalments commencing 1 January 2007 and carries interest at 11% fixed. The balance of £80,000 carries interest at LIBOR plus 3% and is repayable in six quarterly instalments commencing 1 February 2009.

Finance leases

Future minimum payments under finance leases are as follows:

	2008 £'000	2007 £'000
Within one year	31	35
In more than one year, but not more than five years	302	243
After five years	25	37
Total gross payments	358	315
Less finance charges included above	(48)	(34)
	310	281

The total value of leases repayable by instalments any part of which falls due after more than five years is £24,184 (2007: £35,875).

UK GAAP Ltd

Debentures issued

The company issued the following debentures during the year.

Class	Amount Issued £'000	Consideration received £'000
7% unsecured redeemable 2008/2009	337	337
10% unsecured redeemable 2014/2015	68	68

Preference share capital Authorised issued and fully paid	2008 £'000	2007 £'000
75,000: 3.5% Cumulative preference shares of £1 each at 1 January 2008	75	75

The 3.5% cumulative preference shares carry a fixed cumulative preferential dividend at the rate of 3.5% per annum, payable half yearly in arrears on 31 December and 30 June. The shares have no redemption entitlement. On a winding up the holders have priority before all other classes of shares to receive repayment of capital plus any arrears of dividend. The holders have no voting rights unless the dividend is in arrears by six months or more.

Note: Although not applicable for UK GAAP Limited, companies that elect not to adopt fair value accounting for certain financial instruments must give additional disclosures relating to their derivative financial instruments. The following disclosure is required for each class of derivative financial instrument:

- *the fair value of the derivatives in that class, if such a value can be determined; and*
- *the extent and nature of the derivatives.*

[CA85 4 Sch 45B].

In addition, where:

- *a company has financial fixed assets that could be included at fair value;*
- *the amount at which those assets are included in the financial statements is in excess of their fair value; and*
- *the company has not made provision for diminution in value of those assets.*

The following disclosure must be made:

- *The amount at which either the individual assets or appropriate groupings of those individual assets is stated in the company's financial statements.*
- *The fair value of those assets or groupings.*
- *The reasons for not making a provision for diminution in value of those assets, including the nature of the evidence that provides the basis for the belief that the amount at which they are stated in the financial statements will be recovered.*

[CA85 4 Sch 45C].

18 Provisions for liabilities and charges

	Pending litigation £'000	Reorganisation provision £'000	Environmental provision £'000	Deferred tax provision £'000	Total £'000
1 January 2008	–	–	–	48	48
Charged to the profit and loss account	15	153	72	22	262
Utilised during the year	–	(42)	(34)	–	(76)
31 December 2008	15	111	38	70	234

UK GAAP Ltd   18

Pending litigation

In December 2008 the company received a claim from Customer Limited that green colouring had been found in a batch of bread. A provision of £15,000 has been made for the costs of product recall and loss of profit claim from Customer Limited. The claim is expected to be fully resolved in early 2009.

Re-organisation

A rationalisation of product processes at the company's two factories in London and Bradford was announced on 11 December 2008. This rationalisation involving the introduction of new technology will result in the loss of 15 jobs in total over the next few months. The provision is expected to be fully utilised by 31 December 2009.

Environmental

In April 2008 a spillage of cleaning chemicals contaminated land surrounding the Bradford factory. The company is committed to a policy of environmental protection and immediate action is being taken to deal with the contamination. A provision of £72,000 has been recognised for those clean-up costs, which are expected to be incurred over an eighteen-month period.

Provision for deferred tax	2008 £'000	2007 £'000
Accelerated capital allowances	65	40
Other timing differences	5	8
Total provision for deferred tax	**70**	**48**
1 January	48	21
Deferred tax charge in profit and loss account (note 8)	22	27
31 December	**70**	**48**

Deferred tax asset relating to pension deficit	2008 £'000	2007 £'000
1 January	36	38
Deferred tax credit/(charge) in profit and loss account	–	(4)
Deferred tax credited/(charged) to the statement of total recognised gains and losses:		
– on actuarial loss	22	3
– change in tax rate	–	(1)
31 December	**58**	**36**

The deferred tax asset of £58,000 (2007: £36,000) has been deducted in arriving at the net pension deficit on the balance sheet.

During the prior year, as a result of the change in UK corporation tax rates from 30% to 28% that was substantially enacted on 26 June 2007 and effective from 1 April 2008, deferred tax balances were remeasured. This resulted in a net charge to the 2007 profit and loss account of £2,000 and a charge to the 2007 statement of total recognised gains and losses of £1,000.

19 Called up share capital

	2008 £'000	2007 £'000
Authorised		
2,640,000 ordinary shares of £0.25 each	660	660
Allotted and fully paid		
2,032,000 (2007: 2,020,000) ordinary shares of £0.25 each	508	505

During the year 12,000 ordinary shares were issued for cash. The nominal value of these shares was £3,000 and the consideration received was £27,000 after deducting expenses of £1,000.

UK GAAP Ltd   19

20 Reserves

	Share premium account £'000	Profit and loss reserve £'000	Revaluation reserve £'000
1 January 2008	120	2,253	177
Premium on ordinary shares issued (net of £1,000 expenses)	24	–	–
Profit for the financial year (note 21)	–	105	–
Actuarial losses on pension scheme	–	(92)	–
Transfer to profit and loss reserve	–	5	(5)
31 December 2008	**144**	**2,271**	**172**
Pension deficit	–	(150)	–
Profit and loss reserve excluding pension deficit	–	2,421	–

21 Reconciliation of movements in shareholders' funds

	2008 £'000	2007 £'000
Profit for the year	**243**	519
Dividends	**(138)**	(52)
Profit for the financial year	**105**	467
Net proceeds of issue of ordinary share capital (note 19)	**27**	50
Actuarial losses on pension scheme net of tax	**(92)**	(87)
Net addition to shareholders' funds	**40**	430
Opening shareholders' funds as previously reported	**3,095**	2,657
Prior year adjustment for amendment to FRS 17	**(40)**	(32)
Opening shareholders funds as restated	**3,055**	2,625
Closing shareholders' funds	**3,095**	3,055

22 Contingent liabilities

The company has given a guarantee in respect of the bank borrowings of a fellow subsidiary, which amounted to £35,000 at 31 December 2008 (2007: £25,000).

The company is a participant in a group banking arrangement under which all surplus cash balances are held as collateral for bank facilities advanced to group members. In addition, the company has issued an unlimited guarantee to the bank to support these group facilities.

23 Pension commitments

The company operates a defined benefit pension scheme with assets held in a separately administered fund. The scheme provides retirement benefits on the basis of members' final salary. On 1 January 2007, the defined benefit pension scheme was closed to new entrants. At the same time, the company established a defined contribution scheme to provide benefits to new employees.

UK GAAP Ltd

20

Defined benefit scheme

An actuarial valuation of the UK GAAP Ltd pension scheme using the projected unit basis, was carried out at 31 December 2008 by Actuary and Actuary, independent consulting actuaries. The major assumptions used by the actuary were:

	2008 %	2007 %
Rate of increase in salaries	4.3	4.0
Rate of increase in pensions in payment	3.0	4.0
Discount rate	5.2	5.0
Rate of inflation	2.8	2.5

The mortality assumptions used were as follows:

	2008 years	2007 years
Longevity at age 65 for current pensioners:		
– Men	19.7	18.4
– Women	22.4	21.3
Longevity at age 65 for future pensioners		
– Men	20.4	19.3
– Women	23.1	22.3

The assets in the scheme and the expected rates of return were:

	Long-term rate of return expected 31 December 2008 %	Value at 31 December 2008 £000	Long-term rate of return expected at 31 December 2007 %	As restated Value at 31 December 2007 £000
Equities	8.2	5,852	8.4	5,341
Bonds	4.9	1,600	5.6	1,500
Total market value of assets		7,452		6,841
Present value of scheme liabilities		(7,660)		(6,970)
Deficit in scheme		(208)		(129)
Related deferred tax asset		58		36
Net pension deficit		(150)		(93)

The equity investments and bonds which are held in plan assets are quoted and are valued at the current bid price following the adoption of the amendment to FRS 17. Previously these were valued at mid price. The effect of this change is that the value of assets at 31 December 2007 has been restated from £6,875,000 to £6,841,000, a decrease of £34,000.

Reconciliation of present value of scheme liabilities

	2008 £'000	2007 £'000
1 January	6,970	6,315
Current service cost	84	90
Past service cost	5	–
Interest cost	505	489
Benefits paid	(51)	(63)
Actuarial loss	147	139
31 December	7,660	6,970

UK GAAP Ltd

Sensitivity analysis of scheme liabilities

The sensitivity of the present value of scheme liabilities to changes in the principle assumptions used is set out below.

	Change in assumption	Impact on scheme liabilities
Discount rate	Increase/decrease by 1%	Increase/decrease by 8.5%
Rate of inflation	Increase/decrease by 1%	Increase/decrease by 5.0%
Rate of increase in salaries	Increase/decrease by 1%	Increase/decrease by 3.5%
Rate of increase in pensions in payment	Increase/decrease by 1%	Increase/decrease by 3.0%
Mortality	Increase by 1 year	Increase by 4.5%

Reconciliation of fair value of scheme assets

	2008 £'000	As restated 2007 £'000
1 January	6,841	6,190
Expected return on scheme assets	550	583
Actuarial gains	16	15
Benefits paid	(51)	(63)
Contributions paid by employer	96	116
31 December	7,452	6,841

Scheme assets do not include any of UK GAAP Limited's own financial instruments, or any property occupied by UK GAAP Limited.

The expected return on scheme assets is determined by considering the expected returns available on the assets underlying the current investment policy. Expected yields on fixed interest investments are based on gross redemption yields as at the balance sheet date. Expected returns on equity investments reflect long-term real rates of return experienced in the respective markets.

The actual return on scheme assets in the year was £566,000 (2007: £598,000).

Analysis of the amount charged to profit or loss are as follows:

	2008 £'000	2007 £'000
Current service cost	84	90
Past service cost	5	–
Expected return on pension scheme assets	(550)	(583)
Interest on pension scheme liabilities	505	489
Total	44	(4)

Of the total current and past service cost, £63,000 (2006: £65,000) is included within cost of sales, and £26,000 (2006: £25,000) is included within administrative expenses.

Actuarial gains and losses

The cumulative amount of actuarial losses recognised in the statement of recognised gains and losses is £536,000.

Actuarial valuation

The full actuarial valuation at 31 December 2008 showed an increase in the deficit from £129,000 to £208,000. It has been agreed with the trustees that contributions for the next two years will be increased by £100,000 to make good the deficit. The total contributions expected to be made to the scheme by UK GAAP Limited in the year to 31 December 2009 is therefore £195,000. Further to this, as the scheme is closed to new entrants, the current service cost will increase as members approach retirement.

UK GAAP Ltd 22

Amounts for current and previous four years:

	2008	2007	2006	2005	2004
Defined benefit obligation	(7,660)	(6,970)	(6,315)	(6,115)	(5,987)
Plan assets	7,445	6,835	6,190	5,990	5,780
Surplus/deficit	(215)	(135)	(125)	(125)	(207)
Experience adjustments on plan assets Amount (£'000)	16	15	50	41	(33)
Experience adjustments on plan liabilities: Amount (£'000)	(22)	21	98	45	66
Total amount recognised in the statement of total recognised gains and losses: Amount (£'000)	131	124	150	245	160

Defined contribution scheme

The cost of contributions to the defined contribution scheme amounts to £12,000 (2007: £4,000).

24 Capital and other commitments

	2008 £'000	2007 £'000
Contracts placed for future capital expenditure not provided in the financial statements	145	226

25 Financial commitments

At 31 December 2008 the company had annual commitments under non-cancellable operating leases for assets other than land and buildings expiring as follows:

	2008 £'000	2007 £'000
Within one year	12	20
Within two to five years	23	12
After five years	95	65
	130	97

26 Other related party transactions

Note: Information concerning transactions with related parties should be disclosed here, if they are not disclosed elsewhere within the financial statements. Information concerning transactions with directors and loans, etc to officers should also normally be disclosed here.

27 Ultimate parent undertaking

The immediate parent undertaking is GAAP UK Intermediate Holdings Limited.

The ultimate parent undertaking and controlling party is GAAP UK plc, which is the parent undertaking of the smallest and largest group to consolidate these financial statements. Copies of GAAP UK plc consolidated financial statements can be obtained from the Company Secretary at GAAP Towers, 2 The Square, London EC4Y 2DE.